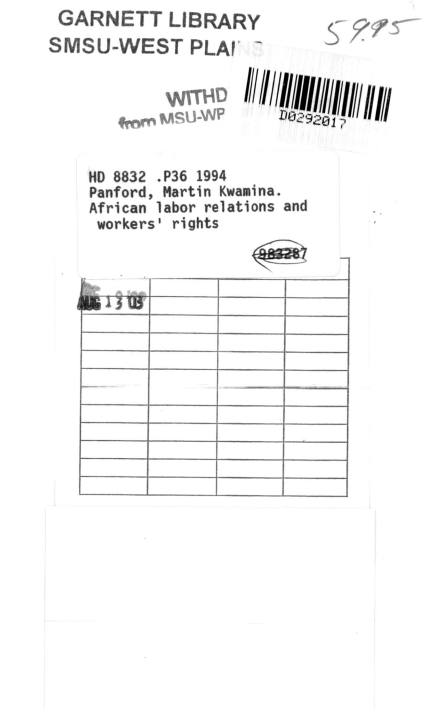

African Labor
Relations and
Workers' Rights

Recent Titles in
Contributions in Afro-American and African Studies

AFRICAN LABOR RELATIONS AND WORKERS' RIGHTS

Assessing the Role of the International Labor Organization

Kwamina Panford

Foreword by W. R. Simpson

Contributions in Afro-American and African Studies, Number 172

GREENWOOD PRESS
Westport, Connecticut • London

Library of Congress Cataloging-in-Publication Data

Panford, Kwamina.
    African labor relations and workers' rights : assessing the role
of the International Labor Organization / Kwamina Panford ; foreword
by W. R. Simpson.
        p.   cm.—(Contributions in Afro-American and African
studies, ISSN 0069–9624 ; no. 172)
   Includes bibliographical references and index.
   ISBN 0–313–29066–0 (alk. paper)
    1. Labor policy—Ghana. 2. Industrial relations—Ghana.
3. Employee rights—Ghana. 4. Labor policy—Africa, Sub-Saharan.
5. Industrial relations—Africa, Sub-Saharan. 6. Employee rights—
Africa, Sub-Saharan. 7. International Labor Organization.
I. Title. II. Series.
HD8832.P36   1994
331′.09667—dc20   94–7431

British Library Cataloguing in Publication Data is available.

Library of Congress Catalog Card Number: 94–7431
ISBN: 0–313–29066–0
ISSN: 0069–9624

First published in 1994

Greenwood Press, 88 Post Road West, Westport, CT 06881
An imprint of Greenwood Publishing Group, Inc.

Printed in the United States of America

∞™

The paper used in this book complies with the
Permanent Paper Standard issued by the National
Information Standards Organization (Z39.48–1984).

10 9 8 7 6 5 4 3 2 1

To Araba and Esi for your keen sense for hard work and humor and to my parents ("Auntie" and "Paapa") for their eternal optimism, dedication to public service and our family.

Contents

Foreword

Under the Treaty of Versailles of 1919, the International Labor Organization (ILO) was charged with the enormous responsibility of protecting and improving the condition of workers, mainly through the adoption of international instruments, or Conventions and Recommendations as they are called. It is, however, the Constitution of the Organization itself that contains the basic principle of freedom of association and collective bargaining, a principle which states, on becoming members of the Organization, are bound to respect. So important is the principle of the right to organize and collective bargaining that two famous Conventions were adopted, in 1948 and 1949 respectively, to specify in greater detail the rights and guarantees that workers and employers and their organizations should enjoy. In addition, special supervisory bodies were set up to examine allegations that the principle of freedom of association was being infringed.

These principles and standards in the field of trade union rights have posed many problems for African ILO member states and confronted them with a number of dilemmas as regards their implementation in law and practice. In this book Kwamina Panford addresses these problems and dilemmas by discussing the internal and external constraints which African member states of the ILO have to face in their attempts to apply Convention Nos. 87 and 98. He carefully draws attention to the close relationship that exists between trade union rights and the particularly fragile economies and unstable political systems that prevail in many countries of Africa.

Panford has effectively drawn on the wealth of professional and personal experience he himself has acquired, as well as that of many others who are familiar with the supervision of ILO standards and their application, and African labor laws and social policies, in order to examine in a systematic way the relationship between worker rights and socio-economic development in Africa. He has also been able, in his analysis, to draw on some unpublished material of the ILO, and some material from African governments and labor organizations, to identify the national and international factors that have shaped African industrial relations and worker rights. His book offers practical policy recommendations to meet the problems that are identified as obstacles to the rapid development of African labor relations.

The author provides useful research and a practical framework for the further examination of the components and conditions for sound labor management relations, worker rights and efficient human resource utilization in Africa. The book is, accordingly, a valuable addition to existing literature on the ILO and other international human rights organizations. It evaluates the strengths of the ILO and the positive contribution it has made to the evolution of worker and human rights and what Panford calls its "delimitations," referring to the constraints within which the ILO operates.

This book is an informative and practical reference work for both practitioners and academics interested in the national and international, historical, social, legal and economic factors that have influenced the labor laws, practices and policies in post-independence Africa and other developing regions. Panford has collated and analyzed information on the application of ILO standards in Africa and provided an in-depth analysis of the activities and programs of the ILO and their impact on African labor relations.

In evaluating and analyzing the labor policies and labor relations systems of post-independence African countries such as Ghana, Kenya, Nigeria and Zambia, Panford's book will be of particular relevance and interest to the newer independent countries such as Namibia and Eritrea, and even South Africa as it emerges from the apartheid system. This publication is also timely since it contributes to the objective assessment of what has been called "Africa's Second Wave of Independence or Liberation," or the attempts that are being made to create more democractic institutions and good governance in Africa.

Panford's book is a welcome addition to the debates over worker rights and their compatibility with economic development not only in Africa but also the rest of the developing world. The author not only provides a book-length study on the subject, but also contributes to the emergence of a much-needed alternative framework for future labor relations and workers' rights policies, laws and practices that are appropriate to meet the challenges of development in Africa.

December 1993   W. R. Simpson
ILO, Geneva, Switzerland   Director, Industrial Relations and Labor
                                            Administration Department and Secretary,
                                   International Industrial Relations Association

Preface

This study assesses the influence of the International Labor Organization (ILO, also referred to in this book as the Organization) over African policies, laws and practices that affect workers' rights to form labor unions, to collectively bargain with employers and to strike to protect their occupational interests. This book derives its significance from the treatment of its subject matter. Although the United Nations Organization (UN), through the ILO and other international agencies, seeks to promote simultaneously economic development and improved human rights conditions in Africa, no book-length study has been conducted and published exclusively on the subject. This book is therefore the first to evaluate systematically the role of any international organization in the promotion of both human rights and development in Africa or any region of the Third World. It is also the first long-term study that utilizes the professional experience and practical insights of key participants in the workers' rights and labor relations fields — ILO, African government and diplomatic personnel and labor leaders — to analyze post-independence labor policies, legislation and actual practices, and their outcomes. This study utilizes these sources to prescribe appropriate solutions to the labor problems identified.

Recent developments in Africa have contributed to the significance of this book: the anticipated end of apartheid in South Africa; the emergence of newly independent African nations such as Eritrea (formerly part of Ethiopia) Namibia and Zimbabwe; the resurgence of movements to end one-party or military rule in several countries such as Ghana, Kenya, Zambia and Nigeria; and massive debates about the future of African economies and democracy have all pushed to the forefront of discussions centering on Africa the connection between human rights, development and democracy.[1]

This book may assist in resolving some of the controversial issues connected to the debates on democracy, human rights and development by evaluating the role of the ILO, the major UN agency responsible for the global protection of workers. In view of Africa's persistent economic difficulties and governments' subscription to the Economic and Structural Adjustment Programs (ERPs/SAPs) of the International Monetary Fund and the World Bank that erode workers' and human rights, the need to reassess the roles of the ILO, workers and trade unions in Africa's development has become more urgent.

This publication is the product of several years of research involving field work in Ghana and a year's employment at the ILO's Geneva (Switzerland) Head Offices. I therefore wish to thank the Institute of International Education, Washington, DC, for making my professional internship at the ILO possible; Messrs K. T. Samson, W. R. Simpson, N. Rubin and E. Kane of the ILO, and Mr. Kwodwo Nyamekye (Deputy-Director, UN Human Rights Center, Geneva) for my exposure to the actual delicate efforts of the ILO and other organizations to protect workers worldwide. Ghana's Diplomatic Representatives in Geneva and other African Labor Department and trade union officials shared selflessly with me their first hand knowledge about Ghana's labor and international affairs connected to the activities and programs of the ILO. They all furnished crucial data and information used in this study.

Several others helped me to complete this book. Professors Tom Koenig (Sociology Department, Northeastern University) and Mike Rustad (Suffolk Law School) helped me to devise an appropriate multidisciplinary methodology and Professor Philip Alston (Harvard University Law School and Tuft's Fletcher School of Law and Diplomacy) used his experience as an International Human Rights Expert to help me fashion a critical perspective on the role and impact of the ILO on African workers' rights. To two of my Cornell University Professors — J. P. Windmuller and Sam Bacharach — I wish to say "thanks" for initiating me into Organizational Behavior and Comparative/International Labor Studies at the Graduate School of Industrial and Labor Relations. My thanks also go to Professor Tayo Fashoyin of the University of Lagos, Nigeria, for his comments on Nigerian labor legislation. I also wish to acknowledge the support of the Office of the Provost and the Dean, College of Arts and Sciences, Northeastern University in the completion of this book.

October 1993, Boston   Kwamina Panford

NOTE

1.   Issues such as the compatibility of human rights, economic efficiency and growth which were popular in the 1950s and 1960s are being re-evaluated after a lull. For a sample of publications see Shivji (1990); ILO (1992); Cohen and Goulbourne (1991); Kothari (1989); Panford (1992).

Abbreviations

AFL	American Federation of Labor
AFRC	Armed Forces Revolutionary Council (Ghana)
CFA	Committee of Freedom of Association (ILO)
COTU	Central Organization of Trade Unions (Kenya)
CPP	Convention People's Party (Ghana)
DC	District Commissioner
ERP	Economic Recovery Program
FNMG	Federal Nigerian Military Government
GCSA	Ghana Civil Servants' Association
GNAT	Ghana National Association of Teachers
GRNA	Ghana Registered Nurses' Association
ICFTU	International Confederation of Free Trade Unions
ILC	International Labor Conference
ILO	International Labor Organization
IMF	International Monetary Fund
IRA	Industrial Relations Act

KANU	Kenya African National Union
MMD	Movement for Multiparty Democracy (Zambia)
NCD	National Commission for Democracy (Ghana)
NLC	National Liberation Council (Ghana)
NLC	Nigerian Labor Congress
NRC	National Redemption Council (Ghana)
OATUU	Organization of African Trade Union Unity
OAU	Organization of African Unity
PIB	Prices and Incomes Board (Ghana)
PNDC	Provisional National Defense Council (Ghana)
PNP	People's National Party (Ghana)
PP	Progress Party (Ghana)
PSI	Public Service International
SAP	Structural Adjustment Program
SMC	Supreme Military Council (Ghana)
TUC	Trades Union Congress (Ghana)
UKCS	Union of Kenya Civil Servants
UN	United Nations
UNDP	United Nations Development Program
UNIP	United National Independence Party (Zambia)
WFTU	World Federation of Trade Unions
ZCTU	Zambia Congress of Trade Unions

Chronology of Relevant Events

1844   The British established formal colonial rule over Gold Coast
        territories (now Ghana).

1919   The International Labor Organization (ILO) became part of
        the defunct League of Nations.

1938   Cocoa boycott by peasant farmers who refused to sell their
        produce to the expatriate cocoa buying companies that
        monopolized cocoa trade in Ghana.

        First colonial labor ordinance allowing limited unionization
        in Nigeria was promulgated by the British colonial
        authorities.

1941   Trade Unions Ordinance, 1941 (Cap 91), became the first
        colonial labor code to permit unionization in the Gold Coast
        (Ghana).

1945   The ILO became a United Nations Specialized Agency with
        financial autonomy.

1949   The Convention People's Party (CPP) broke from the Unit-
        ed Gold Coast Convention and became one of the premier
        mass political organizations in Africa.

        Zambian trade unionists were given restricted legal rights to
        organize workers under the Trade Unions, Trade Disputes
        and the Industrial Conciliation Ordinances.

1951-1957   Kwame Nkrumah became the Head of Government Busi-
        ness in transition from colonial rule to independence after
        the first elections towards self-government in Ghana.

1957   Ghana officially became an independent nation on March
                6, with Nkrumah as Prime Minister, and joined the ILO.

1958   Industrial Relations Act No. 56 was approved by the Ghana-
                ian parliament to create the Ghana TUC.

1959   Ghana ratified ILO Convention No. 98.

1960   Seventeen African nations became independent, leading to
                an increase in the influx of African governments into in-
                ternational organizations such as the UN and ILO.

                Ghana became a Republic with Kwame Nkrumah as the
                President.

1961   The Sekondi-Takoradi rail strike occurred as the first
                political challenge to the Nkrumah-led CPP's legitimacy as
                a mass political organization.

1963   December, Kenya gained official political independence
                from the British.

1964   Kenya became an ILO member.

                October 24, Zambia joined the community of independent
                African nations and in December, officially became
                an ILO member.

1964-1965   Ghana adopted African socialism as the nation's official
                ideology.

1965   January, a military coup in Nigeria ended the first civilian
                administration.

                September 1, a Presidential Declaration led to the
                establishment of the Central Organization of Trade Unions
                (COTU) as Kenya's first unified central labor organization.

                The 1958 Industrial Relations Act was superseded by the
                1965 Industrial Relations Act of Ghana.

                The Ghana government launched the famous Seven-Year
                Development Plan.

1966   February 24, Kwame Nkrumah and his CPP were over-
                thrown in the nation's first military coup and the National
                Liberation Council government was formed.

1969   The Second Republic under K. A. Busia and his Progress
                Party was inaugurated in Ghana.

1971   Industrial Relations Act of Zambia launched the Zambian
                Congress of Trade Unions (ZCTU) as the country's sole
                labor federation.

                September, the Busia-led PP government dissolved the
                Ghana TUC through a parliamentary emergency bill.

1972   January 13, K. A. Busia was overthrown in the second
                coup in Ghana and replaced by the National Redemption
                Council (NRC) headed by Col. I. K. Acheampong.

                Decree No. 22 by the NRC restored the TUC as the only
                labor federation in Ghana in February.

1973   Thirty-one African labor federations established the
                Organization of African Trade Union Unity (OATUU) in
                Addis Ababa (Ethiopia) as the labor wing of the
                Organization of African Unity (OAU).

1975   The NRC of Ghana was replaced by the Supreme Military
                Council (SMC) still led by Acheampong, now a general.

1978   The SMC underwent a leadership change with General Fred
                Akuffo displacing Acheampong and the SMC II being
                founded.

                Industrial Relations Act by the Federal Nigerian Military
                Authorities created the Nigerian Labor Congress with 42
                Industrial Union Affiliates.

1979   June 4, junior army officers overthrew SMC II and launched
                a "house cleaning" exercise (anti-corruption purge) under
                the Armed Forces Revolutionary Council (AFRC). First
                coming of Flt. Lt. J. J. Rawlings into power in Ghana.

                September, Ghana entered the Third Republic after elections
                won by the People's National Party (PNP) led by President
                H. Limann.

1980   Zimbabwe, the former Southern Rhodesia, became
                independent.

1981   December 31, Ghana's Third Republican Constitution was
              suspended by the second coming of Rawlings who led
              the Provisional National Defense Council (PNDC).

1982   June, the PNDC launched a World Bank- and IMF-inspired
              Economic Recovery Program (ERP).

1985   Ghana's ERP was revamped and turned into a Structural
              Adjustment Program with continued World Bank and
              IMF support.

              August, General Ibrahim Babangida ousted General
              Muhammadu Buhari from power to head a new Nigerian
              military government.

1986   Ghana ratified five ILO Conventions in May.

1988   The Federal Nigerian Military rulers temporarily dissolved
              the Nigerian Labor Congress.

1990   March 21, Namibia (the former South African-occupied
              South Western Africa) became the fifty-second independent
              African nation.

              November, multiparty general and presidential elecions
              were held in Zambia leading to the defeat of the
              Kenneth Kaunda-led UNIP by the Movement for Multiparty
              Democracy Party headed by ZCTU's Frederick Chiluba.

1991   Zambia adopted a new constitution through Act No. 1 of
              August 24, 1991 that permitted multiparty rule.

1992   November 3, Ghana held presidential elections towards the
              Fourth Republic. December, Ghana held elections for 200
              Parliamentary seats.

1993   January 7, J. J. Rawlings was sworn in as President of
              Ghana under the administration of the National Democratic
              Convention Party (NDC).

              Eritrea successfully broke from Ethiopia through a ref-
              erendum to become the fifty-third independent African
              country in April.

African Labor
Relations and
Workers' Rights

Chapter 1

Introduction

1. 1   African Workers' Rights Versus Economic Growth?

Towards the end of World War II when Asian and African decolonization began to accelerate, debates emerged concerning the extent to which the exercise
of workers' rights, including the freedom to organize trade unions, to voluntarily bargain with employers and to strike in support of their claims, would affect the economies of the newly independent nations. Several authors (Mehta,
1957; De Schweinitz, 1959; Lewis , 1957) took the position that union autonomy[1] would aggravate developing nations' problems. These development
economists therefore prescribed the imposition of restrictions on unions because in their view, unions' unrestrained activities would result in the excessive consumption of goods and services which in turn would create shortages
in the capital needed for rapid industrialization and economic growth. On the
contrary, a minority of authors (Fisher, 1961; Caire, 1977) were of the opinion
that unions' activities should not be suppressed because they would not lead to
capital deficiencies. They argued that unions would facilitate industrialization
and social development by providing channels for workers to express their
economic grievances and social interests and hence facilitate both economic
growth and the emergence of democratic practices. Their position was that
autonomous and democratic unions could be the nurseries for generating
leadership skills needed for ensuring democracy in developing countries.
Thus, in their view, labor unions provided societies with broader benefits that
went beyond the workplace.
   The four-decade long debate on the role of unions in developing countries
continues to attract a great deal of attention without much resolution. At a
1982 ILO-sponsored symposium, African governments and employers expressed their concerns over how workers' rights to free collective bargaining,
for example, could impede African economies (ILO, 1983). Zimbabwe's

Minister of Labor, taking a different view of the role of workers at a recent symposium, stated:

> To us, in Zimbabwe, the participation of workers in decision-making is an extremely important component of our overall strong determination to create industrial democracy. In this respect, since independence, the Government has introduced measures aimed at ensuring that the worker fully participates in decision-making through the concept of workers' committees and trade unionism (ILO, 1988).

This book examines Ghanaian and other African countries' labor policies, laws and practices with the view to generating more insights into the contradictory views expressed about labor's role in Africa.

The controversy over the role of unions stems from certain assumptions, values and ideologies which, although have shaped immensely the various authors' opinions, have never been made explicit or examined in either the comparative labor relations or economic development literature. Analyzing the various assumptions , values and ideological preferences of the various authors will generate a fuller understanding of contemporary African labor policies, legislation and actual practices. For example, the critical roles of labor policies such as the utilization and the management of human resources and other economic policies in Africa may be fully appreciated. Thus, the author views this book as an important step towards the creation of a proper understanding of the importance of the various authors' positions and their implicit assumptions through the use of an interdisciplinary study combining historical, sociological, economic and legal analyses of both their relevance and validity in the actual context of labor policies and practices in Africa.

In assessing the role of unions, I will evaluate simultaneously the influence of the International Labor Organization (the ILO or the Organization, as it will be referred to) in developing and promoting workers' rights to free trade unionism and collective bargaining in Ghana. The ILO is the United Nations Organization (UN) agency responsible primarily for globally protecting workers' rights.[2] It has developed a system of international labor standards called "Conventions" and "Recommendations" through which it seeks to shape the contents and impact of its member states' labor policies and practices. Upon joining the Organization and ratifying its Conventions, members agree to make their labor relations reflect the ideals on which it was founded such as:[3]

> Freedom of expression and of association are essential to sustained progress . . . the war against want requires to be carried on with unrelentng vigor within each nation, and by continuous and concerted international effort in which the representatives of workers and employers, enjoying equal status with those of governments, join with them in free discussion and democratic decision with a view to the promotion of the common welfare (ILO, 1982: 23).

1. 2   The Importance of ILO Convention Nos. 87 and 98

The specific ILO standards reviewed in this study are the rights of workers to freely form labor unions, and the right to bargain with employers to determine conditions of employment. These rights are enunciated in two key ILO Conventions, Nos. 87 and 98.[4] Convention No. 87 of 1948 seeks to guarantee workers the rights to organize and to freely determine their activities without government or employer interference. Convention No. 98 of 1949 also recognizes the right to form unions and provides further guarantees to the right to collectively bargain with employers in full freedom. These two Conventions are treated within the Organization as its *raison d'être*. They are considered so crucial that even a country such as Zambia, which has not ratified any of these Conventions, may be required by the Organization to rectify their violation.[5] ILO constitutional provisions grant special status to the principles they embody. The constitution explicitly recognizes the right of workers to freedom of association as essential to the entire Organization. Also, since the 1950s, the ILO has used an elaborate supervisory mechanism to investigate and recommend solutions to their violations (ILO, 1956).

The Status of Strikes in Africa

In Africa, the right to strike remains an important source of conflict between governments and labor unions and, as a result, occupies a central place in labor policy and legislation. In Ghana, for example, since 1958, and in Zambia, beginning in 1971, severe restrictions have been placed on strikes via legislation and cumbersome dispute settlement procedures which have virtually outlawed workers' industrial actions.[6] These limitations on strikes, especially in the large public and "essential service" sectors, have been some of the most frequent causes of alleged African government infringements of ILO standards.

A demonstration of the extremely sensitive nature of strikes was the life imprisonment sentence imposed on 11 Nigerian National Electric Power Authority employees for their roles in strikes which caused a nationwide power outage from October 5 to 7, 1988.[7] A more recent dispute involving Nigerian University lecturers and the federal government also demonstrates how strikes have become thorny issues in African labor relations, especially in state-union relations. On this occasion, the government declared illegal the lecturers' May 3, 1993 strike, designated teaching an "essential service" and stated its intent to discharge all employees who struck.[8]

The ILO and Strikes

There are no explicit Conventions recognizing the right to strike, but the practice within the ILO is that, with few exceptions, strikes are treated as inalienable workers' rights (Caire, 1977; Hodges-Aeberhard and De Dios, 1989; Ben-Israel, 1988). The basic position of the ILO is that strikes provide workers with effective means to back their collective bargaining demands and are, therefore, essential workers' rights. I will thus examine how the Organization has sought to protect workers' rights to strike in Ghana and in other African countries.

1. 3   Geographical Scope and Coverage of African Workers' Rights

I am placing special emphasis on Ghana for numerous reasons. First, focusing on a single country will allow a more in-depth study. Second, Ghana's labor situation, especially in the post-1971 era, presents numerous opportunities for assessing the relevance and the influence of ILO standards in Africa. As K. Ewusi (1984: 13) has correctly stated, Ghana epitomizes the major characteristics of several former British colonial territories. Her experience is, therefore, useful for illustrating developments and future trends in African labor relations. Ghana was one of the first former British colonies in Africa to join the ILO and to ratify the two Conventions reviewed for this study. As a result, since 1959, the ILO's supervisory bodies have reviewed the country's labor statutes and practices to check their conformity with ILO Convention No. 98 (Panford, 1988). The country has remained an active ILO member. In 1961, as a result of a complaint Ghana filed against the Government of Portugal, a Commission of Inquiry investigated Portugal's alleged violation of Convention No. 105 of 1957, Abolition of Forced Labor in Colonial Territories (Alcock, 1971; Osieke, 1976: 328 - 329).

Ghana has also had three cases of alleged violations of ILO standards filed against her. These cases, especially the most recent, Case No. 1135 of the Committee of Freedom of Association involving alleged government interference in internal union leadership problems, offer concrete opportunities for determining how the ILO attempts to ensure that states do not contravene its principles and standards on workers' rights.[9] Also, since the ILO actively intervened to resolve the union leadership crises, the country's recent labor situation provides additional avenues for evaluating the influence of the Organization over Ghanaian and by extension, African labor relations. In terms of the sheer number of standards ratified, Ghana has one of the best African records at the ILO. As of April, 1993, Ghana has ratified 45 Conventions, the last five in 1986.[10] The average ratification for the entire African region is 27 (ILO, 1991). The country is one of 13 African ILO members whose ratifications are above average. Further evidence can be provided to indicate Ghana's active participation in the ILO's activities and programs. In 1969, it hosted the Third ILO African Regional Conference (ILO, 1970) and in May, 1987, the Government of Ghana conducted with the ILO "A Tripartite Seminar on International Labor Standards" in Accra (the Ghanaian capital city).[11] In addition, in the last five years, several ILO advisers have visited the country to promote the ILO's standards dealing with issues such as collective bargaining.[12]

Since joining the ILO in 1957, Ghana has sought and received substantial technical aid (called technical cooperation) from the ILO in the areas of management development and training, workers' education, wage policy formulation (Ewusi, 1984; ILO, 1968; 1962) and legal advice for amending the country's labor legislation to meet ILO standards on workers' rights. Together with the United Nations' Development Program, the ILO is undertaking in Ghana a three-year (1992 - 1995) program to generate employment.[13] Besides, a significant number of Ghanaians have assumed leadership roles within the ILO. A. M. Issifu, a Ghana Trades Union Congress (TUC) Secretary-General (1972 - 1982), served on the Committee of Freedom of Association, and in 1985, Ghana was elected a government representative to the Governing Body (the executive organ of the ILO).[14] Furthermore, one of the three Deputies to the Director General of the ILO, Mary Chinery-Hesse, is a Ghanaian.[15] Thus Ghana has had close to four decades of experience (one of the longest in Africa) in dealing with the ILO's standards and other activities.

1. 4   Ghana's Unique Labor Relations

Ghanaian governments have in their policy pronouncements repeatedly emphasized the need for workers, led by the TUC, to make rapid national development a priority. Under Kwame Nkrumah, the first sub-Saharan African President, and the Convention People's Party (CPP), by 1965, Ghana had become one of the first nations to officially adopt "African Socialism" as a national ideology (Ninsin and Drah, 1987).[16] The Kwame Nkrumah era of 1951 to 1966 deserves special attention because of its long-term impact on not only Ghana but also the rest of Africa. In Ghana, as K. Shillington (1992: 4) has observed, "the foundations for Ghana's future development were laid during this period." Shillington (*Ibid.*) also captures the true essence of Ghana and Nkrumah's influence all over Africa:

> In those early years of independence Ghana was indeed the Black Star of Africa. Ghana's route to independence . . . set the trend for other aspirant African leaders to emulate . . . . Nkrumah was inspirational in the African struggle against the new economic imperialism which stretched far beyond the formal end of empire. His striving for economic self-reliance through some form of socialist central control of the economy laid the foundations for a new African economic order. Even those emergent African leaders who were philosophically firmly in the capitalist camp were influenced by Nkrumah and Ghana's apparent economic self-reliance. Kwame Nkrumah's interests stretched way beyond the confines of his own country, Ghana.

In the labor sphere, during Nkrumah's rule, attempts were made to convert labor unions into organs of the state with emphasis on their productionist roles — assisting national development by restraining excessive wages and the disruption of production (Friedland, 1968: 20). The agenda of the Nkrumah administration also included turning the country's labor relations (especially relations between the Ghana TUC and the CPP's industrialization program) and into models to be copied by other African nations.[17] Thus in the late 1970s, when the Federal Nigerian Military Government sought a new trade union structure to end excessive factionalism within the Nigerian labor movement, it turned its attention to Ghana's union structure erected through the 1958 and 1965 Industrial Relations Acts.[18]

The Ghanaian State and Labor

The socialist ideology of the Nkrumah government, coupled with the adoption of an import substitution industrialization strategy, has had profound repercussions on the role of the state in Ghana's labor relations. For example, in spite of past and recent policies to trim the size of public sector employment,[19] the state has remained the largest employer[20] because his socialist policies led to massive public expenditure on not only social infrastructure, but also commercial ventures like state-owned factories for consumer and capital goods. As the leading employer of wage labor, the state has developed a direct vested interest in the outcomes of labor unions' pure economic activities, such as collective bargaining. As noted earlier, the state is also highly sensitive politically to the protest actions of workers and their organizations, especially with regards to strikes. The point being emphasized is that because of the state's direct stake in labor relations, it has opted for policies that often include interfering in internal union affairs, such as union organizing, the structure of workers' associations and the selection of trade union leaders.[21]

Various Ghanaian governments have also sought to protect their interests in labor relations by using the coercive organs of the state — mostly the police — to control workers. For example, the military *cum* police administration of the National Liberation Council (NLC), which toppled the Nkrumah regime, did not hesitate to use the police to shoot striking mine workers in 1969 (Hutchful, 1987: 219 - 229). Intimidation and physical violence by the state were used to reinforce the cooptation of union leaders, especially those who in the views of governments had proved recalcitrant. Cooptation ploys included ensuring that favorites or persons personally connected to a particular government became national union leaders or using TUC leaders as "Personal Advisors to the Head of State" on national policy or political matters. The latter was aimed at insuring that the unions cooperated with governments in power. All these control mechanisms are employed allegedly to channel workers' activities into what, since colonial times, have been called "responsible trade unionism" and which since independence has been declared as speeding up national integration, industrialization and economic growth.[22] The argument offered in defense of the state's control of unions was that developing nations, particularly those in Africa, could least afford the alleged adverse economic consequences and the politically divisive tendencies and ideological struggles inherent in autonomous labor organizations.

In light of actual labor developments in Ghana, I view the examination of the roles of the Ghana TUC — the central labor federation — and the state as crucial to understanding fully the country's labor situation. I deal extensively in this study with the role of the state, not only because it has played, and continues to occupy, a central role in labor matters, but also due to the fact that the intensity of its involvement far exceeds what may be observed in western capitalist countries such as the United States or Britain. I also emphasize the significance of the Ghana TUC because it has virtually remained the exclusive representative of organized labor for both domestic and international labor affairs. It has, for example, represented Ghana's workers since the country joined the ILO in 1957. In addition, through government consultations, it has represented workers in deciding some major national policies. Finally and importantly, it has been the main target for labor control because of its conspicuous role as the single most important labor organization in the country. Thus, in this study both the TUC and the state are treated as critical labor relations actors.[23]

1. 5   Diversity and Similarity in African Labor Relations

Besides focusing on Ghana, I will whenever appropriate refer to the labor relations situations in other English-speaking African countries mainly Kenya, Nigeria and Zambia. The inclusion of these countries is to ensure that this study has practical policy utility beyond Ghana. C. Cambridge (1984: 130) aptly summarizes the advantages derived from the inclusion of other countries:

> The former colonies of Britain in subSaharan Africa provide us with a rich array of industrial relations practices that can shed some light on the questions raised by earlier studies. . . . When these countries became independent from Britain, the leaders in these societies were concerned with the development of industrial relations systems that would assist in the rapid economic development; of their countries. Moreover, these countries and the industrializing elites that ran them, attempted to fashion industrial relations systems that would be appropriate to their particular cultural and environmental circumstances.

All the four countries selected, like most African nations, have legislatively or administratively fashioned single national federations like the Ghana TUC, the Nigerian Labor Congress (NLC), the Kenyan Central Organization of Trade Unions (COTU) and the Zambia Congress of Trade Unions (ZCTU).[24] These federations have monopolized and dominated their respective countries' central labor organizations.[25] In addition, these federations have at times been restricted or banned from joining international labor federations like the eastern-bloc supported World Federation of Trade Unions (WFTU) and its western archrival, the International Confederation of Free Trade Unions (ICFTU).[26] In the case of Nigeria, for instance, Decree No. 35 of December, 1989, barred the NLC and its 42 industrial unions from affiliating with unions outside Nigeria with the exception of the Accra-based Organization of African Trade Union Unity (OATUU) and the trade union organization of the Economic Community of West African States. In the view of the ILO such a ban violated workers' rights.[27] The ILO is of the opinion that such restrictions deprive African unions of the benefits of international labor solidarity and material support from labor organizations such as the ICFTU and the WFTU.

Abundant evidence shows that there have also been significant variations, at least in the timing of policy responses, to the common labor problems identified in the countries selected. Cambridge (1984: 130) provided a valid assessment of the situation when he pointed out that: "while most of the former British colonies have a common denominator, a tradition of industrial relations practices inherited from Britain, the contemporary scene shows considerable divergence from this heritage." A comparison of Ghana, Nigeria, Kenya and Zambia's post-colonial labor situation in terms of chronological developments confirm Cambridge's view. For example, in Ghana, only a year after independence, a monopolized union structure, with the TUC at its apex and in close alliance with the CPP, was erected via the Industrial Relations Acts, 1958 (Panford, 1988). In the case of Zambia, on the other hand, overt attempts by the state to incorporate the unions with the ruling party were delayed until 1971 (Kalula, 1988). In Nigeria, the state's *laissez-faire* posture resulted in noninterference in union organizational structures until Decree No. 31 of 1973 was passed, and subsequently implemented by Decree No. 22 of 1978, which led to the establishment of the NLC as the sole federal labor center.[28] As noted by W. Ananaba (1979: 38) in the case of Kenya, although there was a long history of labor and political party collaboration in the struggle which culminated in independence in December, 1963, the government of Kenya did not move as quickly as, say, in Ghana or Tanzania to intervene in union structures and other internal matters. That changed in 1965 when presidential authority was used to found COTU as the sole labor federation.

There are also some substantial differences in the actual labor practices of the selected countries. In Ghana, beginning with the Industrial Relations Acts of 1958, and in the case of Zambia with the passage of the 1971 Industrial Relations Acts, compulsory collective bargaining became a national labor relations feature. While in Ghana, the laws do not expressly prohibit senior staff or management from joining the TUC, such a practice is discouraged in Nigeria (Kusi and Gyimah-Boakye, 1991). Also importantly, for the purposes of this study, the fact that both Ghana and Nigeria have ratified ILO Conventions Nos. 87 and 98; Kenya, only the latter and Zambia, none of the two, will permit me to distinguish in my assessment of the ILO's influence any differences between its impact on the countries which have ratified the two conventions and those which have not.

The inclusion of other countries will therefore permit an exhaustive description and analysis of their diverse labor experiences, which will in turn make it possible to offer alternative national labor policies and industrial relations practices to assist in finding solutions to the enormous labor and socioeconomic problems that are identified in this study. It may be appropriate to cite a few examples of the usefulness of other countries' labor experiences. During my fieldwork, I observed that before the mid-1980s, because the Zambian government promptly submitted to the appropriate authority standards adopted by the ILO, it did not have to contend with the problems other African members had with delays and the failure to conform to such an important ILO constitutional obligation.[29] Other African governments might learn from Zambia effective methods for complying with such an important membership requirement to enhance their participation in the Organization. Also the 1983 decision by the Zambian government to allow ZCTU to participate in International Monetary Fund (IMF) negotiations over the country's fiscal crisis (Lungu, 1986) offers a useful model for resolving a thorny contemporary labor issue — how African nations deal with IMF/World Bank terms of financial relief, including wage freezes and job cutbacks — without excessively antagonizing labor and generating more union-state conflicts. In this area, Zambia's experience might be particularly relevant to finding practical solutions to Ghana, Nigeria and Kenya's problems with meeting IMF-type conditionalities under their respective Economic Recovery and Structural Adjustment Programs.[30]

Key Issues

My choice of the topic for this study was influenced by G. Caire's (1977) survey of the relationship between workers' rights and socio-economic development. He concluded that workers' rights were not only compatible with, but also necessary for, sustained social progress. In this study, therefore, I am evaluating Caire's views on workers' rights by addressing two basic related issues in the Ghanaian context. These are:

1. An assessment of the influence of the ILO in the development and application of standards concerning workers' rights and the role of the Organization in limiting the restrictions governments place on unions, and
2. To identify and describe the results of past labor policies and practices by examining their impact on the ability of the Ghana TUC to protect its members' interests. By addressing these issues, I will attempt to contribute to filling a critical gap in the literature, which is the need to evaluate systematically the practical usefulness and relevance of the ILO's conventions in Ghana and other African countries.

1. 6   Practical Policy Implications

This section summarizes the major problems in the literature on the role of workers in development and how they have contributed to the failure of both labor and development policies in Africa. Two basic problems exist. First, no single study has focused exclusively on the topic. Second, the prevailing research is heavily value-laden, making it difficult to assess objectively the relationship between the exercise of workers' rights and economic growth in developing countries. There are also several additional shortcomings in the literature. No existing theory adequately describes and explains the precise relationship between labor union rights and economic growth (Fisher, 1963: 102). Instead of a coherent body of knowledge which may be treated as a theory, the topic is saddled with several contentious opinions and policy prescriptions without adequate empirical basis. Besides, the research is scattered in a disarray of several journal articles and other short publications or studies.[31]

Even though Caire (1977) dealt specifically with the two ILO Conventions (Nos. 87 and 98) which are the subjects of this study, he reviewed them in relation to socio-economic development in virtually all developing areas — Africa, Latin America and the Middle East. In another survey of ILO standards on workers' rights, J. A. Erstling (1977: 2) admitted that his "study describes the legal situation in the countries reviewed (all ILO members) and does not assess the practical application and the effects of the legislation." A third survey, Cambridge's (1984: 131) analysis of the ratification records of former British colonies of Africa, revealed more fundamental deficiency in the existing research. He equated the mere ratification of standards with total compliance with ILO norms: "The ratification of ILO Conventions by an English-speaking African state is a *prima facie* evidence of that country's commitment to certain international labor standards." As will be shown in this book, however, the ratification of a standard may not always be equated with full implementation. Cambridge also shares with other authors a research deficiency common in the literature — not thoroughly assessing the relationship between the ratification of standards and actual policies and practices or the broader socio-economic and historical contexts required for a fuller understanding of such a complex subject.[32]

In addition to the problems alluded to, there is profound disagreement between the two opposing groups of authors which have emerged around the subject. The first, represented by A. Mehta (1957), K. de Schweinitz (1959) and A. Lewis (1957), opposed the granting of full union liberties on the grounds that they would inhibit economic growth and industrialization. The second (as noted above, a minority) comprises supporters of workers' rights, including P. Fisher (1961) and Caire (1977), who argued that unions do not only perform important economic functions, but also fulfill necessary socio-political roles in democratic societies. They, therefore, endorsed government encouragement of unionization. Before the practical policy implications of each opposing view are examined I will present briefly a characterization of each view by selecting a representative author.

The Productionist View of Unions workers' right

Mehta's (1957) work, which was on Asia, proposed a role for unions in new nations that was radically different from their role in western capitalist nations. He argued that unions in developing nations should be deterred from engaging in voluntary collective bargaining and similar activities aimed at winning economic gains for their members because such economic claims would obstruct economic growth. He contended that because developing societies lack high rates of economic growth, unions should be made to subordinate their occupational interests, especially wage gains, to national development objectives. He also called for severe restrictions to be imposed on strikes because they could disrupt industrialization and, hence, economic growth. In addition, he argued that wage claims by unions would discourage investments by increasing labor costs, reducing entrepreneurs' profits and, therefore, slow down the rate of capital formation.[33] His basic premises here were that industrialization was the only correct path to economic growth and rapid capital accumulation was the *sine qua non* for successful industrialization.

Fisher (1963: 105, 144) explains the major implications of the views of Mehta and his associates. According to him, their policy prescriptions for solving the problems of economic growth meant that developing nations in Asia and Africa had to devote at least 12 to 18 percent of their gross national product (GNP) to capital formation to ensure self-sustaining growth. With such ambitious rates of investment, the need for suppressing unions seemed to have been made more urgent by the opponents of free trade unions. Commenting on the debates on the role of unions, Fisher (1963: 109) added:

> Our understanding has. . . . progressed. More than a decade of observation and experience revealed that capital is not the only strategic factor affecting the rate of economic progress. . . . the rate of economic development; itself has been found dependent upon men, their skills and their institutions. . . . economic development cannot proceed without favorable economic, social and political climate.

Fisher's observation leads to the problems connected with the assumptions of writers who advocate tight control of workers and their organizations. From both practical and theoretical standpoints, Mehta and his associates erred by emphasizing exclusively rates of capital accumulation.

As A. Cairncross (Caire, 1977: 124) concluded, capital alone cannot guarantee and maintain efficient industrialization. Cairncross' view is supported by B. Callaway and E. Card's (1971: 83) explanation of why Ghana, for example, has failed to industrialize. Among the problems they listed were factories being idle due to lack of raw materials caused by scarce foreign exchange, which in turn was partially due to unprofitable state owned enterprises. I might add the unreliable revenues from the sale of primary African exports. I may thus observe that Mehta, Schweinitz and Lewis seemed to have discarded a basic economic axiom that labor is only one of numerous factors of production and, hence, successful industrialization programs. Fisher and Cairncross have noted other factors that act as crucial milieus for successful industrial growth — political stability, appropriate technology and industrial organization, and efficient human resource utilization. Thus, the causes of successful industrial programs are more complex than the simple view that strict labor control leading to a dampening of labor demands, especially wages, will spur rapid industrialization. Finally, I may add that any analysis that hinges on the assumption that labor control *per se* will ensure rapid industrialization will not reflect or capture the true role of labor in socio-economic development.

There are more unproven and erroneous assumptions associated with the position of the advocates of union control. Although not made explicit, these authors assume that all forms of industrial conflicts are inherently dysfunctional. An example of the practical adverse effect of such an assumption is T.

M. Yesufu's (1968) recommendation to the Nigerian government to stamp out all forms of workers' protests, including strikes. This kind of policy recommendation is underpinned by the incorrect assumption that all strikes are motivated by the unadulterated selfishness of organized labor. But as information from the Ghana Labor Department indicates, some strikes have been caused by workers' genuine desire and demands that incompetent and corrupt managers in state-owned enterprises be dismissed. As shown in Table I, workers have struck in Ghana for reasons which cannot be attributed solely to their "strike-prone nature." These include management's failure to pay government-approved minimum wages and fringe benefits such as canteen (cafeteria) and transportation allowances.[34]

Authors who oppose workers' rights to voice their discontent also neglect a basic fact of industrial relations: There are differences between the interests of workers and managers/state and that other than suppressing unions, there are alternative means, including institutionalized dispute settlement, through which industrial conflict may be managed more efficiently (Roberts, 1964: Nwubueze, 1975, 1981; Kerr et al., 1955).

The advocates of restrictions on workers additionally fail to incorporate in their analyses the crucial consequences of, for example, the chronic economic planning problems in past economic efforts. A perennial problem is the shortage of reliable data/information for planning purposes.[35] The absence of such critical inputs for economic planning is a common phenomenon in Africa. A typical example can be found in Nigeria, where it has remained difficult to compute the national popuation.[36] Even granting that the economic planning process per se has been efficient, the implementation process has not because of disruptions caused largely by political instablitiy. Most development plans in both Ghana and Nigeria never reached full term because military interventions led to their abandonment. Even when plans were not abandoned, their exceedingly ambitious economic growth targets of over five percent per annum were never achieved.

More evidence demonstrates that wage claims and strikes are not to blame for Africa's socio-economic problems. Factors such as inadequate feasibility studies for expensive commercial projects; excessive political interference and management incompetence and/or corruption may also have led to unsuccessful industrialization and economic planning in Africa (Ewusi, 1976; Calloway and Card, 1971). Three failed Ghanaian state-owned corporations will support my point. Within a short span of 27 months of operation, the State Farms incurred a loss of $17.3 million (Levine, 1975: 102) due largely to embezzlement and large scale underemployment of workers. Recently, both the Ghana Airways and State Fishing Corporations have resorted to using expatriate management services because of inefficient management.[37]

Table I
Major Causes of Strikes in Ghana

Demand for:

1. Arrears of pay approved by the government and management
2. Overtime allowance, current or overdue
3. Review of expired collective agreements
4. Delayed approved bonuses
5. Payment of government sanctioned minimum wages
6. Government approved housing allowance
7. The implementation of existing collective agreements
8. Food subsidies
9. Improved working conditions such as safety
10. Tax exemption on overtime wages
11. Transport subsidy
* 12. The removal of corrupt/incompetent management

Source: Ghana Department of Labor, 1987.

*Workers in publicly owned companies demand efficient and honest management on the grounds that as taxpayers, they have the right to ensure that state owned enterprises are managed properly.

On a practical level, since the opponents of workers' rights propose policies which have serious implications for workers' role in African societies, one cannot treat their views lightly. Important policy dilemmas are left unresolved. For example, who will determine if sufficient economic growth has been accomplished to permit union autonomy in the future? Is it government, employers or other sections of society? If labor control is necessary for successful industrialization, who benefits from the fruits of the process? And last, but not least, if unions are currently perceived as immature, irresponsible or irrational, how do they become socially responsible if they are not permitted to operate to attain maturity since practice makes perfect? Furthermore, there is the hidden assumptions that by excluding workers from participation in national policies the state can unilaterally solve all problems and single-handedly determine the best path to social progress. These questions have grave practical consequences and therefore need to be addressed. C. Kerr, *et al.* (1955: 234) provide additional bases for my rejection of the assumptions, views and policy prescriptions of the opponents of union rights. They successfully indict the antagonists of union autonomy by pointing out that their analyses do not meet basic research criteria for handling complex issues such as the relationships between union freedoms and socio-economic development. Their arguments were narrowly focused and, thus, too limited in the explanation of the "need" for labor control. Kerr (1955: 234) and his colleagues provide the essentials for an appropriate theoretical framework and how researches may enhance their contributions to the topic:

> Labour economists, and indeed social scientists in general, must become
> more conscious of the variety of experiences and the range of factors shaping
> the labour problems in the course of industrialization if they are to play a part
> in developing understanding as basis for policy. The framework of analysis
> must be expanded to comprehend a wider range of factors operative in the
> industrialization process if social scientists are to make useful contributions
> to the labour problems of our times.

A theoretical framework — one that satisfies most of the conditions stipulated
by Kerr, *et al.* — is provided by Caire's (1977) study of the relationship
among workers' rights, industrialization and socio-economic development.
An additional strength of his survey is the employment of an interdisciplinary
perspective:

> . . . . a study of this subject must look beyond legal problems of freedom of
> association or the economic aspect of development. Instead, a conscious ef-
> fort must be made to maintain an interdisciplinary approach so as to overlook
> none of the political considerations or ideological aims that may be involved,
> nor the institutional peculiarities of the countries concerned, nor even the
> philosophical overtones of a subject in relation to which the clash of systems
> of values is sometimes decisive. In other words the interdisciplinary nature
> of this study should be precisely that which colours industrial relations,
> which have been described as "a crossroads where a number of disciplines
> have met — history, economics, government, sociology, psychology and
> law. . . ." (Caire, 1977: 11).

As I have noted, because Caire's work was a survey, he did not analyze any
particular country's labor legislation, practices and situation. To compensate
for this delimitation, I am using the case of Ghana, supplemented with materials from other African nations, to study the influence of the two ILO
Conventions I have selected. My approach will allow a thorough examination
of the major complex contextual factors for labor relations and workers' rights
as suggested by Kerr, *et al.* I also employ the interdisciplinary approach Caire
has recommended to shed more light on why several African governments
have difficulties in fulfilling ILO standards which they have voluntarily
agreed to uphold (through the ratification of Conventions and membership of
the ILO) by granting workers their right to form unions and to bargain for
conditions of employment voluntarily and to strike to back their claims without fear of reprisals from the state or employers.

1. 7   Methodology and Sources

This section provides a summary description of the methods used to collect data and other information for this book. The location of key documents
such as various African labor statutes is provided to facilitate the work of re-
searchers working on this topic. I used a multi-research methodology in my
data and information collection to accomplish two objectives:

1. To illuminate the complex socio-historical and economic events which culminated in the enactment of labor statutes and policies which contravene ILO standards and principles and which may also diverge from typical industrial capitalist labor practices, and
2. To assess critically the procedures employed by the ILO in its attempts to make African labor policies, laws and actual practices conform to the ideals and principles embodied in the Organization's Constitution and the two labor standards selected for this study — Convention Nos. 87 and 98.

The research techniques I employed were:

1. In-depth interviews;
2. Open-ended questionnaires (See Appendices 4 and 5);
3. Participant observation; and
4. Content analyses of both primary documents and published materials from African governments and labor organizations and the ILO.

The field work for this study was done in two phases. The first part which was at the ILO's Head Offices in Geneva, Switzerland, from July, 1985 to July, 1986, provided insights into the organizational behavior and processes within the ILO itself. In the International Labor Standards Department (called *NORMES*, in French) where I was employed, I concentrated on the evolution, application and supervision of standards. From key members of this department — Department Heads and Advisers responsible for the African Region — I learned first hand how the ILO sought to accomplish the complex task of the global protection of workers and their organizations. Working in Geneva provided me with valuable access to most Geneva-based ILO and European human rights and diplomatic activities. I interviewed African government officials such as Ambassadors, Heads of Chanceries, Labor Attachés and Labor Department senior personnel responsible for ILO matters. I also met frequently one-on-one with African labor leaders (including Secretaries-General of the Zambian Labor Federation and Ghana's TUC and Labor Advisers on the ILO and other international relations) who were in Geneva for conferences and other international labor activities. Typically the interviews and discussions with my respondents who stayed in or close to Geneva lasted over an hour and a half.

My sources yielded information, data and unpublished documents on trade unions and government activities connected to the ILO. Both the professional experience and personal insights of my respondents were of tremendous value in my analysis of the difficulties African states face in meeting ILO membership obligations. For example, labor department officials gave me their assessment of the ILO's standards supervising system and made suggestions which contributed to my recommended policies for improving workers' rights and labor administration in Africa.

To observe first hand organizational behavior within the ILO — for example how standards were created, adopted or supervised — I attended meetings of key ILO organs such as the Governing Body (the executive branch of the Organization) and the June 1986 International Labor Conference (the equivalent of a UN General Assembly). I observed and recorded the proceedings of these bodies as they unfolded, in their natural setting. My job assignments, which involved reviews of the ratification records of member states, informed me about the ratification status of the countries picked for this study. At the ILO, I also did content analyses of critical primary documents. These included the Constitution of the Organization, case materials and decisions of major standards supervising bodies such as the Committee of Freedom of Association's and the Committee of Experts' published and unpublished comments on member states' performance *vis-à-vis* ratified standards and internal operating documents used to assess member states' compliance with standards at the Organization's head office. In order to fully understand my selected countries' involvement at the ILO, I also focused intensely on original documents, especially correspondence between the Organization and my chosen countries concerning Convention Nos. 87 and 98. I, for example, studied Ghana's replies to the ILO's inquiries about why its labor laws were not in total harmony with the provisions of the two Conventions it had ratified. In the case of Zambia, I was interested in why it has not ratified any of the two international labor instruments selected for this book. My review of the correspondence and national reports helped me to develop a more in-depth perception of the genuine administrative or technical hurdles African countries need to overcome to meet ILO requirements and the sheer excuses or pretexts used to divert attention from failure to meet membership obligations.

To remedy a deficiency in African labor relations research methodology — the scant use of original data sources such as records of the deliberations of the legislature in passing labor laws and the examination of actual contents of labor statutes, case law and administrative decisions — I procured from the Ghana Labor Department and the University of Ghana Libraries in Accra copies of Ghanaian Parliamentary Hansards dealing with the adoption of the Industrial Relations Acts of 1958, which was superceded by the Act of 1965, and their subsequent amendments.[38] The National Assembly records were used to determine the nature of the debates that preceded the adoption of the key labor legislation. These debates were useful in indicating the official Ghana government position on the need to adopt new or amend existing labor legislation. They were helpful in understanding the major historical, economic and political circumstances that accounted for changes in the laws. In analyzing these official Parliamentary records a critical issue I pursued was the extent to which the ILO influenced or was mentioned as being responsible for the promulgation of labor statutes in Ghana. Their contents in addition revealed the precise legal restrictions Ghanaian governments imposed on unions.

The second part of my field work was completed in Ghana in the summer and fall of 1991. I collected materials to complement my research at the ILO and interviewed Ghanaian politicians, labor and government officials, especially those who were the architects of the country's labor policies, laws and trade union structures. These respondents, including former ministers in the Nkrumah administration, used their intimate knowledge and active involvement in Ghana's labor and international affairs to shed light on the polemical and politically sensitive issues raised in this study.

Because the majority of these politicians have retired from active politics they did not feel inhibited to go on record about their views on the origins of Ghana's labor laws, industrialization strategies and policies which although adopted several decades ago, still impact on workers' rights and the relations between the Government of Ghana and the TUC. By going on record, these politicians and the pioneers of modern Ghanaian trade unionism may be contributing to the eradication of certain persistent erroneous views in the relevant literature that, for example, the Nkrumah-led CPP unilaterally imposed severe restrictions on workers rights via the new union structure that was created as a result of the 1958 Industrial Relations Acts. Both the labor and party leaders I interviewed revealed to the contrary that the 1958 Act was in fact initiated by the Ghana TUC. This revelation has serious implications for the research on the evolution of workers' rights and workers' role in the Ghanaian society.[39]

NOTES

1.   B. A. Bentum (1967), a former Ghanaian labor leader, defined union autonomy as the ability of unions to control their internal activities, especially in the election of leaders and being free from government interference.

2.   The ILO was founded in 1919 and became a UN Specialized Agency in 1945 (Swepston, 1984).

3.   Ghana joined the ILO in May, 1957 through a letter to the ILO's Director-General by Kwame Nkrumah, the then Prime Minister, and ratified Convention Nos. 87 and 98 on June 2, 1965 and July 2, 1959, respectively. Article 22 of the ILO's Constitution (1988: 17) requires all countries to report to the Organization their application of ratified Conventions. See Appendix 1.

4.   See Appendices 2 and 3 for texts of two Conventions.

5.   Although Zambia has not ratified these two Conventions, in 1981, the ILO initiated investigations into the government's alleged violation of union rights by detaining four union leaders. The investigations were terminated when, upon the orders of the High Court of Zambia, the leaders were released (Kalula, 1985). Again in 1990, Case No. 1575, alleging infringement of trade union rights, was filed at the ILO against the Government of Zambia for the passage of a new Industrial Relations Act, 1990, that replaced the 1971 Act. According to the ILO, in the Government's communication of May 7, 1993, the Zambian Parliament had amended the 1990 Act and was awaiting presidential action.

6.   In its communication of March 20, 1990, the Ghana Labor Department informed me that the laws of Ghana do not outrightly prohibit strikes. But for strikes to be legal, workers have to exhaust a lengthy dispute settlement process.

7.   The workers were granted presidential pardons in 1990 and subsequently permitted to be reemployed in the government sector. "President Gives Pardon," *West Africa*, Nov. 19 - 25, 1990: 2871.

8.   "Industrial Action Banned" and "Teachers at it Again," *West Africa*, May 17 - 23, 1993: 819 and 829.

9.   Details of this and other cases may be found in ILO (1985a).

10.   Ghana ratified these five Conventions through a letter dated May 22, 1986 from the Provisional National Defense Council's (PNDC) Secretary (Minister) for Labor and Social Welfare to the Director-General of the ILO.

11.   ILO, International Labor Standards Department, *Mission Report*, Ghana, May 3 - 10, 1987; *West Africa*, June 6, 1987.

12.   Kusi and Gyimah-Boakye (1991).

13.   Information from the Ghana Labor Department, Dec. 9, 1992.

14.   Communication received from the International Labor Standards Department. I observed Ghana representing ILO member states at Governing Body meetings between July, 1985 and July, 1986.

15.   ILO "Staff List," ILO, Washington Branch Office, dated March 12, 1993.

16.   On the origins and nature of African socialism, see Friedland and Rosberg (1964).

17.   During my research and employment at the International Labor Organization's (ILO) Head Offices in Geneva (1985 to 1986) several African and Third World labor leaders expressed their admiration for the Ghana TUC. Respondents described the TUC as one of the best worker organizations in developing countries.

18.   The Adebo Commission of Nigeria prescribed to the Nigerian government the adoption of a trade union structure similar to Ghana's as the solution to the chronic problems of lack of unity within Nigeria's labor movement (Panford, 1988).

19.   On at least three occasions, Ghana governments have retrenched public sector employment. The first massive cutbacks occurred between 1966 and 1969, when over 60,000 jobs were lost (Hutchful, 1987; Agyeman-Badu and Osei-Hwedie, 1982: 21); the second was implemented between 1969 to 1971; and the third is the result of the IMF- and World Bank-inspired Economic Recovery Program (ERP), which has been implemented since 1983. Under a Structural Adjustment Policy adopted in 1986, the public sector job retrenchment continued.

20.   The Ghana government employs at least 50 percent of the country's wage-earning work force (Ewusi, 1984; Kraus, 1979). Government employment peaked in 1965 - 1966 when it exceeded 71 percent (Arthiabah, 1985: 6). In Nigeria, nearly two-thirds of wage labor is in government employment (Damachi and Fashoyin, 1989: 319).

21.   As shown in subsequent chapters, the 1958 Industrial Relations Act of Ghana was partly aimed at regulating the country's entire labor movement by designating the TUC as the sole legally recognized federation. The union structure that developed facilitated the CPP's control of unions affiliated with the TUC.

22.   Similar arguments were used by political leaders to justify the proliferation of monolithic political structures, such as the one-party systems which banned plurality in political organization in some African countries from the mid-1960s to the late 1980s.

23.   Ghanaian private employers (for example, the Ghana Employers' Association and the Chamber of Commerce and Mines) are excluded because they had little direct input into the creation of the relevant labor statutes. The Ghana Employers' Association was founded one year after the passage of the 1958 Act. Employer groups which were mostly foreign were not permitted to influence post-independence labor legislation, largely because the TUC and its allies in the Kwame Nkrumah government used the laws to improve workers' bargaining position *vis-à-vis* employers. Information from interviews with Ako Adjei, Ghana's first Minister for Labor, John K. Tettegah and Joe-Fio Meyer, the premier Ghana TUC Secretary-

General and Chair of the Executive Board respectively. Accra, Ghana, summer and fall 1991. See also Sawyerr (1978) and Ghana Labor Department (1961).

24.   Although before its ouster, the Kenneth Kaunda administration passed a new Industrial Relations Act, 1990, ZCTU was allowed to retain its status as Zambia's sole labor federation. See Zambia, Industrial Relations Act (No. 36), 1990, dated Jan. 23, 1991, Part III, Section 28. Unless otherwise noted, copies of all labor statutes cited may be obtained from the ILO's Head Offices, Geneva, Switzerland or the Washington, DC Branch Office.

25.   Union monopolies exist *de facto* and *de jure* where single labor organizations represent exclusively and permanently a class of workers (Erstling, 1977).

26.   Ghana is one of the few African countries whose labor laws are silent on the right of workers to affiliate internationally. However, I observed during my field work in Geneva that members of the TUC were active in organizations like the ICFTU's International Trade Secretariats, such as the Public Service International and the International Woodworkers' Association.

27.   International labor affiliation was a politically sensitive issue during the Cold War because it involved attempts by several African nations to insulate their domestic labor relations from East-West tensions (Ananaba, 1979). T. Fashoyin (1981) also argues that in the view of African governments, trade unions' international affiliation could compromise their nonaligned positions in world politics. As recent as 1990, Case No. 1530 was filed against the Nigerian government at the ILO for barring international trade union affiliation via Decree No. 35, 1989. The ban was rescinded by Decree No. 32 of 1991. ("Ban Lifted," *West Africa*, Aug. 19 - 25, 1991: 1380 - 1381). Similarly in Kenya, the Presidential Declaration of 1965 that led to the birth of COTU outlawed international trade union affiliation (Amsden, 1971). The ILO has repeatedly emphasized to African states the need to amend their laws to permit international affiliation on a permanent basis. At its Fourth Quadriennal Congress, the Ghana TUC resolved to affiliate formally with the ICFTU (Report of the Resolutions Committee, Fourth Quadriennal Congress, TUC, Cape Coast, August 26 - 29, 1992: 5). In its proposals on amendments to Ghana's labor laws of April 7, 1993, submitted to the Ghana National Labor Advisory Committee, the TUC endorsed the right of labor to join international organizations.

28.   According to Fashoyin, the implementation of Decree No. 31 of 1973 was delayed until the passage of Decree No. 22 of 1978, which led to the actual restructuring of the Nigerian labor federations. Personal discussions, New York, Dec. 1988 and correspondence dated March 29, 1989.

29.   Article 19 of the ILO's *Constitution* (1988) requires members to submit to their competent authorities (for example, Parliaments or National Assemblies) instruments adopted by the International Labor Conference. See Appendix 1.

30.   Heightened tensions between the TUC and the Nigerian Labor Congress and their respective public authorities may be largely attributed to attempts by the governments to impose austere economic measures, including layoffs of public sector employees and wage freezes. In Nigeria, for example, the military government's efforts to reduce the national budget have led to withdrawal of subsidies on gasoline, which has sparked worker and student demonstrations, which in turn have aggravated relations between the unions and the government. On new labor tensions in Ghana, see Panford (forthcoming, 1994) and on Nigeria's problems, see Bangura and Beckman (1991).

31.   Exceptions are Caire (1977), Erstling (1977) and Ben-Israel (1988). These surveys, however, did not study actual labor practices and their effects in a particular country or region. Even in its own study of its influence on Nigerian legislation, the ILO admitted that it did not "attempt to analyze the whole Nigerian labor legislation ....

Nor is any detailed assessment made of the practical impact of the legislation concerned" (ILO, 1960: 26; 41).

32.   Cf. Zeytinoglu (1986) and Cambridge (1984).

33.   Similar arguments were made by African employers and government representatives as recent as 1982 (ILO, 1983b).

34.   In Nigeria, salary arrears of more than two years resulted in lawsuits by employees of the Project Development Institute and the Railway Corporation. In the latter case, a court ordered the payment of back salaries from January, 1988 to December, 1991 (*West Africa*, April 20 - 26, 1992: 683 and March 25 - 31, 1991: 448).

35.   Others identified by African labor, government and employer representatives were: declining export revenues, expensive oil imports for nonoil producers, and since the early 1970s, severe world recessions (ILO, 1988: 7). G. Mutahaba (1982: 38) adds the neglect of the strategic importance of labor or human resources management in Africa.

36.   *West Africa*, Oct. 1985: 2097.

37.   T. Cooke, "Aerial Mismanagement, "*West Africa*, Oct. 12, 1987: 2013 - 2014; B. Ephson, "Fishing for Investment," *West Africa,* Aug. 29 - Sept. 4, 1988: 1571.

38.   Copies of Ghanaian statutes are available at the University of Ghana Balme and Law School Libraries, Accra, and the ILO's Head Offices, Geneva, Switzerland and the Washington, D C Branch Office.

39.   It additionally raises policy dilemmas for the ILO and the supporters of free trade unionism in not only Ghana, but also in the other countries selected for this study. These dilemmas are treated with respect to Ghana and Nigeria in Panford (1988).

Chapter 2

African Labor Relations in the Context of International Workers' Rights: The Setting (Background Information on Ghana and the ILO)

2. 1   Inside the ILO: The Evolution of International Workers' Rights

The Functions of the ILO

This section is an overview of the major functions of the ILO, with emphasis on the process for creating standards on worker's rights to freedom of association and collective bargaining, as a prelude to understanding how it has attempted to influence its member states, including Ghana, to incorporate the standards into their domestic labor relations practices and laws. The ILO was founded in 1919 as part of the defunct League of Nations. It became a United Nations (UN) Specialized Agency, that is, with financial autonomy in 1945 (Swepston, 1984).[1] As of 1992 the ILO had 160 members, a third of whom were independent African nations. Its jurisdiction within the UN is the improvement and regulation of national labor conditions through the adoption of international standards and technical cooperation (ILO, 1984). Technical cooperation refers to the material and financial aid the ILO provides to member governments through bilateral and multilateral aid programs.[2] These are often related to standards, but may also at times be connected to other development projects aimed at, for example, employment creation.

The two related objectives of the Organization are the engendering of humane working environments and the promotion of social justice. Thus, the ILO rejects the notion that labor is a pure form of commodity and emphasizes a social, as opposed to a highly economistic treatment, of labor (that is, it is not an ordinary factor or input of production). The work of the ILO can be grouped into three interconnected functional areas:

1. The creation of a body of international labor instruments that deals with issues like workers' rights;
2. International technical cooperation involving, but not limited to, joint efforts with other countries or international development agencies like the United Nations'

Development Program (UNDP) and the World Bank, to launch programs aimed at
improving socio-economic conditions in member states; and
3.   Research, publications and other media such as seminars, conferences and
symposia dealing with issues that fall within its areas of competence (ILO,
1984).[3]

Technical cooperation and research activities are perceived as means to
achieving the Organization's primary aims — the adoption and promotion of
labor standards to ensure social justice. Through its standards which are supplemented with technical services, it seeks to create both ideal and practical
labor policy guidelines for its members. Thus, the policy formulation of
international labor instruments may be correctly described as the
Organization's primary function since its inception.[4]

In the last 70 years, the ILO has created a substantial code of labor standards, rules of law and practices dealing with the application of these standards, especially those on workers' rights and the adjudication of disputes
over their practical implementation. Several international labor law commentators acknowledged that the Organization has remained a pioneer in developing standards which are fairly well recognized in a highly contentious field —
the international regulation of national labor relations and workers' rights
(Tikriti, 1982; Alcock, 1971; Osieke, 1976; Shotwell, 1934; Valticos, 1984).
Officials of the ILO will not describe it as "a supranational judicial organ,"[5]
but it has in many respects been relatively successful in creating a body of
principles and practices which lay down legal rules and procedures for settling
international labor questions that are often accepted by most countries
(Shotwell, 1934: 12). Thus, although its founders never intended it to acquire
a judicial character, it has in practice become a quasi-judicial body, responsible for international labor issues. Tikriti's observations on the nature of the
ILO support the characterization of the ILO as a pseudo-judicial body:

> The unplanned and unexpected became the organ for the protection of trade
> union rights and built up a body of international trade union judgments that
> may prove to be of pioneer importance in the quasi-judicial process of a body
> of accepted international doctrine of crucial social and industrial issues,
> which profoundly influence legal developments in many countries and may
> at some stage, harden into customary international law (Tikriti, 1982: 311).

Conventions and Recommendations

The ILO's comprehensive standards number over 350 separate instruments contained in 173 Conventions and 180 Recommendations dealing with
complex issues ranging from workers' rights to form unions and to voluntarily
negotiate with employers to determine conditions of employment; labor mi-
gration; occupational safety and health, unemployment and personnel training;
social security; hours of work to minimum wages and labor administration.[6]
As of June, 1992, the total ratifications for all conventions was 5,622.[7]

The Organization's standards supervisory bodies have developed a substantial case law dealing with workers' rights concerning issues like the cir-

cumstances under which workers may legally strike or protest against government policies.[8]   The Committee of Freedom of Association of the Governing Body has accumulated 1,710 cases of alleged government and employer infringements of workers' rights to free trade unionism, to collective bargaining and to strike.[9]

The large code of labor principles and guidelines is incorporated into Conventions and Recommendations. The latter, as the name denotes, are not ratified and, thus are nonbinding. They are used as guidelines or ideal conditions, which member states are encouraged to aspire to in their labor policies. Conventions, on the other hand, upon ratification, possess some legal force which binds ratifiers to conform to them according to the practices of the ILO. Hence by ratifying both Convention Nos. 87 and 98, the Ghana government has undertaken to allow the ILO periodically, or as the situation may require, to examine its domestic labor laws and practices to assess their conformity with the standards laid out in the two Conventions.[10] As an ILO member, under Article 22 of the Organization's Constitution, Ghana is legally obligated to report on its labor practices and laws as requested by, say, the Committee of Experts.[11] If, Ghana was not satisfied or disagreed with the findings and recommendations of any of the ILO's bodies, the government could as the last resort seek redress from the International Court of Justice — the World Court, as it is popularly known (ILO, 1986: 9; 1984).

In terms of international legal norms and practices, an important consequence of the ratification of Conventions is that member states surrender part of their national sovereignty to the ILO to allow it to examine their laws and practices connected to the relevant Conventions (Alcock, 1971: 260). This is especially the case when a member violates an instrument it has voluntarily ratified and, therefore is committed to uphold. Under such a circumstance, the member is expected to consent to its internal labor affairs being examined by "outsiders" — ILO officials (such as the Director-General or his representatives such as senior employees of the International Labor Standards Department) and government, worker and employer representatives from other countries. Thus, for example, a Zambian worker member of the Committee of Freedom of Association will be part of a group of individuals who will probe, say, Ghana's alleged violation of the TUC's rights to operate freely. One of the strengths of the supervisory system is that by having nonnationals investigate violations, the fear of government reprisals does not prevent the Organization from drawing attention to government violations. Members of supervisory bodies whose countries are involved in cases are excused and replaced by substitute members. This is a typical practice by the Committee of Freedom of Association (ILO, 1984). Hence reliance on internationally composed committees allows the ILO to reduce the danger of committee members being intimidated by a particular government.

Classes of Conventions

There are several classifications of ILO standards, but for the purposes of this study, only two will be identified: technical/administrative and human rights instruments. The first group of standards deals with public policies and regulations pertaining to specific working conditions. Examples include Conventions on employment and training, labor administration, the collection of labor statistics, and the fixing of minimum wages and hours of work. The second set, as its name suggests, are instruments designed to define and promote acceptable guidelines for the free exercise of workers' and other civil rights (ILO, 1985). Examples are the two Conventions selected for this study (Nos. 87 and 98). Others deal with issues such as forced labor and discriminatory employment practices.

The significance of human rights Conventions and the controversies surrounding them stem from their close relationship to the human rights conditions in member countries (ILO, 1969). Thus, in supervising these standards, the ILO has had to go beyond the traditional confines of labor relations. A case for illustrating this point is that of allegations that the Ghana government had not provided trade union rights including the safety of TUC leaders during the 1982 - 1985 leadership crises (see Chapter 5 and Case No. 1135 of the Committee of Freedom of Association, ILO, 1985). The ILO urged the government to generate a national civil rights situation within which the safety of TUC leaders would be assured. The Committee on Freedom of Association emphasized to the Ghana government its responsibility for maintaining law and order to prevent government security agencies or any group in the society from intimidating trade unionists. In a more current case against Malawi (Case No. 1638) the ILO was of the opinion that the government should engender conditions in which the civil rights of workers including due process rights like access to attorneys during detention and the right to speedy trials in courts of law are respected.[12]

Within the ILO, the two Conventions selected for this study, together with other human rights standards, have attained special status. The two Conventions were often referred to as the "pillars" of the Organization.[13] The handling of these two instruments by ILO employees is deeply influenced by views expressed by delegates to the International Labor Conference of 1948, who affirmed during preparatory work on Convention No. 87 that:

> Freedom of Association constituted a universal and indivisible principle. While certain instruments, for example, social insurance or regulations concerning hours of work, could be introduced gradually in a country, this was not possible in the case of freedom of association.[14]

Thus, the position within the ILO is that the two Conventions embody not only indivisible, but also inalienable workers' and trade union rights, which should be applied without any exceptions to all nations. They are accorded privileged treatment because the general perception in the Organization is that without workers' rights, tripartism — a prerequisite for the survival of the ILO — will be inoperative.[15] The view, for example, is that if workers were not free to associate, they would not be able to meaningfully participate in domestic and international labor activities. The two Conventions are, therefore, specifically aimed at providing safeguards against state or employer encroachments upon workers' rights. Thus Convention No. 87 established the fundamental principles of workers' rights and Convention No. 98 was designed to yield specific practical modalities for concretely accomplishing the social ideals contained in the former (Alcock, 1971: 258).[16]

The Structure of the ILO's Standards Supervisory System

Before turning to how the ILO supervises its instruments, I will briefly describe the structure of its supervisory organs. There are three key bodies:

1. The International Labor Conference,
2. The Governing Body and
3. The International Labor Office (the Office or Head Office).

The International Labor Conference (the Conference or ILC) is the supreme legislative and policy-making unit. It is comprised of representatives of all the 160 governments and their nongovernmental counterparts from labor organizations and employers' associations. It is responsible for adopting the texts of all Conventions and Recommendations and sets the goals of the entire Organization. The Governing Body (which is similar to the Security Council at the UN) is the executive branch in charge of translating the broad policies set by the International Labor Conference into concrete programs and activities. The Governing Body is composed of representatives of all the three major labor relations actors — governments, capital and organized labor. Whereas the Conference meets annually (in June), the Governing Body is convened three times a year. It acts as the liaison between the International Labor Conference and the Office. The Office ("the Bureau" in French) which is the main secretariat headed by a Director-General is responsible for servicing the key bodies and their committees. It is staffed by several international civil servants. The International Labor Standards Department ("NORMES," as it is known in French) and its three branches — Applications, Freedom of Association and Legislative Series — are responsible for administratively assisting the Organization in adopting, implementing, promoting and supervising standards.[17] All the organs, committees and employees of the ILO are expected to be guided in their actions and deliberations by the Constitution (of the Organization) and the Declaration of Philadelphia, 1944 (Alcock, 1971). Thus, for example, officials of the International Labor Standards Department are required to demonstrate allegiance to the Constitution and the organs and committees they serve when they assist in the adoption and supervision of standards in member countries.

The ILO and International Tripartism

A special feature of the ILO's mode of operation and structure is tripartism at the international level. It is the only international organization that practices tripartism which is the cooperation of governments, employers and workers. It means that both in practice and in principle, "Governments, work-

ers and employers share in making the decisions and shaping its policies"
(Shafritz, 1980: 156). Constitutional provisions and practices at the ILO seek
to guarantee full tripartism. Article 4(2) of the Constitution of the ILO denies
voting rights at the ILC to incomplete delegations. A country's delegation is
deemed incomplete if it is missing worker or employer delegates.[18] To insure
full tripartitism, governments are required to finance the participation of both
employer and worker representatives. The only activity devoid of tripartism
is the payment of periodic membership assessments (dues). Only governments pay these assessments. Tripartism is not only essential to the legitimacy of the Organization in its spheres of competence as a UN Specialized
Agency, especially with respect to protecting workers' rights, but it also reflects its origins as an organization born out of the struggles of the international trade union movement (Alcock, 1971). In order to encourage tripartite
participation, governments are obligated to submit all reports on standards to
bona fide employer and worker associations for their comments before submission to the ILO. The comments, technically referred to as "Observations"
(ILO, 1984) are mandated to institutionalize worker and employer inputs and
to check the validity of national reports. The rationale here is that workers'
and employers' scrutiny of reports may motivate governments to report objectively on prevailing national labor conditions which would in turn facilitate
the Organization's supervision and evaluation of the application of international labor standards.

    In spite of its insistence on international tripartite labor relations and so-
lutions to common labor problems, the Organization also maintains the position that workers should be permitted to pursue their separate sectional or occupational interests. Thus, while the ILO subscribes to the ideal of concerted
efforts by all the three labor relations actors, it still acknowledges diversity in
their needs.

*The Special ILO Supervisory Machinery: The Committee of Freedom of
Association*

    This section briefly outlines the supervisory mechanism used to institu-
tionalize tripartism and to protect workers' interests.[19] The salience of the
effectiveness of the standards supervisory machinery is clearly articulated by
David Morse, former Director-General of the ILO:

> The adoption of conventions and recommendations is merely the first stage
> in a lengthy process. The practical value of international standards depends
> on their application in the law and practice of member countries (Tikriti,
> 1982: 275).

Delegates from the World Federation of Trade Unions (WFTU) and the
American Federation of Labor (AFL) who attended the International Labor
Conferences of 1948 and 1949 that adopted Convention Nos. 87 and 98,
demonstrated their awareness of the potential gaps that could exist between
member states' laws and practices and the provisions of the two Conventions

when their concerns led to the creation in the 1950s of a special committee of
the Governing Body. That body is the Committee of Freedom of Association
which oversees the implementation of these two Conventions. It was established to reinforce the roles of the regular standards supervisory bodies — the
Committee of Experts on the Application of Conventions and
Recommendations (the Committee of Experts) created in 1927 which is responsible for the legal and technical interpretation of all international labor instruments and their application, the Governing Body and the International
Labor Conference Committee on the Application of Conventions and
Recommendations (Alcock, 1971).[20]

The work of the latter reflects the true value of the tripartite supervision
of ILO standards. At this relatively open forum, workers from different regions of the world are offered rare opportunities to assist the ILO to identify
and find solutions to violations of workers' rights within national labor practices and laws. Although ILO officials do not accept references to the
Committee's as a "court of law," I observed during the Conference of June,
1986 that its methods of inquiry into member countries' laws were not different from those of a regular court of law. At this forum, in particular, governments provided both written and oral testimony about their labor practices.
Unsatisfactory answers often led to further inquiries which subtly pressed governments to open up their domestic policies and laws to further examination
by "outsiders" (delegates from other countries).

The Committee of Freedom of Association, through its accumulated and
considerable "case law" involving 1,710[21] instances of government or employers' violation of workers' rights — typically, unlawful arrest and detention and the forced exile of union leaders; the torture and murder of workers;
the unlawful seizure of trade union funds/assets and illegal searches of
premises[22] has tremendously assisted the ILO in supervising standards by
furnishing concrete examples of labor violations unacceptable to the
Organization. It, thus, provides useful practical guidelines to what constitutes,
for example, illegal (according to international labor standards) government
restrictions on workers and their associations. The ILO has been relatively
successful in managing a complex area of international law — the tendency of
most governments not to yield their sovereignty to scrutiny by external agencies.

Through several provisions, especially Articles 19 and 22 of its
Constitution, it has proved relatively capable of getting the cooperation of
most governments in reviewing their internal labor practices and legislation.
Article 19 of the Constitution of the Organization empowers it to periodically
require governments which have not ratified particular Conventions to furnish
information on the prospects for and obstacles to ratification. The ILO uses
this opportunity to encourage members to improve labor conditions to meet its
standards. Thus, even though Zambia has not ratified Convention No. 87 or
98, it is still obliged to report to the ILO measures it is taking to insure ratification in the future. Article 22, on the other hand, mandates those who have
ratified Conventions (whom I call "ratifiers") to submit reports at periods determined by the supervisory bodies. Article 22 reports for Convention Nos. 87

and 98 are due biannually. Hence, every two years, Ghana and Nigeria (which have ratified Convention Nos. 87 and 98) are required to report on the status of these two Conventions. Countries which have not ratified them and are therefore not required to report their application. Under the Constitution, however, the latter are still liable for violations of basic workers' rights enunciated in these two Conventions.

Member states that fail to submit reports due or persistently do not amend policies, laws and practices that in the opinion of the ILO transgress the spirit and letter of ratified Conventions may face a relatively benign pressure which relies on the opinion of the international community to embarrass violators. Several of my respondents spoke of their embarrassment by their governments' failure to change laws and practices that did not meet ILO standards. At this juncture it may be appropriate to observe that through the creation of standards and technical cooperation and a combination of "a wide range of enforcement devices including the use of good offices, diplomatic persuasion, public exposure and criticism" (Hannum, 1984: 15) of nonconforming countries, the ILO has attempted to create, in over seven decades, standards which may be correctly viewed as containing fairly tangible guidelines in an area which several international legal experts agree is fraught with international tensions and complex national sovereignty issues — the international regulation of domestic labor relations. The influence of the ILO in this area, in the African context with emphasis on Ghana, is the subject of the next three chapters.

2. 2   Ghana: Workers' Rights in an Unstable Political and Economic Environment

In order to understand the effects of Ghana's political environment on the country's labor relations and the capacity to meet ILO standards, I present a brief political profile of the country.[23]   A bane of post-independence Ghanaian society — political instability — is borne out by the relatively high rates of successful military interventions, so far numbering four, plus the excessive number of unsuccessful or attempted military takeovers. For example, within a short period, December, 1981 to January, 1985, the country witnessed at least nine coup attempts (Ray, 1986: 103 - 113). The officially acknowledged "abortive" or failed coups may grossly underestimate the real threat to the country's political stability emanating from military interventions because the official records do not include what are popularly dubbed "hushed up" coup attempts — coups that the public hears of only through rumors and about which official information is suppressed. The significance of these successful or unsuccessful attempts by the military to wrestle power is that they may be indicative of the failure or problems of elected civilian and constitutional governments to meet the expectations that rose on the eve of independence or on the birth of each new civilian administration that the country would experience improvements in socio-economic and political conditions. On the birth of independence, for example, there was the expectation that a government that was genuinely representative and responsive to pressing human needs, concerned about ameliorating social inequities and improving access to services such as health, education and public transportation, would emerge (Lofchie, 1971: 4 - 5; Hansen and Ninsin, 1989).

Ghana began independence in 1957 with a Westminster (British Parliamentary) style of government. The only difference was that Ghana had a unicameral legislature, that is, a single National Assembly or Parliament. The first independent Ghanaian government was led by Kwame Nkrumah (as the Prime Minister), whose Convention Peoples' Party (CPP) won the majority of all pre-independence elections from 1951 to 1957.[24] The country also had a legally recognized parliamentary opposition party. Hence, Ghana had a multiparty system of government. By 1964, however, through a referendum, the country was turned into a one-party state under the tutelage of Nkrumah and the CPP (Archer and Reay, 1966). From 1964, all non CPP-affiliated political groups were banned.[25] In addition to proclaiming a single-party system, the government launched an ambitious development program with a socialist orientation. The state became the primary generator of investment capital through the establishment of state-owned air and shipping lines, manufacturing and retail/wholesale concerns (Ray, 1986; Botchway, 1972).[26]

The socialist experiment did not last long. In 1966, a military and police junta toppled the Nkrumah government and formed the first military regime — the National Liberation Council (NLC) — the precursor to a spate of military takeovers, both successful and unsuccessful ones. The NLC which was anti-Nkrumah and backed by western nations (mostly the United States and Britain) adopted IMF prescribed austerity policies, including the massive layoff of public employees. It is estimated that through privatization and cutbacks in the public sector, including state-owned enterprises, between 60,000 to 80,000 workers lost their jobs (Hutchful, 1987). Claiming to be a "caretaker government," the NLC announced its plans to include "revitalizing" the economy and restoring democratic civilian rule. But before it could hand over the country's administration to a new civilian regime, the country was jolted in 1967 by an abortive coup, which led to the death of a member of the NLC.[27]

In 1969 (with the NLC still in power), elections were held and won by the K. A. Busia-led Progress Party (PP), which formed the majority party with 104 out of 140 seats in parliament. The PP was formed out of the remnants of the opposition party that was outlawed in 1964 and, was thus fiercely anti-Nkrumah. Although on the eve of the birth of the PP administration, once again expectations rose, these expectations were dashed only 27 months later. The PP regime was swept out of power because of the personal ambitions of certain military personnel and the party leaders' intolerance of judicial independence and other civil liberties, including the right of organized labor to express its views on public policies.[28] Busia failed to uphold democratic principles as much as his political nemesis, Nkrumah. On abrogating the Second Republic's Constitution of 1969, upon which the PP was established as the ruling party, the National Redemption Council , a military government was established and led by Col. I. K. Acheampong. The NRC ruled from January,

1972, to October, 1975, and then changed its name to the Supreme Military Council (SMC), still led by Col. Acheampong, but this time as a General. Claiming to revive Nkrumah's programs and ideas, the NRC/SMC allied itself with the TUC and its 17 national affiliates (See Appendix 8 for the names of these unions). One of the first proclamations of the NRC was the restoration of the TUC as the sole legally recognized labor federation. By 1978, however, due largely to sheer incompetence, widespread state sponsored corruption and the failure to tackle the country's long-term structural economic problems (Ray, 1986; Pellow and Chazan, 1986), the government was pressured by students, professional associations and the Protestant and Catholic Churches to hand over the reins of government to a civilian administration. Conspicuously absent from the opposition to the NRC/SMC was the TUC. It was one of the few social groups that refrained from protests against the SMC. It did not demand the SMC's ouster because Acheampong restored it as the sole central labor organization and gave it financial relief by writing off its debts (Gray, 1981). Additionally in the final months of this bankrupt regime, A. M. Issifu, the TUC Secretary-General, was appointed a Personal Adviser to the Head of State.[29]

Under intense pressure to resign, Acheampong proposed "Union Government" (infamously referred to as "Unigov"), a nonparty coalition government made up of the representatives of identifiable social groups such as the army, police, academics, churches and businesses (Agyeman-Badu and Osei-Hwedie, 1982). To gain support for Unigov and also to retain power, the SMC launched an expensive campaign which was fiercely opposed by students and their allies. Desperate to retain power at all costs, the SMC resorted to violence using armed police and paid thugs to physically assault opponents. Although the true outcome of the subsequent referendum could not be determined because of electoral fraud by the SMC and its attempts to kidnap the Electoral Commissioner (for refusing to rig the referendum on behalf of the government), the overwhelming opinion in Ghana was that Unigov was an expensive political hoax perpetrated by Acheampong and his associates.

After the Unigov referendum, opponents of the SMC stepped up their pressure through strikes involving nurses, doctors and public utility workers in Accra and other regional capitals. Schools and courts were boycotted by students and lawyers, respectively. Due to the mounting attacks, the SMC itself underwent an abrupt change. In a palace coup of July, 1978, Gen. Fred Akuffo replaced Gen. Acheampong as the head of the SMC I.I. The Akuffo-led SMC II hurriedly scheduled general and presidential elections for a return to civilian/constitutional rule. But two weeks before the elections, a group of junior army officers toppled the new SMC. They formed the Armed Forces Revolutionary Council (AFRC). In its short reign of four months, the AFRC declared a national "house cleaning" exercise aimed at ridding the army and society of excessive corruption and reckless dissipation of national resources (Ray, 1986; Krause, 1982; Panford, 1980).

The AFRC permitted elections scheduled by the SMC, which led to the rise of H. Limann and his People's National Party (PNP) to power in September 1979. Thus was born the Third Republic with a rekindling of national hope that political instability, engendered by frequent military coups, authoritarian rule and abuse of the public trust by governments would subside. As usual, with the inauguration of a new civilian government, the constitution was expected to be an effective buffer against the causes of frequent military interventions. But as D. I. Ray (1986: 16) correctly summarized post-1979 events: "The military's taste of power and the PNDCPNP's ineffectiveness in solving Ghana's economic crises led to Limann's fall on the last day of 1981." The military again cut short the reign of a civilian government and returned to power under the auspices of the Provisional National Defense Council (PNDC), once again led by Flt. Lt. J. Rawlings.

Upon assuming power, the PNDC was confronted by two basic problems:

1. Amelioration of structural economic deficiencies such as collapsing social and economic infrastructure; decreasing state revenue in the face of increased expenditures; shortage of foreign exchange due to low export capacity and low prices for exports and excessively high rates of inflation, and
2. The search for a suitable political system that would arrest mounting political corruption and public apathy towards government institutions.[30]

The PNDC also had its share of internal leadership turmoils. For example, according to Ray (1986), nine coup attempts occurred from December 31, 1981 to January 31, 1985. Besides, there were heated debates within and outside the government (in public fora) about whether Ghana should adopt a socialist or capitalist ideology.[31] The debates were indicative of the fact that Ghana's search for a suitable form of government, which began four decades ago, has not ended.

Labor policies and practices have thus evolved in a highly volatile political environment. The lack of political stability, which has been ignored in the relevant literature, as will be shown in subsequent chapters of this study, has had a significant impact on TUC-Ghana government relations. For example, because the TUC relied on alliances with specific regimes (like the CPP and NRC/SMC), it has had conflicts with the regimes that toppled them. Recent TUC-PNDC relations, which were mutually suspicious and often conflict-ridden, could be traced to organized labor's close links with the NRC/SMC and more especially, labor's endorsement of the generally unpopular "Unigov" concept (Panford, 1988; Yeebo, 1991). Political instability may also have inhibited the government's capacity to plan and implement a coherent PNDClabor policy to meet the ILO's standards and national needs. For example, the Ghana Department of Labor informed the ILO that there had been instances in which government documents used to process the Organization's reports had been lost because of abrupt changes in government.

The often disruptive turnover in governments in Ghana has increased the cost of political unionism based on alliances with particular governments as a TUC strategy for meeting its members' needs. At the macroeconomic level, abrupt succession in government leadership may also be largely responsible for the country's failure to engage in any meaningful long range planning to overcome its economic problems. Since these political developments have often led to the abandonment of even viable and necessary economic projects, disruptive changes in government have frustrated the effective harnessing of the country's relatively abundant natural and human resources (including the potential economic and social contributions of workers). These political developments therefore need to be factored into the analyses of the country's contemporary problems, including those connected to domestic and international labor matters to make them more useful to labor, public policy and international human rights researchers and practitioners.

NOTES

1.   See Shotwell (1934) and Alcock (1971) for a detailed history of the ILO.
2.   Since the 1960s, when large numbers of independent African nations joined the ILO, 50 percent of its technical cooperation has gone to Africa (ILO, 1988).
3.   Through the creation and supervision of standards, research and publications dealing with labor matters involving 160 countries, the ILO has become the foremost "international clearing house" for information pertaining to labor policy, legislation and practices in the world.
4.   According to A. Alcock (1971), one of the first accomplishments of the ILO was the adoption of standards on hours of work, the employment of women and child labor. Technical cooperation, on the other hand, emerged on a large scale only after World War I.I. More recently, with mounting global recession and the adoption of austere policies in the form of ERP/SAPs with attendant unemployment problems, the ILO's research and publications have centered on world employment problems (ILO, 1984).
5.   ILO officials I interacted with during my field work and employment in Geneva emphasized that the standards supervisory units of the Organization were not "courts of law."
6.   Information from the Washington, DC, ILO office dated March 17, 1993. For an exhaustive classification of standards, see ILO "Official Titles of Conventions Adopted by the International Labor Conference," and "Classified Guide to International Labor Standards Adopted up to the 79th Session of the International Labor Conference 1992." These are available from the International Labor Standards Department, ILO, Geneva or the Washington, DC Branch.
7.   Information from the ILO, Washington, DC Branch Office, April, 1993.
8.   In Malawi's case, No. 1638, the ILO concluded that the detention of trade unionists, a raid on their premises and the resulting fears of arrest among workers' leaders were not in conformity with the due process of law and ILO standards (ILO, 1993: 147).
9.   ILO, Geneva communication dated April 19, 1993.
10.   Some of the mechanisms used are the persistent written and oral comments issued concerning discrepancies between national laws and ratified standards, and requests to governments to report on particular labor practices deemed to be inconsistent with the Organization's principles. For example, in the case of Ghana, with respect to Convention No. 98, the ILO has since 1959 recommended changes in the relevant statutes. Also, in Case No. 1135, the Committee of Freedom of Association specifically drew the PNDC attention to ensuring that TUC leaders operated in full freedom within the country. Facing possible diplomatic embarrassment, which could soil its in-

ternational image, the government responded by creating conditions under which the TUC was able to hold elections and function normally (see ILO, 1985; Yeebo, 1991: 90 - 91).

11.   See Appendices 2 and 3, ILO Report Forms for Convention Nos. 87 and 98.

12.   ILO, *286th Report of the* Committee of Freedom of Association (March 1993).

13.   Point expressed repeatedly by the heads of the International Labor Standards Department and the Freedom of Association Branch.

14.   International Labor Conference, 1948, San Francisco, "Record of Proceedings": 480.

15.   The two instruments are deemed the very core of the ILO, and since the 1920s, the key principle embodied in them — freedom of association — has remained an integral part of the Constitution and operating principles. Its importance was reiterated when the Declaration of Philadelphia (1944) was incorporated into the Preamble to the Organization's Constitution (Alcock, 1971).

16.   It is appropriate to point out that Convention Nos. 87 and 98 seek to guarantee both employers' and workers' rights. However, because of the scope of this study, issues and rights pertaining to employers and their organizations have been excluded. For full texts of these two Conventions, see Appendices 2 and 3.

17.   The Secretariat comprises the bureaucratic structures which together with the ILC, the Governing Body and other organs and institutes, constitute the International Labor Organization.

18.   Typically, a complete Ghanaian delegation to the annual ILC comprises the following. on the government side, the Minister for Labor and the Ambassador and Permanent Representative to the UN in Switzerland, and one or two Counsellors; employers' delegates are the Executive Director, Ghana Employers' Association with one or two Advisors and workers; the Secretary-General of the TUC accompanied by the Head of the International Relations Department of the TUC and an Advisor (ILO, "Delegations," ILC, June 21, 1991: 53).

19.   Details of the ILO's standards setting and supervisory activities are provided by Alcock (1971), Servais (1984), Pouyat (1982), Valticos (1984), Samson (1979); Ben-Israel (1988).

20.   At its March, 1992 meeting to review the application of international labor standards, the Committee of Experts comprised 19 members, out of whom three were Africans from Nigeria, Madagascar and Senegal. A total of 10 were from the Third World. The typical member is an internationally renowned juror with experience in labor law and human rights. The Senegalese, for example, had served on the World Court. See ILC, Committee of Experts Report, 1992 for other details. The Conference Committee on the Application of Conventions and Recommendations is made up of workers, employers and government delegates who assess the application of standards in member states.

21.   Statistic from the ILO's Head Office, Geneva, April 19, 1993.

22.   Personal communication from heads of International Labor Standards Department and Freedom of Association Branch. See also, ILO (1985) for complete details of these cases. These reflect the gravity of the violations leading to loss of life, family disruptions and job losses. For a relevant recent case, see Case No. 1638 against Malawi cited above.

23.   This section aims at furnishing a summary description of the types of government and the turbulent environment in which labor relations has evolved, and to familiarize the reader with the names of key political figures in the post-colonial Ghanaian state up to January, 1993. On January 7, 1993, Flt. Lt. J. Rawlings (the Head of the PNDC) was sworn as Ghana's head of state under a new constitution ushering

the country into its "Fourth Republic." Rawlings' party won both the presidential and parliamentary Elections of November and December, 1992 (A. Yeboah-Aferi, "Enter the Fourth Republic," *West Africa*, Jan. 18 - 24, 1993: 52). For detailed presentations of the country's pre- and immediate post-colonial political history, see Kimble (1963) and Austin (1964); on 1970s and 1980s political and economic developments, see Panford (1980), Hug (1989), Chazan and Pellow (1986), Ray (1986), Hansen and Ninsin (1989), Ninsin (1992) and Shillington (1992).

24.   The CPP was one of the first most successfully organized political parties in Africa. It won all elections held towards independence because of its mass appeal and promise to convert political independence into improved material conditions for all Ghanaians, but most especially for workers (Botchway, 1972; Padmore, 1953).

25.   According to Twumasi (1980), media, labor, youth, market womens' and farmers' organizations were all appended into different wings of the CPP.

26.   See Section 3.2 for details.

27.   This coup attempt marked the bloody nature of coups and countercoups against civilian and military governments.

28.   Due to serious disagreements over national economic policies and personal animosities between the PP and TUC's leaders, the PP passed the Industrial Relations Amendment Act, No. 383 of 1971, to dissolve the TUC.

29.   The implications of the TUC's position are explored in Section 5.1.

30.   The PNDC established the National Commission for Democracy (NCD) to collate opinions about appropriate political structures and processes.

31.   M. Barnor, "The role of the NCD," *West Africa*, Jan. 12, 1987: 67; Y. Graham, "Democratic Meanings," *West Africa*, Jan. 12, 1987: 65; Ninsin and Drah, 1987.

Chapter 3

African Labor Laws, Policies, Practices and Problems at the ILO

3. 1   Constraints on African States and Workers' Rights

Several African countries, soon after gaining independence in the late 1950s and 1960s, joined the ILO.[1] As a result, African nations currently constitute a third of the 160 total membership of the Organization. Because of the huge influx of African states, it has become necessary to examine how these countries' labor policies, laws and practices conform to the Organization's standards, especially those embodied in Convention Nos. 87 and 98.[2] Since it is not feasible to thoroughly review the labor situations of all 53 African countries in a single study, I am focusing on Ghana with brief comparisons with other English-speaking African countries: Kenya, Nigeria and Zambia.[3]

Ghana is the main focus because its union-state relations from 1971 to 1985 yielded developments which provide opportunities for assessing the relevance of the ILO's position and standards on workers' rights. Nigeria, too, is useful because its labor situation depicts the classic conditions which may be conducive to government violation of the two Conventions being studied. Kenya has ratified only Convention No. 98 and Zambia has not ratified either of the two Conventions under review. Thus, Zambia and Kenya may be used to explain national circumstances which deter ratification of such key Conventions. Since Ghana and Nigeria have ratified these two Conventions — or only one, as is the Kenyan case — their relevance to this study lies in their obligations under Article 22 of the ILO's Constitution to report periodically their application to the Committee of Experts.[4] Currently, to permit the standards supervisory bodies of the Organization ample time to review the laws and practices of ILO members, reports on the two Conventions are due biannually. Even in the case of Zambia, which has not ratified either of the two, and of Kenya, which has not ratified No. 87, these two countries are still obligated under Article 19 of the Constitution to submit reports requested by the Governing Body. These reports constitute the basis of the process used by the ILO to measure the extent to which ratifiers apply Conventions, and in the case of a nonratifier like Zambia, to establish dialogue which may lead to technical assistance to overcome domestic conditions responsible for nonratification.[5] As demonstrated in the rest of this section and in Chapter 4, the application of the two selected Conventions in Ghana and in other parts of Africa presents some of the most intractable technical/administrative, legal, political, economic and international relations problems, which require equally complex solutions. African members, during various International Labor and Regional Conferences, have voiced the opinion that their complex problems should lead to their exemption from the rigorous application of these Conventions. A typical explanation offered is that of the dangers inherent in excessive union multiplicity if the provisions of both instruments are strictly applied to permit the proliferation of labor unions.

The ILO's unequivocal response is that while Conventions like those dealing with the creation of workers' social security systems, hours of work and the purely technical aspects of labor administration (such as, the compilation of statistical data) may be implemented progressively, in the case of Convention Nos. 87 and 98, no exemptions can be made. Even nonratifiers are still accountable to the ILO for how they treat workers.[6] The firm ILO position is that the rights in these Conventions are inalienable because, without them, there will be no other workers' rights.[7] The insistence on strict compliance with Convention Nos. 87 and 98 presents problems which all ILO members have to grapple with, almost without exception. However, African members such as Ghana, Kenya, Nigeria and Zambia have had to deal with relatively more complex policy dilemmas largely because of their unique national labor conditions.

A host of complex colonial and contemporary political and socio-economic problems have, at times, genuinely hindered African governments' full compliance with the relevant ILO provisions and their full participation in the activities of the Organization. Some states lacking the resources to sponsor delegates' travel and other expenses are not able to insure full involvement in all ILO activities especially those conducted in Europe. Zambia's response to these bottlenecks has been total avoidance of the ratification of the two instruments because it does not want to be liable for not implementing them (Kalula, 1985). Kenya's strategy was to ratify only No. 98, which is less complex to fulfill.[8] In the cases of Ghana and Nigeria (which have ratified both Conventions) they have contended with numerous problems related to their laws, policies and practices and how they impacted on workers' rights. On three separate occasions since independence, the Government of Ghana has had cases of alleged violation of workers' rights filed with the Committee on Freedom of Association.

Workers' rights issues that Ghana, Nigeria, Kenya and Zambia have had difficulties with (from the ILO's point of view) include government interference in internal union affairs like the structures and principles of union organizing, requirements of prior administrative or legislative authorization to form and operate unions, restrictions on collective bargaining and workers' rights to strike. The nature of Ghanaian statutes and practices and how they have led to restrictions on workers' rights problems are the subject of the next five sections of this chapter. Section 3.2 consists of a summary description of aspects of Ghanaian labor laws dealing with the two Conventions, and Section 3.3 describes in detail the nature of the problems the country and other African states have had to contend with in meeting international labor commitments.

3. 2   Ghana's Labor Laws, Policies and Practices

The objective of this section is to familiarize the reader with the salient aspects of Ghana's labor legislation, policies and practices as a step to discussing the problems African governments face in meeting their membership obligations at the ILO.

Labor Union Monopoly

A chronically problematic feature of African labor law and practice is the persistence of what the ILO's standards supervisory organs have dubbed "the single union" or "monopoly union" system (Erstling, 1977; ILO, 1983a; Panford, 1988). W. Ananaba (1979: 167) provides three concrete examples of union monopoly situations in Africa. The first originated from a collective bargaining agreement between the Mine Workers union of Liberia and the Iron Ore Company Limited which came into effect on November 20, 1975. In a similar agreement dated January 1, 1974, Ghana's state-owned shipping company, the Black Star Line, conferred on the Union of Seamen an exclusive collective bargaining agency. In the case of Kenya, the government officially recognized the Union of Civil Servants (UKCS) as the only body legally permitted to represent all civil servants.

These single-union systems may not be in conformity with ILO principles, especially those embodied in Convention No. 87 which require governments to take measures to grant and protect the right of workers to organize and join trade unions in full freedom. The imposition of single unions may violate workers' rights where they restrict workers' choices and force them to join only state approved unions. In some of these situations, workers have only two choices. They either join organizations sanctioned by the state or they cannot join any unions at all.

The monopoly union structures predominant on the African labor scene are erected in two basic ways. They may be created, as is common, via instruments such as parliamentary acts or military or executive decrees.[9] These are then reinforced by administrative practices and decisions, such as the dissolution of rival unions. The net effects of such acts of state are that in most African countries, unions which are not actually approved by the state are not allowed to register or operate as *bona fide* workers' associations. Ghana's post-independence labor union structure (at local and national levels) can legitimately be described as both a *de jure* and *de facto* single union system because the laws, public policies and practices have virtually banned (with the exception of the brief period of the dissolution of the Ghana TUC from September, 1971 to February, 1972) all unions except the TUC and its 17 National Unions and their local affiliates. Thus, the TUC, for over 30 years (1958 to 1993) has dominated the country's labor organizations.[10] Since the legislative inception of the Ghana TUC and the other nations' central labor organizations, these federations have enjoyed exclusive representation of their respective countries' entire labor movement. In Ghana, for example, TUC officials represent workers on the boards of directors of state-owned corporations and at the ILO annual labor conference and other activities. It is also often consulted by the government on national economic and political issues.[11]

In spite of the repeal of the Industrial Relations Act, No. 56 of 1958 by the Ghanaian Parliament as a result of the repeated recommendations of the ILO,[12] remnants of *de jure* monopoly labor organization exist as long as the First Schedule and section 1(1) of the current statute (Act 299 of 1965) retain the TUC and its affiliates as the only unions legally permitted to operate in Ghana. Section 1 of the 1965 Act states inter alia:

1. (1) The body which immediately before the commencement of this Act was known as the Trades Union Congress shall be continued in existence under the same name subject to the provisions of this act until dissolved or otherwise constituted in accordance with rules made under this section 2.
    (2) The Congress shall be a body corporate with perpetual succession
         . . . .
    (3) Unless and until otherwise decided by the trade unions or any appropriate organization of workers, the Congress shall act as the representative of the trade union movement in Ghana.

The original First Schedule of this Act listed 10 "Constituent members of the Trades Union Congress." However, as a result of an amendment of January, 1966, the number of national unions increased to 17. The result of this act and its subsequent amendment in effect has been the determination of the number of national unions in the country by the National Assembly.[13]

The TUC's monopoly situation in Ghana was reinforced by statutorily assigning to it special privileges and roles in the country's labor relations. It was not only the sole representative of Ghana's workers at international fora like the ILO, but it has also remained the leading workers' spokes organization for national labor, social and economic policy policy formulation. Additionally, it plays a significant role in union recognition, registration and certification as bargaining agents. Section 3(1) of the Industrial Relations Acts, 1965, makes the TUC an important intermediary for all unions seeking to operate in Ghana. Without the TUC's endorsement a union cannot be registered for collective bargaining:

The Congress shall on application by a trade union request the Registrar to issue a certificate appointing that trade union as the appropriate representative to conduct on behalf of a class of employees specified in the certificate collective bargaining with the employers of such employees, and subject to subsection (4), the Registrar shall be bound to comply with such a request.

Exclusive Bargaining Agency

Section 3(4) of the Industrial Relations Acts of 1965 granted exclusive bargaining agency status to unions the TUC intervened to get registered:[14]

> More than one certificate may be issued under this section in respect of the same trade union . . . . but the Registrar shall not appoint a trade union under this section for any class of employees if there is in force a certificate under this section appointing another trade union for that class of employees or any part of that class.

The real consequences of the special status conferred on the Ghana TUC and other national labor federations may be fully understood by establishing its practical significance in the areas of union registration and certification to permit representing workers at the bargaining table. In Ghana, for example, according to the Department of Labor, it is totally illegal for trade unions which are not registered and expressly certified to engage in collective bargaining and, more importantly, to strike.[15]

Exclusive bargaining agency and the mandated requirement that only certified unions can engage in collective bargaining and legal strikes have combined to make the privileged position of the TUC more critical to the survival of other unions. That may have induced other unions to affiliate with it to win its approval and ultimate endorsement for registration and certification. Thus, one prominent feature of the legal provisions establishing single union systems and exclusive bargaining agency in a country like Ghana is that the laws circumvent the rights of workers and their associations to join organizations of their choice. Organizations representing labor today are sanctioned by the state and exclude all others not approved. In other words, without government authorization, new unions cannot be registered and certified to represent any group of workers in any of my selected countries.

Compulsory Collective Bargaining in Ghana

Ghana, like most African countries, has an elaborate legal framework for collective bargaining. As stated above, Section 3(1) of the Industrial Relations Acts, 1965, requires unions to be certified as a condition for bargaining with employers. Furthermore, the law stipulates that employers and their employees should set up "Standing Negotiating Committees." Within each bargaining unit, according to Section 5(1) of the relevant act:

> It shall be the duty both of the trade union appointed in a certificate issued under section 3 and of the employer of the employees of the class to which the certificate relates to nominate representatives authorized to negotiate on their behalf and such representatives shall be members of a standing

negotiating committee which shall be set up to negotiate on matters referred
to them under this Act.

To enforce this provision, Sections 8(1) and 9 empower the Attorney General
to impose fines enforced by the law courts if, within 14 days, an employer and
the union concerned fail to create these committees for bargaining purposes.
The compulsory aspects of the relevant statute are revealed in the legally imposed duties of the labor relations parties. Sections 5(2) and 6(1) specify in
detail the obligations of the "Negotiating Committees," including submission
of copies of their proceedings to the public authorities through the Registrar of
Unions:

>   5.   (2)   A negotiating committee referred to in subsection (1) shall make
>   rules governing its proceedings a copy of which rules shall be
>   supplied to the Registrar for his information.
>
>   (3)   A standing negotiating committee set up under this section shall
>   have the power to appoint subcommittees to which it may delegate
>   any of its functions under this Act.
>
>   6.   (1)   Negotiations on all matters connected with the employment or
>   nonemployment or with the terms of employment or with the
>   conditions of labour of any of the employees of the class specified
>   in a certificate issued under section 3 shall be conducted through
>   the standing negotiating committee set up under section 5.

Copies of all collective agreements are also mandated to be deposited
with the registrar "for his information." The provisions cited are not the only
ones imposed by the state. The laws are so exhaustive that they even determine the minimum duration of labor agreements. Section 11(11) of the
Industrial Relations Acts, 1965, requires that: "every collective agreement . . .
. shall be for a term of at least one year." All these examples demonstrate
how through legislation, the public authorities in Ghana intrude into the
structure and scope of collective bargaining between unions and employers.

The "Powers of Extension" of the Minister of Labor

An innovative provision in Ghanaian law not found in the other African
countries included in this study is the "Powers of Extension" under Section 20
of the 1958 Industrial Relations Acts and Section 13(1) of the 1965 statute
currently in force. This section allows the Labor Minister to apply to workers
and their employers the terms of collective agreements to which they were not
original parties:

>   13. (1)   Where it appears to the Minister that all or any of the terms of a
>   collective agreement under this Act are suitable for application to a
>   class of employees who are engaged in the same kind of work, or
>   who work in the same area, as the employees to whom the
>   collective agreement applies and that the parties who concluded
>   that agreement were sufficiently representative of the employees to
>   whom it is proposed to apply the agreement and their employers,
>   he may by legislative instrument make an order directing that those

> terms of the collective agreement shall apply in relation to that
> class of employees and their employers as they apply in relation to
> employees of the class prescribed in the certificate and their
> employers.

This is one of the several discretionary powers given to the minister to intervene in labor relations as the government sees fit. To reinforce the powers of
intervention, Section 14(1) of the same act makes the terms of these "extended
contracts" as legally binding as those voluntarily negotiated: "These extended
terms also remain valid until they are varied by the parties."

Compulsory Settlement of Labor Conflicts

In the areas of dispute settlement — conciliation, mediation, arbitration
and strikes — the relevant Ghanaian laws are very exhaustive. For example,
Section 12(1) lays out the precise procedures for adjustments:

> Every collective agreement under this Act shall contain a provision for final
> and conclusive settlement, by arbitration or otherwise, of all differences be-
> tween the persons to whom the agreement applies concerning its interpreta-
> tion.

Once again, the Minister of Labor is accorded immense discretion. By law, he
is authorized, based on his personal or his government's judgment, to initiate
proceedings for compulsory arbitration. He is permitted under Section 17(1)
of the Act of 1965 to appoint conciliation officers after any one of the parties
notifies him about an impasse. Subsection (2) of this section vividly depicts
his discretionary role in labor disputes:

> The Minister shall not take any action under this section if it appears to him
> that effective steps have been taken for the reference of the dispute to
> arbitration or for the use of conciliation procedure, unless and until he is
> satisfied that the steps so taken are not likely to lead to a settlement of the
> dispute.

This subsection, in particular, amply illustrates the absence of any legal
checks on the minister in resolving labor conflicts. As it were, he is responsible to only himself or to his government and relies on his own personal judgment.

All the above, however, do not end the discretionary role of the minister.
As the sole judge of the nature of industrial conflicts, even if only one party
agrees, he can order compulsory arbitration under Section 18(1):

> In the circumstances mentioned in section 17 the Minister shall serve on the
> parties a notice —
> (a) stating what are in his opinion the issues between the parties; and
> (b) asking the parties whether they agree to those issues being referred
>   to and determined by arbitration; and

(c) notifying the parties that, if one of them consents and the other
     does not, the Minister has power to give a direction that the issues
     shall be so referred and determined without the consent of the other
     party;
and where only one of the parties so consents the Minister may, if he thinks
fit, give such a direction.[16]

To complement his immense powers, the minister is empowered to give final
approval to the outcomes of all arbitrated disputes. Without his confirmation,
all awards are not legally binding:

20. (2) Every award confirmed by the Minister shall prevail over any
          contract of service or apprenticeship in force at the time of the
          award and accordingly the provisions of any contract of service or
          collective agreement shall be deemed to have been modified as far
          as may be necessary in order to conform to the award.

When disputes are not settled through arbitration and are likely to lead to
strikes (or lockouts by employers) the minister still wields a lot of discretionary power and influence. Even where workers completely exhaust the
elaborate requirements preceding legal strikes — conciliation, arbitration and
additional conciliation — they are only authorized and become legal if both
parties to a dispute refuse to refer it to the minister. After referral to the minister, workers have to wait four weeks before they can strike because of a mandated 28-day waiting period.[17]
     As an additional measure to circumvent workers' rights to strike, the few
rights to strike that are left are confined to issues which Negotiation
Committees are authorized to deal with. Thus, a strike is automatically illegal
if disputed issues fall outside the scope of the work of these committees.
Section 22 of the 1965 Act permits the state to impose both fines and criminal
penalties, including jail terms, on workers and unions that strike illegally.

The Paradox of African Labor Laws

A paradoxical situation I observed as common in all the selected countries
relates to the adoption of statutes dealing with employer unfair labor practices.
All these countries, under their current labor practices, especially those concerning the state's creation of single labor federations, may be guilty of violating their own laws. Ghana's situation is quite instructive.[18] Section 27 of the
1965 Industrial Relations Acts states:

If a person who is an employer of labour in any trade or industry takes part in
the formation of a trade union or, with the intention of influencing a trade
union, makes any contribution, in money or money's worth, to that trade
union, he is guilty of an unfair labour practice.

Under this particular provision, whenever the Ghanaian government participated in restructuring unions in the state owned sector in which it is also the

employer, it may have violated this section. This was also the case when the Ghanaian and other African governments donated cash and material gifts to their favorite labor federations.[19] One can argue that such gifts or "contributions" may have influenced these labor organizations. In Section 5.1, I explain the actual and potential negative consequences for the TUC for having received favors from the CPP and NRC/SMC regimes.

Dissolution of Unions: The Ultimate Violation of Labor Rights

A final important aspect of Ghanaian labor practice is the actual or potential dissolution of unions via the legislative route. One of the most notorious liquidations of labor unions in Africa occurred in September, 1971 when the Progress Party government dissolved the Ghana TUC.[20] Although this event proved to be temporary, other similar acts, including threats to dismember unions, signify some of the deep-seated practical labor policy dilemmas that result from the statutory creation of single union structures. These features have been the subjects of repeated comments by the ILO's supervisory bodies, requesting countries such as Ghana and Nigeria to modify their laws and practices to make them conform to the Organization's standards and principles.[21] In light of problems Ghana and other African nations have at the ILO, a question that emerges naturally is: Why have these countries not modified their laws and practices to meet ILO standards? Answers to this question are provided in Chapter 4. But before that I will elaborate on how the labor statutes and practices described above have posed persistent major problems at the ILO for not only Ghana but also several other African governments.

3.3   African Labor Problems at the ILO: The Ghana Case

In spite of the frequent changes in governments in Ghana, all governments have expressed repeatedly their desire to make the country's labor policies, laws and practices conform to ILO standards especially those the country has ratified. At its first International Labor Conference (the 40th Session) Ghana's representative stated in unmistakable terms the government's willingness to honor "all obligations entered on behalf" of Ghana by the former British colonial authorities. But even more important he pledged his government's commitment to uphold workers' rights:

> The Government of Ghana will continue to apply the provisions of the Right of Association (Non-Metropolitan Territories) Convention, 1947, and the Labour Inspectorates (Non-Metropolitan Territories) Convention, 1947, pending ratification of the Freedom of Association and Protection of the Right to Organise Convention, 1948, the Right to Organise and Collective Bargaining Convention, 1949[22] . . . .

Furthermore he stressed that Ghana would use ILO standards to guide a review of the country's labor laws:

... in consultation with employersand workers through the national Labour
Advisory Committee, all legislation affecting labour with a view to eliminat-
ing any sections which are incompatible with our changed status and to in-
troduce legislation which is necessary for our advancement.[23]

On a separate occasion, during the National Assembly's review of
Convention No. 87 for ratification, the then Minister of Labor (I. Amoa-
Awuah) reminded his colleagues that Ghana's ILO duties included guarantee-
ing workers:

... complete freedom of association under the law, as well as the right to establish and subject only to the rules of their own organisations, to join organisations of their own choosing without previous authorisation, for the purpose of furthering and defending the interests of workers . . . . The
Convention protects workers and employers' organisations from control by
public or administrative authorities.[24]

During another International Labor Conference, the Commissioner (Minister)
of Labor for the second military government, the NRC, expressed in clear
terms his government's understanding of the responsibilities connected to the
ratification of standards. He indicated Ghana's "wholehearted" commitment
to ensure that its laws were congruent with ILO principles. He even stated
that Ghana was doing all it could to "observe scrupulously" Convention Nos.
87 and 98, which he described as "cardinal principles."[25]

The above cited pledges and official pronouncements are significant in
that they show clearly and consistently the Ghanaian government's awareness
of its obligations as a member of the ILO and also for ratifying the two
"cardinal" Conventions. Getting closer to the recent national scene, the then
PNDC Secretary for Mobilization and Productivity (Minister of Labor, G.
Adamu) in praising Ghana's ratification record (one of 13 African countries
with the highest ratification rates) also made an insightful observation. The
secretary noted bluntly that "ratification is one thing and implementation is
another."[26] He also hinted at some of the technical or administrative bottlenecks that hinder the furnishing of "accurate reports" on the country's application of ILO standards as required by the Organization.[27] Thus, the last
administration (the PNDC) may also be said to have been fully aware of
problems that hinder the country's total compliance with ILO Constitutional
and ratification commitments.

This section analyzes why and how certain features of Ghanaian and other
African labor laws, policies and practices may in the view of the ILO contravene international labor standards such as Convention Nos. 87 and 98. These
standards support the rights of workers to engage in activities to protect their
interests without fear of victimization or other forms of negative sanctions
from either the state or private employers. In examining the problems hinted
at by the PNDC Secretary for Labor, six categories dealing with workers'
rights to form associations of their own choice and their rights to voluntary labor negotiations and strikes are analyzed.[28] These are:

1. The prevalence of single/monopoly union systems (in virtually all African states);
2. Compulsory union membership;
3. Legislatively imposed automatic checkoff of union dues;
4. A ban on international union activities and affiliation (as in Kenya, Nigeria and Zambia);[29]
5. The privileged positions of government-sponsored unions; and
6. As it was in Ghana from 1958 to 1966 and in Kenya from 1988 until 1992, the domination of labor unions by the state or party in power.[30]

Three other common problems relate to limitations imposed by governments over the rights of workers to engage in voluntary collective bargaining; the compulsory and penal aspects of industrial dispute resolution, especially (as shown in Section 3.2 of this book) in the cases of strikes and other protest actions; the dissolution of unions by the public authorities through administrative orders or other legislative mechanisms like parliamentary acts; and civil and trade union rights violations including the arrest and detention, dismissal from office and forced exile of union leaders; the state's security agents' interference (at times resorting to force) in internal union affairs, violation of union premises and meetings, and the confiscation and freezing of union accounts and assets (ILO, 1983a; 1985a).

All of the above are considered violations of fundamental ILO principles by the various standards supervisory organs. For example, the Committee of Freedom of Association considers the incarceration of a union leader for leading a legal strike a violation of the provisions of Convention Nos. 87 and 98. Therefore, in June, 1986, when the Federal Nigerian Military Government arrested about 25 union leaders for planning a protest march against the government's treatment of student demonstrators,[31] the ILO's response was that the Nigerian Labor Congress (NLC), which had led the march, had the legal right (according to the Organization's principles) to peacefully demonstrate against the Nigerian government's policies.[32] From the ILO's point of view, some of the rights violated by African governments adversely impinge upon certain primary workers' and fundamental civil rights , without which no other rights may be exercised. Thus, in 1970, for example, the International Labor Conference (without opposition from any member states including those from Africa) adopted a resolution reaffirming the importance of civil liberties in the nurturing of union rights:

> . . . the rights conferred upon workers' organizations must be based on respect for those civil liberties which have been enunciated in particular in the Universal Declaration of Human Rights and in the International Covenant on Civil and Political Rights and that the absence of these civil liberties removes all meaning from the concept of trade union rights.[33]

Compulsory Unions

As noted in Section 3.2, a characteristic of contemporary African labor relations, in contravention of ILO standards, is the statutory creation of single-union systems.[34] Where they exist, competing unions have been virtually eliminated, as the case is in Ghana, Kenya, Nigeria or Zambia. In Ghana, by law, no unions outside the TUC are allowed to operate. For example, a 1960 amendment to Section 16 (cited below) of the 1958 Industrial Relations Acts created union shops which required employers to offer jobs to only unionized workers. The effect was that workers were compelled to join unions which were TUC affiliates and workers could not exercise any choice in union membership or the organizations they joined. In present-day Ghana, rival unions cannot be founded due to administrative practices, including the denial of registration of nonTUC unions by the Registrar of Unions (currently the Chief Labor Officer). The impact of prevailing statutes and practices is that, with the exception of a brief period (September, 1971 to February, 1972, when the TUC was dissolved by the PP government), the TUC and its affiliates have had virtual monopoly over the representation of organized labor. The TUC, for example, has since 1958 always represented Ghanaian workers at the ILO and at other domestic and international fora. At home, for instance, it has remained the key labor representative for national policy-making.[35]

In Ghana, the statutory creation of state-sponsored union monopolies resulted from Sections 1 and 3 and the First Schedule of the Industrial Relations Acts, 1965. Such statutes infringe upon fundamental workers' rights protected under Article 2 of ILO Convention No. 87, which urges members to ensure that:

> Workers . . . without distinction whatsoever, shall have the right to establish
> and subject only to the rules of the organisations concerned, to join organisations of their own choosing without previous authorisation.[36]

A problem often closely connected to the imposition of single unions emerged in Ghana as a result of Section 16 of the 1960 Amendment (Act No. 7) to the 1958 Industrial Relations Acts. As noted, this section led to a union security practice called "union shop,"[37] which is explained by the relevant amendment:

> 16. No person who belongs to a class of employees specified in a certificate
> issued under the provisions of Part II of this Act but who is not a
> member of the trade union covered by the certificate shall be kept in any
> employment for a period exceeding one month.

The effect of this particular amendment was that it made union membership a condition for continuous employment, and hence, may have compelled employees to join unions. The intent of making unionization compulsory was accomplished by making the employment of nonunion labor a punishable unfair labor practice. Under Section 16(a), an employer violated the law if she or he continued:

> To employ any person who is not a member of a trade union and belongs to a
> class of employees specified in a certificate under Part II of the Act and who
> would share in the benefit of a collective agreement in accordance with section 17 of this Act shall be guilty of an unfair labour practice.

It is important to note that although the ILO permits full discretion of countries over union security practices, in the Ghanaian case, as in other African countries, where union membership is strictly limited to only state approved unions, such union security arrangements may contravene Article 2 of Convention No. 87. The Organization voiced its strong opinion about this problem when the Committee of Experts recalled that: "in the preparatory work for Convention No. 87 it was stressed that freedom of industrial association is one aspect of freedom . . . in general, which forms part of the whole range of fundamental liberties."[38]

The single-union systems of Africa and their associated compulsory union membership requirements were the products of new union "restructuring" or "rationalization" processes through which the state, with the encouragement and full support of unions and their political allies in government, used legislative or executive authority in the form of parliamentary acts (as in the case of Ghana, the Industrial Relations Actss, 1958 and 1965), military decrees (as in Nigeria in 1973 and 1978) and Presidential decrees as in Kenya with the presidential Declaration of 1965.[39]

Mandated Labor Unity

One of the several policy paradoxes posed by the state's micromanagement of internal union affairs to unite competing unions is that in most African countries, the compulsory creation of labor unity is one of the few exceptional labor policy areas over which there is almost unanimous agreement by all the labor relations actors, academics and practitioners. Several examples support this view. In Ghana, for example, the TUC and its allies in the 1980s urged the PNDC government to merge all nonTUC unions (the Association of Registered Nurses', the Ghana Civil Servants' Association and the Ghana National Association of Teachers) with the TUC as a means to enhance labor unity.[40] The circumstances leading to the founding of COTU (in Kenya) and the NLC (in Nigeria) as sole labor federations depict the dire national situations which explain the intervention of the state. The founding of COTU was precipitated by the deaths of three trade unionists and injuries to over 100 during a clash of rival unions (Amsden, 1971: 111; Iwuji , 1979). In Nigeria, repeated attempts to form a single federation were rendered ineffective by excessive rivalry fueled by ethnic, regional, religious and even ideological differences emanating from the Cold War (Fashoyin, 1981).

In his comments on the Nigerian labor scene, R. O. Nwubueze (1981) praised the Federal Nigerian Military Government for imposing unity and order through Decree Nos. 31 and 22 of 1973 and 1978. This highly influential labor practitioner (currently one of three African ILO Experts on the Application of Conventions and Recommendations) was of the opinion that the creation of the NLC was the most important accomplishment of the military government in the area of labor relations and hence an important contribution to Nigeria's national development. With reference to Zambia, E. Kalula (1985) noted that employers, the government and of course, the unions were all solidly behind the unification of all unions under ZCTU. In addition, my observation of ILO activities in 1985 and 1986 revealed that African members were strongly convinced that the creation of single labor centers did not only enhance labor solidarity but was a virtual national or industrial relations imperative. For example, at the 1986 International Labor Conference, Nigerian delegates vehemently argued that the abolition of the NLC or the withdrawal of government recognition would create a chaotic national labor-management situation which would grossly undermine collective bargaining and jeopardize efforts to develop the national economy. The Nigerian Government representative, the Labor Attaché accredted to the Nigerian Embassy in Geneva, stated that modifying the decree founding the NLC to permit more than one labor federation will cause the reappearance of ethnic, regional, religious and ideological factions which had prevented workers from achieving voluntary forms of labor unity.[41]

While expressing its sympathy for and understanding of the problems African nations have with excessive labor union plurality, the ILO takes the strong position that, contrary to the expectation that compulsory unity will alleviate all these problems, it does not. It points out that such acts of state, even if supported by workers themselves, may still constitute a violation of crucial principles embodied in the two Conventions dealt with in this study. It supports its apparent contradictory or unreasonable view by citing the problems workers face when statutory provisions granting monopoly labor union status make it difficult for unions to function as *bona fide* worker associations. Evidence from the countries under review supports the ILO's position in regard to the dissolution of or severe restrictions on unions by African governments (See Chapter 5).

Based on its views about the role of the state in internal union affairs, the ILO, for instance in the case of Ghana, with regard to Convention No. 98, has since 1959 (and, in the case of Convention No. 87, since 1969) urged the government to amend the *de jure* status of the TUC and its 17 national unions. The International Labor Standards Department, with the help of the Committee of Experts, has specifically suggested on several occasions that Section 1(1) and the First Schedule of the 1965 Act may be modified to expunge the last traces of *de jure* monopoly unionism.[42] The cases of Ghana and Nigeria depict the problems these two countries have had to deal with in ratifying the two Conventions but not amending their laws to meet the standards they stipulate.

The situations of Zambia and Kenya (for only Convention No. 87) are significant in drawing attention to how national conditions, particularly the statutory imposition of centralized labor organizations, deter some African ILO members from ratifying both Conventions. The Zambian government admitted that it delayed ratifying both Conventions because provisions of the 1971 Industrial Relations Act — especially those imposing industrial unionism and ZCTU as the sole labor center — did not conform to ILO standards (Kalula, 1985). In Kenya, similar legal provisions prevented the government from being a ratifier of Convention No. 87. Thus, the creation of single union systems in both Kenya and Zambia, plus their attendant violations of ILO principles dealing with fundamental workers' rights, were accountable for the failure of both countries to ratify both Conventions. I may also add that technical/administrative hurdles (analyzed in the next chapter) and, at times, the diplomatic humiliation countries such as Ghana and Nigeria have endured[43] at the ILO for not amending their laws to meet ILO standards, may have acted as deterrence to these two nonratifiers. The persistent efforts of the ILO to seek modifications to African labor laws and the continuous diplomatic embarrassment suffered by government delegates for over three decades may be indicative of the complex legal and international labor relations problems the relevant statutes have engendered. Subsequent sections of this chapter discuss other problems besides single trade unionism evident in African labor relations.

Forced Payment of Union Dues

Another persistent feature of African industrial relations which the ILO deemed incompatible with its standards is compulsory or automatic checkoff of union membership dues. The specific problem here is that legally mandating the deduction of dues from payrolls reinforces the monopoly status of the state-supported unions. In other words, a situation emerges in which workers are compelled to join and then pay membership fees to government-specified unions. In Ghana, the compulsion to join TUC affiliates, coupled with automatic checkoff, guaranteed the TUC permanent financial security. Section 34 "Union Dues" and the Third Schedule of the 1965 Act assure the perpetual financial solvency of the Ghana TUC,[44] because one percent of all wages of unionized workers are deducted as union dues, of which the national unions receive 55 the locals, 20; and the TUC, 25 percent.[45]

A practical policy dilemma compulsory checkoff presents is the tension between the rights of workers to freely unionize and bear the cost of unionization and the problem of "free riders" receiving benefits without financial responsibilities. To African labor leaders and their allies, the solution was the use of the legislative resources of the state to make all workers of unionized employers pay for union services through compulsory checkoff. But to the ILO, such financial arrangements only reinforce the compulsory creation of unions and, hence, result in further divergence between African labor laws and practices and its cardinal principles.[46]

The Most Favored Unions

The final practice relates to the dominant status of the state-designated unions, which may also paradoxically infringe upon these countries' own labor laws, is the granting of both cash and material gifts to these unions. As shown in Chapter 3.2, the Ghana government under Kwame Nkrumah donated a Hall of Trades Union worth a quarter of a million United States dollars to the TUC. Currently, this building houses the TUC's head offices and most secretariats of its 17 affiliates.[47] It also provides substantial revenues in the form of rent. The other central labor organizations discussed in this study

have also received substantial cash and material support from their governments (Bates, 1970: 371; Nwubueze, 1981).

An unanticipated consequence of such apparently benign acts of state is
that, in the cases of Ghana and Kenya, by furnishing their "favorite unions"
with material benefits, these governments violated their own domestic laws,
where the state was also an employer. For example, according to Section 27
of Ghana's Industrial Relations Acts (IRA), 1965, an unfair employer labor
practice occurs whenever an employer makes contributions to a trade union
with the intention of influencing it.[48] Similar provisions exist in Kenyan law.
In addition to violating the laws of Ghana and Kenya, the granting of these
privileges to the government-designated unions also constitutes a violation of
ILO Convention No. 87, especially Article 3, which urges members to desist
from interfering in internal union activities:

1.   Workers' and employers' organisations shall have the right to draw up
     their constitutions and rules, to elect their representatives in full
     freedom, or organise their administration and activities and to formulate
     their programmes.
2.   The public authorities shall refrain form any interference which would
     restrict this right or impede the lawful exercise thereof.

The Ban On International Affiliation

A byproduct of government mandated union restructuring or rationalization which also puts African labor laws and practices at odds with ILO principles, is the ban on international affiliation by workers' organizations. As
noted earlier, Ghanaian laws are silent on this issue because there are no
statutory prohibitions on joining cross-national workers' groups.[49] In order to
formalize their involvement in the international trade union movement, in
1992, the Ghana TUC resolved to affiliate formally with the ICFTU. The situations in Kenya, Nigeria and Zambia are different from that of Ghana.
Decree Nos. 31 of 1973 and 35 of 1989 (Nigeria) expressly banned international trade union affiliation and activities.[50] According to Section 11(1) of
the Kenyan Societies' Act, 1962 (as amended) consent of the Registrar of
Societies is required for membership of foreign-based labor organizations.
Sections 33 and 34 of the Industrial Relations Act, Zambia, of 1971, barred
unions from accepting aid from foreign-based agencies and ministerial approval was required in order to join multinational labor associations.[51] The
only international organizations exempted are the ILO and the Organization of
African Trade Union Unity (OATUU), the African continental confederation
established in 1973 under the auspices of the Organization of African Unity
(OAU) (Ananaba, 1979: 138 - 139, 234).

The above cited prohibitions in Kenya, Nigeria and Zambia violate
Article 5 of Convention No. 87, which states that:

Workers' and employers' organisations shall have the right to establish and
join federations and confederations and any such organisation, federation or

confederation shall have the right to affiliate with international organisations of workers and employers.

The ban on international affiliation has assumed a continentwide problem because, although OATUU enjoys consultative status at the ILO, Article 8 of its charter prohibits African workers from affiliating with nonAfrican based labor organizations, such as the ICFTU and the WFTU. Although in practice this ban not been enforced it illustrates the intractable issues centering on African workers' rights to become members of the international labor community.

Unions and Partisan Politics

Although there are no concrete ILO instruments disallowing the domination of unions by the state or ruling parties, the position of the International Labor Conference, which is backed fully by the Committee of Freedom of Association and the Committee of Experts, is clearly indicated in a 1952 Resolution, which underscored the crucial importance of independent labor unions:

> . . . when trade unions in accordance with the law and practice of their respective countries and at the decision of their members decide to establish relations with a political party or to undertake constitutional political action as a means towards the advancement of their economic and social objectives, such political relations or actions should not be of such a nature as to compromise the continuance of the trade union movement or its social and economic functions, irrespective of political changes in the country.[52]

The Conference further resolved that union-government relations should not hinge on the subordination of unions and not be permitted to result in unions' loss of autonomy through the conversion of unions into auxiliaries of government or the ruling political party.

Labor developments in post-colonial Ghana and Kenya substantially vindicate the ILO's stance towards institutionalized labor union-government alliances. In the case of Ghana, from 1958 to 1966, the CPP subordinated the TUC and its affiliates (Archer and Reay, 1966; Twumasi, 1980). Besides, due to the rapid and often abrupt changes in government, the TUC has had to pay the price for establishing alliances with particular regimes in a turbulent political environment. It faced the hostility of governments such as the NLC and, to some extent, the PNDC, which toppled regimes that were pro-TUC. The case of Kenya similarly illustrates the adverse consequences of unions being subjugated as a result of their conversion into labor wings of the ruling Kenya African National Union (KANU) party. As Iwuji (1979: 207) has shown, Kenya evolved a classic situation of government control of unions. Starting in 1965, the President was empowered to appoint from a panel of three the General Secretary of COTU. Then in 1988, together with other social groups, the labor unions were formally integrated with the party and may have lost their autonomy. Under such conditions, as the ILO has strongly asserted and continues to emphasize, it becomes extremely difficult for labor unions to protect adequately the occupational interests of their members. The stage is now set for using Ghana's situation to probe why the ILO's standards supervisory organs strongly disapprove close links between African unions, especially national ones, and their governments.

Government Control of Unions in Ghana

In the opinion of the ILO, several aspects of Ghanaian labor laws, policies and practices depict government control over unions and actual or potential violations of Convention Nos. 87 and 98 which the country has ratified. Here, I will discuss two prominent aspects of Ghana's labor policies which clearly demonstrate government domination of organized labor. Between 1958 and 1966, there were numerous instances in which even CPP leaders openly acknowledged their domination of workers' organizations. The Minister of Labor and Cooperatives (Ako Adjei), in introducing the 1958 Industrial Relations Bill in the National Assembly, bluntly stated:

> The government . . . . agrees with the view . . . . that the needs of the workers and of the nation as a whole would best be served by a strong centralized trade union organization whose central body is recognized by government and is given certain powers and duties; and over which . . . . the government will be able to exercise some supervision to ensure that those powers are not abused.[53]

By 1965, however, the government's need to closely supervise the TUC was turned into a necessity to convert the entire labor movement into the party's labor auxiliary. Here, too, excerpts from the introduction of the Industrial Relations Bill of 1965 in Parliament by the Minister of Labor proved useful in describing the subservient role of the TUC:

> I am sure that I have covered all the points made by Members and I should like to conclude that it is the policy of the Government to ensure that workers and employers in this country work in an atmosphere of absolute industrial peace, because we know that it is only in such an atmosphere that the Development Plan which we have implemented will proceed in accordance with our programme. We require such atmosphere for rapid economic growth and that is the reason for this Bill — a Bill which aims at achieving harmony and good labour management relations. . . . The TUC is a wing of the party and the party has chosen the road of socialism as its goal for better and improved living conditions for the people of this country. It will, therefore, always support the party. And it is for us all to support this Bill to make sure that the working class of the country are adequately protected.[54]

Kofi Baako, a confidant of Kwame Nkrumah, a Cabinet member and a leading CPP ideologue, elaborated on the CPP's objectives and the role assigned to the labor unions in Ghana:

> Ghana is a budding nation having socialism as her goal; and all the integral wings of the dynamic Convention People's Party including the Ghana Trades

Union Congress are aware of their obligations as enshrined in the Constitution of the party. As a one-party State they should be guided by the party's Constitution . . . . Our party bases its policy on . . . . endeavours to deepen awareness in the consciousness of the workers so that the satisfaction of their personal interests in the first place depends on social progress in the comprehensive building of socialism. The draft Bill therefore falls in line with our aspirations. It is not opposed to our African and International Policy, neither does it untie the bond between the party and the Government and the Trades Union Congress.[55]

Through the declaration of a one-party state and the "new structure" of labor organizations adopted as a result of the 1958 and 1965 Acts, the CPP's membership card, for example, replaced union cards for employment purposes (Archer and Reay, 1966). In fact, the party's song and flag superseded the country's original national anthem and flag after it was declared the sole legally recognized political organization.[56] The CPP exerted direct control over TUC affairs by first ensuring that J. K. Tettegah, a staunch CPP member, became the first full-time Secretary-General in the mid-1950s and after 1962, the party's Central Committee (the most powerful political organ outside the President's Office), appointed directly the next Secretary-General. Tettegah was replaced by two party appointees — first, Kwaw AmpahGhana TUC, a party "stalwart," and then Magnus-George, a former Government District Commissioner (D. C.).[57]

Based on the union-party relations I have described, I may comment that while in Ghana, official and direct government control of unions, especially over their internal matters, ceased with the ouster of the Nkrumah government, events in Nigeria and Zambia, indicate stepped up government efforts to bring unions under tighter control, in spite of the repeated objections of the ILO. I am referring to middle to late 1980s developments in Nigeria and in Zambia in the early 1990s. In Nigeria in 1988, the government resorted to the ultimate weapon of union control — the dissolution of the NLC as means to silence organized labor's opposition to the austere Structural Adjustment Program policies. Then in 1989, it passed a decree disallowing the NLC and its 42 industrial unions the right to affiliate internationally. But before all this, the government incarcerated 25 unionists in 1986 for leading massive demonstrations against its economic policies.[58] In Zambia, the government arrested ZCTU leaders, including the President and the Secretary-General in 1981 (Kalula, 1985). By 1990, mounting pressure on the Kenneth Kaunda-led United National Independence Party (UNIP) to turn the country into a multiparty democracy caused the government to retaliate against ZCTU for its leaders' involvement in the opposition party, the Movement for Multiparty Democracy (MMD, by replacing the already restrictive IRA of 1971 with a more restrictive 1990 IRA which came into force in January, 1991.[59]

The Dilemmas of Labor-government Collaboration in Africa

My examination of TUC documents, including its 1958 Constitution and position papers, revealed its total endorsement of "the aims of the CPP."[60]

Such labor endorsements complicate the labor problems identified in this study by raising a relevant issue which is: To what extent can the ILO deem state actions inappropriate and not in the interests of labor, if labor itself voluntarily supports such acts of state? The issues of state control get murkier in instances in which as, in the case of Ghana, the initiative for worker-state cooperation, which resulted in the relative domination of the TUC by the CPP, in fact, came from the unions' leaders and not the government.[61] In the Ghanaian case, the ILO objects to state control of labor, on the grounds that labor's support does not necessarily diminish its harmful effects on workers. The evidence I gathered from my research and presented in Section 5.1 dealing with the practical outcomes of post-colonial labor policies supports the views of the ILO at least in the Ghanaian context.

Restrictions on Collective Bargaining

Collective bargaining in Africa is another labor relations area where several problems are encountered in the application of ILO standards, especially Convention No. 98 which encourages governments to create machinery for voluntary negotiations to determine conditions of work. Article 4 states:

> Measures appropriate to national conditions shall be taken, where necessary, to encourage and promote the full development and utilisation of machinery for voluntary negotiations between employers or employers' organisations and workers' organisations, with a view to the regulation of terms and conditions of employment by means of collective agreements.

This article creates a number of interesting paradoxes for Africa. The essential ones in Ghana include: the compulsory features of collective bargaining (outlined in Section 3.2); the government specifying the minimum duration of collective agreements; the "Powers of Extension" vested in the Labor Minister, which allow him to apply collective agreements to workers and employers who are not original parties (which has already been referred to in Section 3.2) and compulsory arbitration. There is also the common practice in most African countries of government-mandated maximum wages, which cannot be exceeded by voluntarily negotiated wages. The significance of all these provisions and policies lies in their chilling effect on voluntary negotiations. A case in point is that of Zambia. The ILO observed that, because all wages and labor agreements have to be approved by the Industrial Courts, the labor partners are not genuinely motivated to engage in meaningful voluntary collective bargaining. They often negotiate with the expectation that the outcome will be modified by the labor courts. In Ghana, the role of an income regulatory body such as the Prices and Incomes Board (created in 1972 and now dormant) resulted in confusion over the role of collective bargaining in determining wages in the country. The Ghanaian and Zambian situations illustrate how in Africa, government policies to regulate wages may have stifled voluntary bargaining.

Government intrusions into collective bargaining in Africa may intuitively look appealing and useful to society. On the one hand, one might argue they serve to stabilize not only labor relations but also national economies by putting tight reins over wage-induced inflation. Apparently also, the argument could be made that if employers are forced under the law to negotiate wages and other terms of employment that would beyond any doubt be in the interest of workers. Here, too, the ILO takes a position contrary to one's general expectation (that is, the compulsory elements of the collective bargaining laws favor workers). Its basic opinion is that all national laws that do not enhance voluntary negotiations contravene principles enshrined in Convention No. 98. I will now present Ghanaian collective bargaining statutes to examine the extent to which they conform to or deviate from ILO standards pertaining to collective bargaining.

Section 3 of Ghana's 1965 Industrial Relations Acts raises problems about the representativeness of unions because it grants unions exclusive bargaining agency and, hence, deprives workers of their right to designate their own bargaining agents. It raises the question of whether a class of employees may be properly represented by a union they did not appoint or join voluntarily. In addition, there is the issue of unions, after being granted virtual permanent representation rights, becoming complacent and, thus, not protecting their constituents. Other features of Ghana's statutes may also violate the letter and spirit of Convention No. 98. Section 5(1) of the Act of 1965 making the creation of "Negotiation Committees" compulsory clearly violates the principles of the relevant Convention. This section also limits the scope of negotiations by predetermining issues which may be negotiated voluntarily and others which the parties are bound legally to negotiate. Legal strikes can occur only over issues which are defined as negotiable by law. Also, when the law establishes the minimum duration of contracts, as in Section 11(1), workers and their employers cannot on their own free will fix the duration of employment contracts. Thus, in Ghana, it is illegal to have a term of less than a year for a contract. The cumulative impact of such restrictions is that labor and management are not permitted by existing regulations to work out the terms of labor contracts. Instead, these were predetermined by the National Assembly in Ghana or by the Industrial Courts in Zambia (Kalula, 1988).

The ILO, the Right to Strike and Civil Liberties in Africa

A great deal of controversy surrounds the rights of workers to strike to protect their interests and to demonstrate as citizens against government policies. The highly sensitive nature of strikes and workers' protests is borne by the fact that the ILO does not have instruments that explicitly guarantee these rights. The only mention of strikes in standards is in connection with a Convention dealing with forced labor (Hodges-Aeberhard and De Dios, 1987). The Organization, therefore, in relation to strikes, relies on the opinions of bodies such as the Committees of Freedom of Association and Experts.[62] The ILO explicitly avoided endorsing strikes in the form of an international labor standard because it did not want to create the erroneous impression that it instigated strikes (Alcock, 1971: 259). However, the view of the Organization is that it is "one of the essential means available to workers' and their organizations for the promotion and protection of their economic and social interests."[63]

Very significant to the African context in which governments are highly sensitive to open criticisms of public policies, the Committee of Experts (*Ibid.*) adds to workers' rights by emphasizing that their:

> Interests not only have to do with pursuing collective demands of an occupational nature, but also with seeking solutions to economic and social policy questions and to labor problems of any kind which are of direct concern to workers.

The broader definition of workers' rights means that African workers have the right to demonstrate against government policies which affect them. The only condition is that the protests should be orderly or peaceful. These rights exemplify how the ILO seeks to promote other civil rights which may impact upon workers' rights. The ILO, based on these expanded views of workers' rights, rejects African governments' contention that workers, especially civil servants or public employees, should not be permitted to protest against public policies.[64]

In the summer of 1986, when the Nigerian military authorities arrested 25 union leaders for planning a protest march, the ILO declared that these workers had the legal right to demonstrate if they conducted themselves lawfully. In the opinion of the Organization, lawful conduct did not mean the state imposing conditions which were both legally and practically impossible to meet or restricting the right to demonstrate on the grounds that the issues involved were of a political nature. Similarly in its conclusions in a case against Zambia, No. 1575, the Committee of Freedom of Association noted that such a ban on protests:

> Would not only be incompatible with the principles of freedom of association, but also unrealistic in practice, given that unions may, for example, wish to express publicly their opinion on the Government's social and economic policy. . . .[65]

On their part, protesting workers are required to refrain from behaviors which would cause loss of life or destroy public and private property.

In Ghana, as in other African and developing areas, the relevant statutes, policies and practices impose severe restrictions on strikes. A basic policy problem is how to reconcile the rights of a segment of society to withdraw its labor and to protest against public policies and society's needs for order and uninterrupted production of goods and services. In most societies, but more so in Africa with fragile economies and, at times, genuine concerns to accelerate social and economic development;, finding workable and satisfactory solutions to these policy issues has been prolonged and almost intractable. Often it has been argued that extreme national economic and security concerns alone should justify the restrictions imposed on the right to strike and the freedom of workers to express themselves. This was especially the case from the early 1960s and again in the 1980s and 1990s with the application of World Bank and IMF types of economic packages.

The Right to Strike Under Ghanaian Laws

Since Ghana has ratified both Convention Nos. 87 and 98, which are interpreted by the ILO to imply that workers have, with few exceptions, the right to strike, it may be worthwhile to examine the country's laws on industrial actions by workers. An issue to probe is the extent to which, for example, Ghanaian laws and practices meet the ILO's standards set in Article 3 of Convention No. 87 that:

> Workers'. . . . organizations shall have the right to draw up their constitutions and rules . . . . in full freedom, to organize their administration and activities and to formulate their programs.

Article 3(2) adds, "The public authorities shall refrain from any interference which could restrict this right or impede the lawful exercise thereof." To erase any lingering doubts about the state's responsibilities, Article 8 of the same Convention explicitly requires all ILO members to refrain from promulgating laws which circumvent the rights provided in the Article cited above.[66]

In addition to the above cited ILO instruments, African ILO members have unanimously endorsed an appeal to ensure workers' right to strike on the continent. During the First ILO African Regional Conference, a resolution adopted on freedom of association urged all the African members to urgently:

> Examine their legislation and practice afresh, in a thorough and objective manner, so that, in accordance with international standards, there may be recognised in every African State and territory . . . the right of all workers to go on strike in defence of their economic and social interests . . . it being understood that in exercising these rights due consideration must be given to the provisions of Article 8 of the Freedom of Association and Protection of the Right to Organise Convention, 1948 (No. 87).[67]

This resolution is important in two respects. Firstly, it shows that African member states are aware of and accept the ILO's position *vis-à-vis* strikes. Secondly, the members at the conference expressed the view that tensions between workers' rights to strike and societal needs may be reconcilable.

Exceptions to the Right to Strike

The ILO, fully cognizant of national conditions which may not always make feasible the exercise of workers' rights to withdraw their labor, has specified three exceptions to the right to strike. These are: civil and *bona fide* essential service sectors, police and military services, and periods of genuine national emergencies. Thus, for example, army and police personnel and civil servants (those who act as agents of the state) may be legally barred from striking. Here it is worthy to note that the ILO does not accept the exclusion of employees of paramilitary organizations like border patrol or prison services from striking. Thus a government cannot strip a class of workers, say, border or prison guards, of the right to strike by simply converting their organizations into military or paramilitary outfits.[68] With respect to civil servants, the ILO is of the opinion that only personnel directly employed in the true capacity of state agents may be denied the right to strike. Concerning essential services, the ILO goes to great lengths to point out specific services in which workers may not strike. Through the "case law" developed by the Committee of Freedom of Association and the opinions of the Committee of Experts, some sectors have been classified as essential. Typically, they include hospitals, public utilities — water, electricity, sewer services, air traffic control — and other services whose disruption would actually endanger life and health in the community. According to this definition, prison, dock and other services, usually considered by governments to be essential, are not accepted by the ILO.

In cases where governments declare emergencies, the test applied by the ILO is that the state of emergency has to be real and caused by natural calamities such as severe droughts, floods or fires. In situations of human-made disasters, such as those caused by wars, the ILO insists that restrictions on rights can be legally imposed in war-torn areas only and not in the entire country. Thus, for example, during the Biafran war in the 1960s in Nigeria, the government could legally restrict workers from striking in only geographical areas directly affected. In the case of economic emergencies, it is interesting to point out that the ILO applies a *force majeure* test (that is, events beyond the control of the government) to ensure that a government that plunges the economy into bankruptcy (such as the NRC/SMC of Ghana) does not turn around and impose restrictions on workers because of the alleged fiscal crisis of the state.[69] One final note is that in all permissible situations of essential or emergency services, the ILO only allows temporary restrictions of well-defined limits on the duration, tbe areas affected and the specific class and number of workers barred from striking. Whenever a member exceeds the stipulated time or issues a blanket prohibition of strikes, the supervisory organs reject them and call upon the state involved to reinstate the right to strike.

Despite Ghana's participation in the adoption of the resolution calling for workers' rights to strike and the country's ratification of Convention Nos. 87 and 98, the laws in the country have virtually outlawed strikes, even in nonessential sectors of the economy. Under Section 21(1)b of the Industrial Relations Acts, 1965, workers can only strike if they wait 28 days and exhaust an arduous dispute settlement procedure, and if the Labor Minister does not refer the dispute to arbitration. In its observations about the effects of these kinds of provisions, the Committee of Experts remarked that:

> The prohibition of strikes may also result, for all practical purposes, from the cumulative effect of the provisions relating to the established dispute settlement machinery, according to which labour disputes are channeled through compulsory conciliation and arbitration procedures leading to a final award or decision which is binding on the parties concerned; a similar situation may arise in cases where, in the absence of an agreement between the parties, dis-

putes can be settled by compulsory arbitration or decision at the discretion
of the public authorities. Under these systems, it is possible to prohibit or put
a rapid stop to almost any strike.[70]

The point communicated to me during my field work that since independence,
all strikes have been virtually illegal in Ghana, supports the view of the
Committee of Experts. In the public sector, because of the failure to adhere to
the ILO's exemptions from strike, public employees such as teachers, although not employed in the capacity of state agents, are not permitted to engage in collective bargaining lest they strike.[71] Such restrictions violate the
provisions of Convention Nos. 87 and 98 and the principles enunciated by the
Committees of Freedom of Association and Experts.

Essential Services

In dealing with essential services in Ghana, the first problem that emerges
is the long list of services classified by the government as essential and, thus,
within which workers could never strike legally. According to the list furnished by the Ghana Department of Labor, housing and transport industries
are defined as essential sectors, but these are not on the ILO's list. Zambia
has an even more exhaustive list. Under powers conferred on him by the
Industrial Relations Acts of 1971 and 1990, the Zambian President has almost
unlimited discretion to extend the classification of essential services as he
deems appropriate to meet state security needs (Kalula, 1985; ILO, 1992).
The Zambian provisions indicate one of the most critical obstacles to workers'
and other civil liberties in Africa. This is the problem of the broad powers
vested in the office of head of state often with little or no judicial review. A
case epitomizing this serious problem is the appointment and dismissal of
Supreme Court justices in Kenya by the President.[72] Such presidential powers can be utilized to strip the judiciary of all autonomy and to silence judges
who are critical of government policies and actions.
     Whereas in most societies, governments are expected to be interested in
reducing strikes, in the case of Ghana, the government has not covered up its
intent to use labor statutes expressly to stifle them. The Minister of Labor, in
his introduction of the 1965 Labor Bill in Parliament, was candid when he
listed its fifth function as rendering strikes "unlawful." One of his colleagues
correctly summed up its impact by declaring,: "We know that it will be impossible for anyone or a group of persons to go on strike because they have to
pass through a very lengthy process."[73] Besides several legal barriers in the
way of workers who desire to strike, the state has responded harshly to strikes.
Following colonial traditions, the public authorities had fired strikers from
their jobs and in extreme cases killed by the police. Under the NLC, employees of the state-owned Cargo Handling Corporation and hotels were dismissed
en masse for striking and under this regime, striking gold miners were shot by
the police.[74] Other repressive measures resorted to by the public authorities
include invocation of states of emergency as in 1961 and 1978 by the CPP
and SMC regimes, respectively.

In 1961, while President Nkrumah was visiting the former Soviet bloc, the Presidential Commission declared a state of emergency when rail workers struck in the Western Region of the country. The strike leaders were sentenced to six-month jail terms (Drake and Lacy, 1966), which were later commuted by a presidential pardon. Similarly in 1978, the SMC declared a state of emergency when faced with mammoth strikes by public utility workers in Accra and other major cities and towns.[75] Under the Emergency Powers (Proclamation of a State of Emergency) Instrument, 1978, the government did not only reiterate the ban on strikes in the so-called essential service sector, but also sought to detain striking workers indefinitely. In this particular situation, before the ILO was called upon to intervene, the government itself was ousted and the state of emergency revoked (see Section 2. 2).

The repressive measures I have alluded to, however, do not exhaust the wide spectrum of coercive means employed by the state to restrain strikes. For example, the PP, when faced with a wave of strikes and protest rallies denouncing its policies, decided to apply the ultimate weapon to silence the unions — dissolution. Under a guise of ensuring freedom of association to all workers, it rushed through the National Assembly a certificate of urgency and in less than 24 hours adopted the 1971 Amendment to the 1965 Act which led to the temporary demise of the TUC.[76] In a parallel development, although the outgoing Kaunda administration did not outrightly liquidate the ZCTU or its affiliates, it used the 1990 Industrial Relations Act to attempt to institute a tighter rein over the trade union leaders who assumed leadership roles in the opposition parties that emerged to challenge it. Thus, Ghanaian and other African governments' strategies to curtail strikes have ranged from cumbersome statutory requirements and prohibitions to the occasional use of coercive instruments such as the police and other security agencies. In Ghana, the Busia-led PP, through statutory dissolution, hoped to deal the TUC a blow from which no recovery was anticipated.[77] Organized labor in Nigeria had to contend with a similar fate when in 1988 the NLC and its 42 affiliates were banned by the Federal Nigerian Military Government. But as it happened in Ghana, the ban proved to be temporary.[78]

The state's use of violence to regulate strikes or labor demonstrations raises further questions of trade union and civil rights violations in Africa. State actions, especially the killing or injuring of workers, arrest of union leaders without trial and their indefinite incarceration, or forced exile are all deemed severe infractions of not only ILO norms, but other international human rights instruments. In relation to that, the ILO has on several occasions pointed out the close links between general civil rights conditions and the exercise of workers' rights. It, for example, refers to the fact that in 1970, without any opposition from member states, a resolution was adopted to protect both the civil and trade union rights of workers.[79] Additionally, in its examination of workers' rights, in Case No. 1135 against Ghana, the Committee on Freedom of Association emphasized the need for the government to employ both statutory and practical measures to guarantee workers' safety in the exercise of their occupational and civil rights . The Committee of Experts also emphasized that: "the body of existing laws and regulations, together with national practice, cannot fail to have a decisive impact on trade union rights" (ILO, 1983a: 16).

Therefore, the Organization's position is that all members are obligated to generate conditions in which workers can exercise the rights designated in Convention Nos. 87 and 98. In this connection, it draws attention to provisions in these two Conventions that bar national laws from impeding workers' rights. The Committee of Experts, for example, is convinced that all freedoms are meaningless if member states do not respect essential civil rights like freedom from arbitrary arrest, the right to free speech, and to demonstrate against government policy (Ibid.: 16 - 19). Regarding the use of force in labor relations, the organization takes the view that it may be used only under very extreme circumstances: situations in which workers do actually threaten life, safety and the health of the community. Thus governments, in the view of the ILO, are not permitted to physically assault or intimidate workers under the guise of protecting life, health and public safety. Even where the use of force is considered appropriate, the ILO urges extra caution to avoid maiming or killing workers. Upon the use of force, the ILO requests prompt, thorough and impartial investigations of any deaths or injuries.

A reiteration of key ILO opinions on the rights of workers to strike will conclude this section. The ILO's Committees of Experts and Freedom of Association are of the view that anti-union state actions, like the violent suppression of strikes through police shootings and the arrest and jailing of strike leaders, may all be prejudicial to the rights of workers, especially when their conduct is legal or orderly. The Organization is also of the strong opinion that penal sanctions deter workers from effectively protecting their bona fide occupational interests which member states have agreed to preserve through the ratification of Convention Nos. 87 and 98 and their membership in the Organization. Furthermore, the denial of the right to strike and to dissent publicly from government policies, actions and programs which have an impact upon the working class can lead to an erosion of all other workers' rights. including collective bargaining. A basic premise of the ILO's position is that the right to strike is a sine qua non of all workers' rights — without the right of workers to withdraw their labor without fear of government retribution, all other rights become irrelevant. J. Hodges-Aeberhard and A. O. De Dios (1987: 556 - 557) aptly sum up why the ILO is extremely concerned about these rights especially when they apply to union leaders:

> . . . adequate protection against all acts of antiunion discrimination . . . including reprisals for strike action — is particularly desirable in the case of trade union officials because, in order to be able to perform their trade union duties in full independence, they should have a guarantee that they will not be prejudiced on account of the mandate they hold from the union's members
> . . . .

In spite of the ILO's unequivocal position on the right of workers to strike, the evidence from Ghana, Nigeria, Kenya and Zambia shows that both ratifiers and nonratifiers of Conventions on workers' rights implement policies which tend to contravene the Organization's basic principles.

NOTES

1.   Examples are: Ghana became independent on March 6, 1957 and joined the ILO on May 13, 1957; Kenya's independence and membership occurred in 1963 and 1964, respectively; Nigeria acquired independent status in October, 1960 and shortly after joined the Organization; and Zambia became a Republic on October 24, 1964 and an ILO member on December 8 of the same year.

2.   See Appendices 2 and 3 for the texts of the two Conventions.

3.   There are 22 African ILO members which use English as the official language. (ILO, Washington DC Branch Office, April, 1993). These are listed in Appendix 7.

4.   See Appendix 1 for texts of Articles.

5.   From a researcher's standpoint, these reports furnish immense insights into why countries such as Zambia and Kenya have not ratified both Conventions. Thus, in Section 3.3, I relied, to a large extent, on the ILO's comments (both published and unpublished) on my selected countries' labor policies and practices *vis-à-vis* workers' rights to freely associate and to pursue their occupational interests.

6.   Although Zambia has not ratified Convention No. 87, the ILO requested the government to explain the circumstances that led to the detention of ZCTU leaders in 1981 (Kalula, 1985). In Case No. 1575 of 1990, the ILO urged the Zambian authorities to void provisions of the new 1990 Industrial Relations Act (No. 36) which came into force in January, 1991 and restricted the rights of ZCTU and its affiliates.

7.   This is reflected in the deliberations of ILO bodies such as the Governing Body and the Conference Committee. Also, the Committee of Freedom of Association (which oversees workers' rights) has repeatedly emphasized similar opinions in its decisions concerning alleged violations of trade union rights. See, for example, the Committee's Case Nos. 1135 against Ghana, and 984 and 1189 against Kenya (ILO, 1985a). For recent cases, see Case Nos. 1530 of 1990 against Nigeria, 1575 of 1990 against Zambia and 1638 of 1992 against Malaw.i.

8.   Because Convention No. 98 has less stringent requirements, most ILO members have found it relatively easy to meet its provisions. Thus, for example, Ghana ratified No. 98 only two years after independence, but waited until 1965 before ratifying No. 87.

9.   An example of the former is the Industrial Relations Act of 1958 or 1965 of Ghana; of the latter, the 1978 Decree establishing the Nigerian Labor Congress and the 1965 Presidential Declaration which created COTU of Kenya.

10.   Ghana was the first sub-Saharan African nation to institutionalize a single national union framework. She was followed by Zambia in 1965, Kenya in 1966 and Nigeria in 1978 (Ananaba, 1979: 143). In Kenya, 1966 is indicated as the year for founding a single-union federation because, although the Presidential Declaration authorizing its formation was issued in September, 1965 COTU was actually founded in 1966.

11.   It is worthy to point out that although the TUC and its affiliates are the only recognized unions under Ghanaian law, in practice other labor associations — typically the Ghana National Association of Teachers (GNAT), the Ghana Registered Nurses' Association (GRNA) and the Ghana Civil Servants' Association (GCSA) — also enjoy consultative status in their respective sectors. For example, since 1985 representatives of all these associations have on regular basis participated in the deliberations of the National Advisory Committee on Labor.

12.   One of the reasons why the 1965 Act was passed to supersede the 1958 Act was that the Ghana government wanted to meet ILO standards embodied in Convention No. 87. Therefore, immediately following the passage of the former Act, the country ratified that Convention (Ghana, "Parliamentary Debates," *Official Report*, May 21, 1965, "The Industrial Relations Bill": column 190).

13.   In other African countries, similar legislation was used to create central labor organizations and their affiliates. In the case of Nigeria, for instance, Decree No. 22 of 1978 led to the founding of the NLC and reduced the national unions from 71 to 42.

14.   An exclusive bargaining agency situation exists when labor laws or practices result in a single union having the exclusive privilege of representing a group of employees for collective bargaining purposes. According to the ILO, this does not violate its standards *per se* . It does so only when exclusive agency is conferred permanently to the exclusion of all other unions.

15.   In Ghana, union registration (official recognition as a workers' association) is distinguished from certification for collective bargaining. Hence, although the GNAT and the GCSA are registered, they cannot legally engage in direct labor negotiations over wages and terms of employment or embark on strikes because under existing labor regulations they cannot be certified as bargaining agents. As noted above, these organizations, together with the GRNA, do, however, participate in consultations with the government and several of their members have struck on numerous occasions to back their wage claims. Cases in point were massive strikes by civil servants in 1978 and 1979 against the Acheampong regime and more recently a spate of strikes by nurses, teachers and civil servants, especially towards the end of the PNDC's reign in 1991 - 1992 and in 1986 to reinstate leave allowance (Nimo, "Ghana: Civil servants in revolt: Breaking a tradition," *West Africa*, August 10 - 16, 1992: 1346 - 1347; N. Alabi, "Labor Front: Cold comfort for workers," *The Independent*, September 23 - 29, 1992: 8; N. A. Y. Asamany, "Salary Disparities and Strikes," *People's Daily Graphic*, September 28, 1992: 5).

16.   He has additional powers by being solely responsible for appointing individual or panels of arbitrators.

17.   Information from the Ghana Department of Labor, Accra, 1987. See also Appendix 4, Ghana Labor Department Questionnaire.

18.   For how and why this paradox has emerged in Ghana and Nigeria see Panford (1988).

19.   Cases in point are cash and material donations such as the gift of the Halls of Trade Unions (valued at U. S. $250,000) given to the TUC by the Kwame Nkrumah government in 1962; the million naira seed money the Federal Nigerian Military Government gave to the NLC in 1978. Similarly, ZCTU and COTU received substantial cash advances from their governments (Bates, 1970).

20.   This dissolution was, however, temporary because the NRC, which overthrew the PP government, restored the TUC as the sole labor federation in February, 1972 (Jeffries, 1978; Gray, 1981). See also NRC Decree No. 22 of 1972.

21.   See, for example, ILO, "Report of the Committee of Experts, General Report and Observations Concerning Particular Countries," International Labor Conference, 71st Session, 1985, and Committee of Experts Observations Concerning Ratified Conventions, 1992: 215 - 217, dealing with Ghana's problems with Convention No. 87.

22.   ILO, International Labor Conference, 40th Session, 1957 *Record of Proceedings* (Provisional): 11.

23.   *Ibid*. This statement also meant that the government was committed to abide by the ILO's tripartite principles concerning domestic and international labor affairs.

24.   Ghana National Assembly, Parliamentary Proceedings, "Official Record on Motions," ILO Convention, May 21, 1965: columns 205 - 207. Hansards used in this study were obtained from the University of Ghana Law School and Balme Libraries, Accra (Ghana).

25.   ILO, International Labor Conference, 59th Session, 1974, "Report of the Director General (Discussion)," *Provisional Record*: 6/13 - 14.

26.   ILO International Labor Standards Department, "Mission Report," Ghana, May 3 - 10, 1987; *West Africa*, "Labor Seminar," June 6, 1987.

27.   Under Articles 19 and 22 of the ILO's Constitution (1988), members are obligated to submit periodically reports detailing their status with respect to Conventions and Recommendations. See Appendix 1 for full texts of these articles. These problems are treated in Section 4. 3.

28.   These categories are used to facilitate my analysis and therefore do not necessarily exhaust the broad spectrum of problems. They represent the common obstacles I observed during my field work.

29.   Ghana's laws are silent on rights to affiliate internationally. But in practice, the TUC and its nationals participate in cross-national labor activities and in organizations such as the ICFTU and its International Trade Secretariats (ITS). At its 1992 Quadriennial Congress, the TUC adopted a resolution to formally affiliate with the ICFTU.

30.   In 1988, COTU was officially designated the ruling party's (Kenya African National Congress, KANU) labor wing (*New York Times*, Oct. 5, 1988: 11A).

31.   Nigeria, "Police Stop Union 'Confrontation'," *West Africa*, June 9, 1986: 1234; "Control of Human Rights," *West Africa*, June 16, 1986: 1250 - 1251. These protests were in connection with the imposition of IMF- and World Bank-style structural adjustment by the Federal Nigerian Military Government.

32.   Based on its principles that workers had the right to protest against public policies (if such protests are orderly and peaceful), the ILO, in conjunction with other international human/workers' rights organizations, such as the British Commonwealth Association of Trade Unions, requested and secured the release of these 25 union leaders by the Nigerian government.

33.   ILO, International Labor Conference, 54th Session, 1970, "Record of Proceedings": 733. The Committee of Freedom of Association remarked that Malawi's trade unions had the right to express their views on national political developments such as a return to a multiparty government (Committee of Freedom of Association, Case No. 1638, 286th Report, March 1993: 145 - 147).

34.   At the ILO, concerns over this issue led to my analysis of related problems (Panford, 1988). See also Erstling (1977) for a comprehensive treatment of these problems.

35.   That has been accomplished through the creation (via the legislative route, that is, the 1958 and 1965 Industrial Relations Acts) of a highly centralized union structure, with the TUC at the apex as a powerful organ formulating policies, directing trade union operations and coordinating government relations from its head offices in Accra. Parallel situations exist in other African states. I may note, however, that in Ghana, increasingly since the mid-1980's, although the GNAT, GNRA and GCSA are not officially designated as collective bargaining agents, they have been encouraged by the government to participate in deliberations concerning labor such as attempts to overhaul Ghana's labor laws and in the meetings of the National Advisory Committee of Labor.

36.   ILO, *International Labor Conventions and Recommendations 1919 - 1981* ILO, Geneva (1982). For a full text of this Convention, see Appendix 2. As indicated in the full text, the ILO also seeks to protect private employers' rights, which are be-

yond the scope of this study. This and other conventions cited may be obtained from the ILO, International Labor Standards Department, Geneva, or the Washington DC Branch Office.

37.   This is an arrangement under which all employees within a bargaining unit are required to join the union representing workers in the unit within a specified time, say, one or two months, as a condition for continuous employment (Sharfritz, 1980: 349).

38.   ILO, 1983a: 16.

39.   To further examine the details of this "restructuring" and "rationalization," see Nwubueze (1975, 1981); the Republic of Kenya, *The Policy of Trade Union Organization in Kenya*, Government Printer, Nairobi, 1965 and Zambian Industrial Relations Act, 1971 executed through Instrument No. 29 of 1974. Since the published literature is confusing about who actually initiated the New Union structure in Ghana in 1958, and during my Summer and Fall 1991 field trip to Ghana, I investigated that matter. Joe-Fio Meyer, a premier trade unionist and the Nkrumah regime's last Ambassador to Vietnam, and John K. Tettegah, the first TUC full-time Secretary-General, informed me that the union leaders including themselves created the labor bills that the Nkrumah government pushed through Parliament in the form of the 1958 Industrial Relations Act. That was confirmed by Ako-Adjei who oversaw the bill's technical drafting for both the Cabinet and Parliament (information from interviews conducted in Accra, Ghana, 1991). The events narrated by the three respondents were substantiated by the official records of the relevant Cabinet meeting minutes, which I examined during my 1991 field trip. These minutes are available at the Ghana National Archives, Accra.

40.   Ghanaian labor leaders I interviewed in Geneva (from 1985 to 1986) were very passionate in their support for government intervention to provide "a united labor front." In fact several of them expressed strong preference for the use of statutory authority to bring the associations of teachers, registered nurses and civil servants "into the TUC fold."

41.   Similar concerns may have influenced the decision of the Federal Nigerian Military Government of President I. Babangida to decree a two-party system for Nigeria as part of the program for a return to civilian rule.

42.   The status of the NLC has also been discussed periodically at various ILO fora since 1979 and in June 1986 at the International Labor Conference.

43.   Based on in-depth discussions I had with African diplomats and government representatives, and the observations I made concerning the proceedings of key ILO standards supervisory bodies — the Governing Body and the International Labor Conference sessions of 1985 - 1986 — I concluded that these government officials felt embarrassed and pressured by the repeated oral and written requests to explain their countries' situations. This was especially true in situations in which they were called upon at fora such as the Governing Body and various conference committees to explain their governments' positions.

44.   It was therefore not surprising to find it in financial crisis when the PP administration annulled these sections in 1971. It could not pay the salaries of its officials and meet other financial obligations until the NRC reinstated automatic checkoff (Jeffries, 1978; Gray, 1981). The Zambian Congress of Trade Unions' (ZCTU) relative financial success is also attributed largely to a statutory checkoff system activated by the Industrial Relations Act (Zambia) 1971 (Kalula, 1988).

45.   Information from the TUC, March 1987.

46.   In Chapter 6, I describe some of the innovative and practical ways in which this tension has been surmounted without violating ILO norms.

47.   The Mine Workers Union's offices are in Tarkwa and the Rail Workers are located in Sekondi-Takoradi in the Western Region.

48.   In 1972, as part of the "restoration" of the Ghana TUC, the NRC wrote off all debts owed by the former to state agencies (Gray, 1981). The restoration and the financial relief contributed to what the TUC's Research Department described as the TUC's "unflinching support" for this government. Section 5.1 describes the negative effects on the labor movement for this kind of support.

49.   During my field work, I met several Ghanaian union leaders attending International Trade Secretariat meetings in Europe. The Public Service International (PSI) held a one-week course in Accra in conjunction with its local affiliate, the Ghana Civil Servants' Association (ILO, "Mission Report," Ghana, May 3 - 10, 1987). Thus, Ghanaian workers have membership in international organizations.

50.   Under pressure from the ILO, Decree No. 35 was repealed in August 1991. See ILO CFA Case No. 1530 of 1990 (Nigeria), *West Africa*, August 19 - 25, 1991: 1380 - 1381 and ILO, Governing Body, *278th Report of the* Committee of Freedom of Association, ILO: Geneva, May - June 1991: 73 - 76.

51.   Similar provisions were retained in the new Industrial Relations Act (1990) which came into force in January, 1991. As a result of Case No. 1575 of 1991 filed against Zambia, and also because of a change in government, the new Zambian Government informed the ILO that the IRA of 1990 had been amended and awaiting presidential action. (Information from ILO Head Offices dated June 11, 1993. See also ILO, Committee of Freedom of Association, *284th Report*, 1992: 263 - 286).

52.   ILO, 1983a: 62.

53.   National Assembly, *Official Record of Proceedings*, "Second Reading, Industrial Relations Bill, 1958," December 17, 1958, column 546. This statement is also significant for revealing why a centralized union organization was adopted with the TUC playing a critical role. The structure was designed as a mechanism for controlling the entire organized working class. According to Ako-Adjei, features of the 1958 Act which the ILO deemed too restrictive were in fact incorporated by the leaders of the TUC to assure the Ghana government that workers would not abuse the privileges granted to them under post-colonial labor legislation. Interviews conducted at Ako-Adjei Park, Accra, Ghana, Summer and Fall, 1991.

54.   National Assembly, *Record of Proceedings,* "Second Reading, Industrial Relations Bill, 1965," May 21, 1965, column 201.

55.   *Ibid*. The last section of this comment also confirms the opinion that there are still aspects of Ghanaian statutes which contravene the provisions of Convention Nos. 87 and 98, in spite of the 1965 Act being promulgated partly in response to the recommendations of the ILO.

56.   For details of the origins and nature of the one-party state in Africa, see the classic study by Friedland and Rosberg (1964).

57.   Information from the Ghana TUC, March 1987. See also, Jeffries (1978) and Gray (1981). In Zambia, as in Kenya's situation already referred to, through Section 27 of the Industrial Relations Act (No. 36) of 1971, the ruling United National Independence Party (UNIP) exercised political leverage over ZCTU and its affiliates by mandating the submission of unions' constitutions for approval by the Labor Minister. UNIP also intruded into union organizational affairs by laying down procedures for resolving, for example, jurisdictional conflicts within the labor movement. Thus although unlike in the Ghanaian and Kenyan situations in which the ruling parties completely controlled unions, in Zambia the party established controls over important internal union processes and activities without officially making ZCTU its labor wing.

58.   The FNMG reinstated NLC as the sole labor federation, and thus the dissolution was temporary. The ban on international affiliation, as noted already, was an-

nulled and the unionists detained were released in the summer of 1986, all due to a combination of factors including the intercession of the ILO, other international labor groups and also, importantly, local pressure on the government.

59.   With the MMD as the new government, the ILO has been informed of pending legislation to void the 1990 IRA passed by the outgoing UNIP government. For details of the struggles centered on government control of ZCTU, see Hamalengwa (1992).

60.   See, for example, John K. Tettegah, *Towards Nkrumaism: The building of socialist Ghana, the role and tasks of the trade unions,* Report on Doctrine and Orientation Presented to the First Biennial Congress of the Ghana TUC (March 26 - 30, 1962) Accra: Education and Publicity Department of the TUC (Ghana), no date.

61.   As indicated above, Ghana government and TUC officials such as Tettegah, Meyer and Ako Adjei, who were directly involved in the TUC's relations with the CPP, were unanimous in stating emphatically to me that the 1958 Act was proposed by the TUC and the government's role was limited to the technical drafting and passage in Parliament. See Tettegah, 1958; Cowan, 1960.

62.   ILO, 1983a; 1985a.

63.   ILO, 1983: 62. The Organization's definition of strikes includes what in Africa may be called "go slows" (work-to-rule), sit-down and short strikes lasting a few hours or days. Its definition is comprehensive enough to incorporate any form of withdrawal of labor to protect workers and demonstrations (marches) to voice their concerns in public.

64.   An additional instrument designed by the ILO to seek further protection of the rights of public employees is Convention No. 151, which has been ratified by Zambia, for example. Ratifiers are obligated to permit civil servants to protest against unpopular government policies.

65.   ILO, Committee of Freedom of Association, *284th Report,* 1992: 283. In its more recent report, this committee made similar remarks about attempts by the Malawi government to stifle trade unions' political activities. See ILO. Case No. 1638, Committee of Freedom of Association, *286th Report,* March, 1993.

66.   For a complete text see Appendix 2. The ILO's rationale is that societies can avoid the excesses of labor disruptions if governments permitted the development of speedy, just and reliable methods for resolving labor conflicts.

67.   ILO, First African Regional Conference, Lagos, Nigeria, 1960.

68.   Among the few groups of workers the ILO allows to be restricted from striking are the police and army. Even with these groups, after they acquire the right to strike, governments may not take away such rights.

69.   For a complete list of essential services as defined by the ILO, see ILO, 1985a; 1983a: 78 - 85; and Hodges-Aeberhard and De Dios, 1987.

70.   ILO, 1983a: 63.

71.   As I have already pointed out, the Ghana National Association of Teachers (GNAT) is not a legally certified bargaining agent. Therefore, under Ghanaian law, it cannot strike. However, as recent industrial actions by nurses, teachers and other public sector employees have demonstrated, such bans have not prevented public sector strikes. On the contrary, in the last two years of the PNDC, the country witnessed massive increases in strikes and anti-government demonstrations (see Note 15).

72.   J. Perlez, "Kenya Threatens to Curb Churches," *New York Times,* October 5, 1988: 11A.

73.   Ghana National Assembly, 1965 Industrial Relations Bill, *Parliamentary Record of Proceedings,* columns 192 and 195.

74.   This was, however, more of an aberration in post-colonial Ghanaian labor relations because as much as most regimes have sought to repress strikes, rarely have

workers been shot (Hutchful, 1987). The dismissal of these employees was reported
to the ILO as Case No. 578 against Ghana. These workers were reinstated in 1969, just
before the ILO's African Regional Conference was held in Accra (ILO, 1970). I may
infer from the timing of the reinstatement a subtle influence of the ILO in the PP government's decision. The government may have been seeking to develop an image as a
respecter of ILO principles shortly before the Regional Conference commenced and
may also have used the reinstatement as a goodwill gesture towards labor.

75.   See Map of Ghana: The Geopolitical Context of Labor Relations, Appendix
6.

76.   Ghana, 1971 Parliamentary Debates, *Official Report*, Second Series, Vol. 8,
Nos. 29 and 30, The Industrial Relations (Amendment) Bill, September 9, 1971:
columns 1531 - 1650 and September 10, 1971: columns 1651 - 1668.

77.   According to the Ghana TUC, before the ILO could take any action on this
dissolution, the PP administration was toppled and the NRC restored it as the sole national labor federation. See NRC Decree No. 22 of 1972, which read in part that the
TUC has been restored as if nothing happened to it.

78.   According to the ILO's information to me dated April 19, 1993, the ILO
Director General's intervention contributed to the restoration of the NLC and its organizations.

79.   ILO, 1970a. This view was re-echoed in the conclusions of the Committee
of Freedom of Association in Case No. 1638 against Malawi.

Chapter 4

Why African Governments Have Difficulties Implementing ILO Standards

4. 1   How Colonialism Retarded African Labor Administration and Workers' Rights: British Colonial Labor Relations

The Relevance of Colonial Labor Policies

This subchapter is devoted to the role of colonial labor laws and policies in contemporary African governments' predisposition to use ILO standards as labor policy guidelines. It depicts, for example, how foreign domination has constrained the capacity and willingness of post-independence African nations to grant workers rights enshrined in ILO Conventions and Recommendations. In addition, this chapter evaluates the views of several authors on the role and impact of British rule on contemporary labor relations in Africa with emphasis on Ghana and my other selected countries.

The role of the Ghanaian or any African state in current labor relations can be better understood by putting trade union-government relaions in their proper historical, political, economic and social contexts. British rule is considered significant because modern-day African labor affairs show that, although the countries under review have been independent for at least 30 years, their policies, laws and practices continue to be substantially influenced by colonial labor policies and laws. This is especially the case in public sector labor relations.[1] What I refer to as the "British labor legacy" constitutes what in the post-independence period has become so influential that in several respects it may be equated with having set strong precedents which African governments have found too difficult to resist or conveniently used to their advantage. D. Otobo (1987: 49) furnishes a classic example of this situation in Nigeria:

> . . . the original 1938 Trades Union Ordinance. . . reinforced in all subse-
> quent legislation governing the formation and administration of trade unions,
> has been used by successive governments to prevent or slow down the rate of
> unionisation, to neutralise those sections of organized labour considered too
> radical or troublesome and to influence the composition of union leadership,
> particularly at the centre.

The British legacy together with two other factors — the geopolitical location and activities of unions and technical and or administrative bottlenecks
— explain why Ghanaian and other African laws and practices may not be
compatible with ILO provisions regarding workers' rights. (See subsequent
subunits of this chapter.) On the whole, although one cannot attribute every
African labor problem to British rule alone, colonial economic and political
activities have been strong catalysts to or severe constraints on contemporary
African labor policy choices.[2] British hostility and patronizing attitudes contributed to the emergence of weak African unions. The pioneers of modern
day unions accepted or initiated government intervention in the form of the
1958 Industrial Relations Acts in Ghana and similar provisions in Nigeria,
Kenya and Zambia[3] to overcome the excessive and counter productive union
multiplicity situation which one labor commentator described as: ". . . a good
deal of jealousy between rival unions and each will outbid the other trying to
gain support from the unfortunate rank and file" (Roberts, 1964: 190). As will
be shown, the extremely fragile unions depicted by Roberts were the products
of deliberate British labor policies and laws.

The profound impact of British colonialism on the capacity of the African
state to meet ILO standards may be assessed in terms of its short- and long-
term effects on the functions of trade unions. Of much concern here is the institutionalization of labor organizations as the representatives of workers' aspirations. This is the acceptance of unions as legitimate and integral parts of
the industrial relations. It implies the creation of conditions by the British in
which unions are encouraged to thrive, because they are perceived to be socially beneficial. The institutionalization of unions has important implications
for any country's membership of the ILO. This is because one important assumption within the Organization is that members can fully participate in activities and programs if they fulfill another important condition — they have
to take steps to insure that unions operate in full freedom and are indeed the
true voices of the working class. It is implied further that trade unions can
function legitimately only when they enjoy a great deal of autonomy. And as
noted in earlier chapters, to be effective, trade unions should be able to use
strikes to back their claims. Contrary to these conditions described by the
ILO, because of British domination, African unions until recently were weak,
restricted and could barely rely on pure economic pressure to defend their interests.

Although, as in the case of Ghana, the British had ratified Convention No.
84 (the equivalent of Convention No. 87 for colonial territories) on behalf of
the Gold Coast (now Ghana), their activities often did not comply with the
provisions of that Convention which required them to ensure free trade unionism.[4] In this respect, the British, by not abiding by international labor laws set

inappropriate examples for African ILO members to follow. Subsequently, on the eve of independence, the industrial relations situation which Africans inherited from the British was highly unsuitable for countries such as Ghana, Kenya, Nigeria and Zambia to fulfill adequately their ILO membership requirements. Besides the typically fragile unions, the labor departments they had created were not intended to and capable of performing the technically complex duties associated with ILO membership such as providing elaborate reports on the national economy and labor situation. I will now turn to a number of substantive areas to demonstrate how the colonial legacy made it extremely difficult for Africans to institutionalize labor relations and workers' rights as prescribed by ILO standards and principles.

4. 1. 2   The Alleged Liberal Dimensions of Colonial Labor Policies

Persistently false views in the literature often lead to the incorrect conclusion that colonial labor policies were rooted in principles of "voluntary" or "liberal" trade unionism in the exact image of metropolitan labor relations. Advocates of such views include B. C. Roberts (1964), C. Cambridge (1984) and I. Davies (1966). Cambridge, for example, alleged that the British left a tripartite system of labor relations in all the African countries he studied. Based on the definition of tripartism, that meant that at the time of Ghana's independence, unions were permitted to participate fully with employers and government to make policies impacting on labor. Roberts' alleged existence of voluntary trade unionism implied that the British nurtured unions which were not only independent but truly defended organized labor.

The benign views of British colonial labor practices are rejected in this book because their authors failed to comprehend the real context of British colonialism in Africa, or they simply discounted as inconsequential the nature of colonialism as an exploitative system which had adverse impact on both pre- and post-independence union evolution. Roberts' description of colonial labor policies contradicts his own favorable impressions of the British legacy. A more valid assessment of British policy may be garnered from a thorough examination of the relevant British statutes *per se*, the roles of British labor advisers, the labor departments created and other practices of the British authorities. Since practices are more telling than policy pronouncements, a critical reexamination of actual British measures in the labor area needs to be provided. The actual outcomes of the practices also need to be reviewed in depth. Finally, and equally important, one needs to be reminded that these labor practices took place within the confines of a much broader phenomenon — colonialism. Hence to appreciate the colonial labor experience, one needs a comprehensive understanding of the broad socio-political, legal and historical contexts of British colonialism in Africa.[5]

4. 1. 3   Oppressive Colonial Labor Legislation

The British role is treated in four categories for convenience:

1. The passing of colonial labor laws, called "Ordinances," such as the Gold Coast (Ghana) Trades Union Ordinance, 1941. It deals with trade union organization — membership, registration and certification for collective bargaining purposes and strikes;
2. The establishment of rudimentary labor departments (or ministries);
3. The employment of British Labor Department and TUC officials as labor advisers in the colonies; and
4. The application of force often involving the police to suppress strikes and other workers and civilian protests.

All of the above, especially the use of force were aimed at colonialism's dual objective of exploiting the human and natural resources of Africa and the forced retention of British domination. As Otobo (1987: 13) has perceptively observed, force was an indispensable component of colonialism because the colonial authorities lacked legitimacy and thus operated as occupying forces.

The U.S. Department of Labor (1958: 16) made two insightful comments about the colonial labor laws Ghana inherited form the British. It described the restrictions in the 1941 Trades Union Ordinance to include a compulsory requirement that unions "register and keep financial records." The second referred to how the Conspiracy and Protection of Property (Trade Disputes) Ordinance of 1941 treated strikes by workers as criminal breaches of contract. The Department described the ordinance as dealing with:

> . . . . malicious breaches of contract by persons employed in essential services. Declares illegal strikes. . . designed to coerce the government or having any object other than the settlement of a labor dispute. Otherwise the right to strike and picket peacefully are allowed. Suits for damages for acts committed during a labor dispute may be taken to court under certain conditions.

These comments draw attention to some of the control mechanisms the British used to channel union activities into what they conveniently called "responsible unionism" (Roberts, 1964). That, for example, meant using official registration to permit only weak unions to operate in safeguarding British economic and hegemonic interests.[6]

Thus under British rule, even successfully completing the tedious process of union registration could not guarantee the survival of trade unions because the threat of decertification and dissolution always plagued them. The long-term impact of such legal provisions were demonstrated in recent African labor situations: the 1971 dismemberment of the Ghana TUC by the PP government, the dissolution of the Kenyan Civil Servants' Association[7] and the 1988 "temporary suspension" of the Nigerian Labor Congress (NLC). These illustrate how colonial labor practices, as it were, remain entrenched in African policies and practices today.

Extensive Essential Services

The unusually broad definition of essential services which led to the exclusion of workers in virtually the entire public sector from forming unions and from striking provided extra avenues for the British to restrict the rights of workers in Ghana and elsewhere in Anglophone Africa.[8] The excessively comprehensive definition of essential services and the denial of public employees the rights to freely join unions and to strike contradict the assertion that the British modeled colonial labor relations on a liberal policy in the image of metropolitan labor practices (Roberts, 1964; Cambridge, 1984; Davies, 1966).

As O. Agyeman (1980) observed, there was an inherent double standard in the practices of the British administration at home and overseas. For example, in Britain, the laws did not completely deny workers the right to strike. In the colonies, on the contrary, public sector employees were totally denied this fundamental right. He also noted that even if the British laws in the metropolis repressed workers in essential services, these laws were modified later. But long after, in the colonies, they were applied through the invocation of "states of emergency," as was the case in 1950 concerning the joint TUC-CPP declaration of a "General Strike" and "Positive Action" campaign conducted to force the British to end colonial rule in Ghana. By declaring states of emergency and broadly defining essential services, the British sought to immunize the colonial government from strikes by African workers. That worked because another arbitrary aspect of British practice was the immense discretionary powers of the Governor to extend the list of essential services to exclude more employees from striking. These powers proved helpful to the British during declared states of emergency.

The Discretionary Powers of the British Registrar of Unions

In addition to the excessively restrictive aspects of the relevant statutes, the 1941 Trades Unions Ordinance conferred on the Registrar of Trade Unions (an employee of the colonial government) immense powers to interfere in internal union matters. He could, for example, summarily order audits of union accounts, and was allowed to refuse union registration on the grounds that their activities were illegal (Agyeman, 1980). In his work he was solely accountable to his employer, the British colonial authorities. The discretionary powers of the registrar were aimed at ensuring that unions behaved in ways deemed "appropriate" by the British. The registrar was also the Chief Labor Officer or the Commissioner of Labor, the head technocrat in the labor departments. The registrar's role leads us to the functions of the colonial labor departments set up in the countries under review.

Colonial Labor Departments

Ghana's Department of Labor was established by the British on April 1, 1938.[9] There are two conflicting schools of thought about the rationale for its

founding. The first, led by authors such as Roberts (1964) and J. F. Maitland-
Jones (1973: 140), argues that the creation of labor departments was aimed at
encouraging Ghanaians to form unions. This group also argues that labor
outfits were established because of the British Colonial Office's overt concern
in the 1930s and 1940s to improve the conditions of workers in the colonies.
The second school, with a less benevolent view of colonial labor administration, takes the position that labor departments were created because of increased economic and political agitation in all the colonies (Jeffries, 1978;
Agyeman, 1980; Ziskind, 1987). R. Jeffries (1978: 39) points out the Colonial
Secretary's reason for setting up Ghana's labor department:

> The recent spread of labor unrest through the British Colonial Empire points
> to the necessity of an organization with accurate knowledge of labor condi-
> tions should the day come when we have to face serious labor disputes in the
> Gold Coast.

Such a candid admission, plus the circumstances leading to the establishment
of the Ghanaian labor department, makes the second school's views on the
origins and role of the colonial labor department more plausible.[10]

4. 1. 4   Local Pressure, Colonial Labor Ordinances and Welfare Acts

As in all spheres of colonial labor activities, the passage of the first ordinances allowing limited unionization and the promulgation of the so called
development and welfare acts are shrouded in factual inaccuracies. Events
immediately preceding and following World War II (1939 - 1945), which influenced the development of labor administration, however, do not in any way
support the contention that the British were magnanimous in promulgating labor laws in the colonies. The timing of the passage of the relevant laws is crucial and their broader contexts of the so-called "Colonial Development" and
"Welfare Acts" need to be reexamined thoroughly.[11]

Roberts (1964) for example, contends that the welfare acts were directly
aimed at improving material living conditions for Africans and the labor ordinances passed around the time of World War II were aimed at the genuine
growth of African unions. He thus repudiates the real circumstances that led
to these new labor and economic development;s. He might also have been
oblivious of the admissions of some colonial administrators regarding the motives behind the changes that occurred. In addition, he might not have taken
cognizance of the total context of British or any other form of colonialism and
its exploitative and racial dimensions. He may also have ignored the crucial
links between capitalism and colonialism as practiced in Africa. As correctly
noted by most authors, colonialism was fueled by the desire to exploit the
human and material resources of the colonial population for the primary
benefit of the metropolis (Agyeman, 1980; Otobo, 1987; Rodney, 1982;
Padmore, 1953).

Exploitation and Racism Equals Colonization

To ensure effective exploitation, the British imposed a colonial system which subjugated Africans by stripping them of basic human rights, including the protections offered by labor organizations. The prime motive behind British laws and practices in all spheres was ensuring reliable supplies of labor for commercial purposes and the least expensive level of public works and administration required. That explains why, for example, the construction of railroads and the other little infrastructural developments that occurred (under colonialism) were confined to a small section of the total land area of Ghana — about one-eight of the geographical area (see Appendix 6). K. A. Ninsin and F. K. Drah (1987: 156) aptly describe the core feature of colonialism:

> The essence of colonisation was the creation of an economic system by which the colonised territory was a producer of raw materials exported to the metropolis and the dumping of cheap finished products from the metropolis on to the underdeveloped colony.

D. Ziskind (1987: 7) adds that the British were no exception in exploiting African resources and rejects the notion that they were more liberal in their policies. On the contrary he argues that they suppressed the civil rights of Africans as much as their Portuguese, French and Italian counterparts:

> All . . . colonial powers had policies favoring white employers by supplying needed African workers, often through forms of conscript or forced labor. Historic actions have been cited to demonstrate national characteristics (as well as exceptions thereto); however, all colonial governments denied meaningful civic participation of Africans and exploited human and material resources primarily for their own benefit . . . .

Available evidence supports Ninsin's, Drah's and Ziskind's views.

Limited Trade Unionism: A Colonial Expediency

In light of the origins and purposes of colonialism, it may be said correctly that a limited amount of weak and insignificant unionization was tolerated in Africa because the British were convinced of the tactical advantages of their new labor policies and statutes. Colonial officers and their counterparts in Britain were persuaded that restricted forms of labor organizing (especially the low-level and nonaggressive types exhibited by the classic company or house unions) would serve the future interests of the British more than the outright prohibition of all worker associations. Besides, as the British realized by the 1930s, it had become increasingly difficult to resist unionization completely. The idea that unions could be used to regulate rising tensions steadily became more acceptable than the absolute denial of trade union rights. The colonial welfare acts were also seen as not capable of hurting but guaranteeing the long-term commercial and industrial interests of the British. Therefore, the British labor and economic policies initiated during World War II can be appropriately seen as a means of defusing increasingly explosive social and economic situations. This potentially explosive situation and how theBritish sought to prevent it from undermining their hegemony are presented below.

As Otobo (1987) correctly argued, the Colonial Development and Welfare Acts and Ordinances adopted in Nigeria were British responses to Africans' protests and attempts to end colonialism. One of the most popular of these was the 1940 Colonial Development Act passed by the British Parliament in London. It stipulated that colonial territories that did not permit some unionization would be ineligible for financial aid from London. Here, too, Roberts' (1964: 187 - 188) views do not agree with his own remarks about the situation in the former British colonies in Africa. He contends that the 1940 Act was a totally selfless action by the British aimed directly at the well-being of Africans:

> The second world war, like the first world war, gave further impetus to the development of colonial labour policy. A landmark in this respect was the passing of the Colonial Development and Welfare Act. This Act was passed in 1940, and it is worthy of special note that men were prepared to turn their minds to the task of building a better future for colonies at one of the black-est moments in British history. The purpose of the Act was to make available to the colonies, over a period of years, subventions from the United Kingdom for approved schemes of economic and social development. On the insistence of a group of Labour M.P.s, who had the close co-operation of the then Parliamentary Under-Secretary of State for the Colonies, the Act in-cluded clauses stipulating that no territory might receive aid under its provisions unless it had in force legislation protecting the rights of trade unions, and unless the works for which the aid was to be used were carried out under a contract which embodied a fair wages clause . . . .

But commenting further on this act, Roberts (1964: 187) revealed that it represented "the first real power" of the Colonial Office in Britain, "to coerce colonial governments into carrying out the labor policies it was recommending . . . ." Thus in his own words, the colonial administrators in Africa had to be compelled to promulgate labor laws and welfare acts. This brings to the forefront the issue of the timing of the founding of the relevant labor departments.

As far back as 1930, Lord Passfield (Sydney Webb), the Colonial Secretary of Labor, had urged the recognition of unions in all territories. But the colonial administrators ignored these orders until the late 1930s and early 1940s. The timing of the passage of the laws recognizing unions may be explained largely by the efforts of Africans to overturn colonialism. Therefore, the ostensible reasons offered as the goals of the welfare acts and the accompanying labor ordinances are unacceptable. Besides, these acts and ordinances were used largely as means to control a situation in which British rule for the first time was directly and seriously challenged by African nationalists.

Based on the description of the circumstances surrounding the new British labor policies, Roberts' (1964) claims that the welfare acts were aimed at enhancing the material living conditions of Africans and that the colonial labor statutes were aimed at genuine union growth could be deemed as ignoring the real conditions that led to their adoption. The fact that the British waited for almost 100 years (after ruling Ghana from 1844) before passing these labor laws and development acts contradicts the assertion that the British intended to assist the development of unions and to improve living conditions of the colonial populations. There is enough evidence to support the view that the British changed their labor policies largely in response to protest actions by Ghanaians to resist British hegemony. One of these protests was the 1937 - 1938 cocoa boycott during which local farmers refused to sell their produce to expatriate monopoly cocoa-buying agencies. Following that boycott, the rail workers of Sekondi-Takoradi (see Appendix 6) conducted the first strike in Ghanaian industrial relations history.[12] These were the kinds of social and industrial unrest that motivated the establishment of Ghana's Department of Labor and the passage of the various welfare and labor statutes by the end of World War II. One British TUC Secretary-General was candid about the selfish aspects of British colonial labor policies:

> I would say that the sooner some people get away from the traditional idea of the bowl of rice, the mango and the coconut being the unit of traditional measurement of the standard of living of colonial peoples, the better for all concerned . . . . I think we should realize that if our exports are to be kept at a high level over a long period (upon which our own standards of living depend) it can only be done by fostering the standards of living in those markets which are likely to absorb the products of our industry to an increasing extent. Vital amongst those markets are colonies and dependent territories.[13]

Further evidence demonstrates how pervasive the selfish intent of the British was. The British Assistant Secretary of State for the colonies, in his introduction to a Colonial Development Bill in the House of Commons (in London) in 1929 explained the benefits reaped by the British:

> The Government gathered in the Debate on Friday that the measure is acceptable to all sections of the House and they are anxious that today's proceeding on the Second Reading may not be unduly prolonged, so that we may start immediately with the means which, we believe, the bill will provide, of colonial development on a very large scale — development which will in turn provide work for our people in this country . . . . The bill is linked with the promotion of commerce and industry in the United Kingdom, and we have good reason to believe that . . . . purchases of materials will come to this country and will assist considerably in the provision of work for our people. There is no doubt that up to now the colonies have purchased materials for their development schemes in this country and we believe that their orders will remain here and will help considerably in the provision of employment in this country. The scheme, based primarily on a far-sighted policy of Imperial development, will no doubt mean a good deal in prosperity to some industries at home.[14]

British Policies in Action

Since actual activities are more significant than policy pronouncements, the rest of this subchapter will illustrate how British activities impacted on workers' rights and labor administration in Africa. The first legacy to be examined is the labor department they set up in Ghana. It is the precursor of today's Ministry of Employment and Social Welfare, formerly called the Ministry of Labor. The colonial labor department was instrumental in the implementation of British labor policies. The U.S. Department of Labor described this department as functioning to ensure the exploitation of Africans through its use as the major labor recruitment agency.[15] It was, therefore, not intended to operate as a neutral organization which mediated disputes or worked to protect workers — the weak group in labor relations — through the enforcement of employer fair labor practices.

The creation of a *bona fide* tripartite labor relations system was not one of the duties assigned to this department as Roberts (1964), Cambridge (1984) and Davies(1966) claim. The British were hostile to African trade unionism and did not seek to promote a liberal trade union tradition in Africa. For example, one Principal British Labor Officer in Kenya, M. P. de V. Allen did not hide his contempt for Africans when he openly stated: "I am not in favor of trade unions for natives; the time is not ripe for this" (Singh, 1969: 129). This is an example of the paternalistic and often racist attitudes of the British, which had important repercussions in the labor sphere.

Policing African Trade Unions

The labor departments the British founded in Africa were for strictly regulating the weak unions that were permitted. A prime task was the depoliticization of unions to prevent them from aligning with nationalist movements. The policing functions of the department over the unions may be typically described as surveillance over:

> Their conduct . . . . socialize union leaders to stay clear of politics and stick to bread and butter organizing and issues, attempt to prevent strikes and other labor protests from occurring and to help end them quickly, give no encouragement to demands on the Government for higher wages and benefits, and, lastly, with the police Special Branch build up informers within the unions in order to keep the Government well aware of union activities.[16]

Such unethical and illegal (according to ILO Convention No. 84, which Britain ratified on behalf of Ghana) surveillance through a network of informers enabled the British authorities to nip strikes at the planning stages. They also directly contradict the view expressed by Roberts, Cambridge and Daviesthat the British encouraged the growth of unions in Africa.

The Role of the British TUC

Another popular myth is that the British TUC was instrumental in the promotion of liberal trade unionism in Ghana and other Anglophone colonies. The view that British TUC advisers helped to establish industrial relations reminiscent of relations in Britain is not only misleading, but also fails to take account of the serious contradictions it gives rise to. First, as Agyeman (1980) has already indicated, there was a huge gap between metropolitan and colonial labor laws and policies. An analogy that comes to mind is the allegation that colonial people enjoyed as much rights as British nationals! Whereas in Britain the TUC fiercely participated in partisan politics culminating in the launching of the Labour Party, in the African colonies, officials of the TUC colluded with their bureaucratic counterparts in the attempt to divert the unions from politics. Roberts (1964: 15) provides an explanation of why British TUC officials colluded with the colonial administration to deter political unionism in Africa:

> The reaction of the TUC to the problems of trade union organization and in-
> dustrial relations has inevitably been heavily influenced by British experi-
> ence, beliefs and values. Since the labor policy of the Colonial Office has
> been influenced by the same factors, it is not surprising that the attitude of
> the British TUC has often coincided with that of the British Government.

Roberts' admission about the role of British trade unionists has several implications for the view that the British were interested in duplicating in Africa British labor relations. It is also worth emphasizing that not only did English labor unionists reflect British values and interests which were incompatible with African interests, but also they became important and active agents of colonial policies. According to Davies:

> The trade union movement has played a unique role in British colonial policy
> which contrasts strongly with French, Belgian and Dutch experience. For
> over twenty-five years the TUC and individual unions have not only been
> consulted on labour relations policy; they have in effect (through the system
> of Labour Officers and participation of the Colonial Advisory Board) been
> part of the Colonial Administration . . . .[17]

Even if we grant (for the sake of argument) the benign intentions of a few TUC officials, their overall activities, as Roberts has correctly stated, fell within the confines of British values and experiences and, I might add, interests. The actions of a few well-meaning TUC officials could not, therefore, have changed substantially the repressive colonial labor laws and practices. As both Roberts and Davies(advocates of a liberal view of British labor practices) have shown, not only did TUC advisers arrive in Africa imbued with British values but also over time became active enforcers of policies they would not have tolerated at home.

Forced Economic Unionism

On the alleged need for African unions to remain pure economic associations of labor, J. S. Patrick, Special Adviser to the Kenyan Labor Department, expressed an opinion widely shared by several of his colonial colleagues: "A trade union is not an organization with political aims. It is an association which has as its main objective, the regulation of relations between workers and their employers" (Jeffries, 1978: 40). According to Otobo (1987), British TUC officials shared with colonial civil servants the patronizing view that African unions, because they were "immature" and "irresponsible," might "fall under the dominance of disaffected persons, by whom their activities may be diverted to improper and mischievous ends." Thus, it was not surprising that I. G. Jones, a TUC official employed by the Labor Department to reorganize Ghanaian unions "in the most appropriate fashion," took his job to mean ". . . assisting to create a . . . nonradical labor situation, stifling the demands of nationalists collaborating with unions to demand national self-determination and absolute control of local resources" (Agyeman, 1980: 70).

Finally, in connection with the role of the British TUC, it is important to note that even if within British industrial relations, labor adopted a more radical stance and, therefore, opposed private capital as being exploitative, in the colonies labor cooperated fully with British, other foreign firms and the colonial governments to exploit the indigenous population (*Ibid.*,: 70 - 71). One British TUC official in charge of international relations was blunt about the exploitative role of the TUC when in 1949 he asked the following rhetorical questions: "It is said that we are closely associated with our own government. Well I ask . . . is that a crime? Is it wrong that we are doing things in cooperation with our own government?" (Agyeman, 1980: 70). Hence Agyeman's apt description of the British TUC as the facilitator — a crucial link between the colonial administration and the expatriate commercial interests that were preoccupied with extracting African resources including timber, bauxite, gold, diamond, cocoa, cotton and tobacco for their own profits.

One needs to add, however, that attempts to stifle labor and African nationalist alliances were abortive because the British authorities and their TUC collaborators failed to understand that in Africa as elsewhere, under colonial domination:

> The status of the employee at work cannot be divorced from his status in society, the establishment of trade unions has .... been a manifestation of concern with issues of social as well as of industrial significance. The link between political activity and trade union organization was inevitably made close when the right of workers to protect their interest by the exercise of collective bargaining was intimately connected with the bringing about of changes in the prevailing political environment (Roberts, 1964: xiv).

Labor's Response to Restrictive Labor Relations

In the case of Ghana, the colonial authorities, the British TUC and the foreign-owned businesses seemed to have succeeded in controlling trade unions and in preventing them from aligning themselves formally with the nationalist movement until the "Positive Action Campaign" of 1950.[18] This was a two-week joint effort by the Ghana labor unions and Kwame Nkrumah's CPP in the form of a general strike and national protest against colonial rule. As noted already, the British swiftly responded by jailing the nationalists involved and firing the trade unionists who led the general strike. The last point leads our attention to the use of coercion and at times not-too-refined union busting and state-sponsored terrorists acts under the guise of keeping law and order. This was especially the case in Kenya where in addition to the huge "arsenal of legislation" (Agyeman, 1980: 58 - 59) the colonial administrators unleashed a suppressive system to separate trade unionism from nationalist struggles. The fact that African labor leaders were subjected to daily government harassment does not corroborate the contention that colonial practices or policies were liberal, as it were, in the image of labor policies in Britain. Woddis (1961: 77) provides a valid summary description of British coercive tactics:

> The . . . forms of daily intimidation, openly being followed by the police, the obvious tempering with the post, the victimization from job to job, the denial of a passport to travel to an overseas conference or to a trade union school, the arrest on a flimsy charge, the smear campaign in the press, the threats from the police or from the Registrar of Trade Unions, or banishment to a remote corner of the territory, cut off from relatives, friends and organizations . . . .

The Ghana and Kenya examples draw attention to another dimension of colonialism often ignored or treated as inconsequential. Although the use of force is often ignored (by authors such as Roberts, 1964; Davies, 1966 and Cambridge, 1984), as Otobo (1987: 13 - 14) emphasized, force was not marginal to but an important feature of colonialism because it was an illegitimate system which could only be retained by the use of coercion. Within this illegitimate system, trade unionists and their nationalist counterparts bore the most brunt because their activities were not only deemed hostile to but also capable of overthrowing it.

In several respects, free and especially radical trade unionism posed a threat to British interests. Firstly, the British were not only the largest employer of wage labor, but were also naturally identified by the African nationalists as responsible for the race and class based exploitation endured by the colonial populations. Secondly, British policies contributed to the emergence of a nascent African working class, which struggled to unionize in their efforts to achieve labor solidarity and to protect themselves from expatriate employers, both private and public (Ewusi, 1984; Gray, 1981: 80). Thirdly, these working classes were the most alienated politically because policies including "Indirect Rule" excluded them from even the rudimentary kinds of local political structures the British created to permit very little local political participation (Agyeman, 1980: 50).

4. 1. 5   Urbanization, an African Working Class and the Rise of Political Unionism

As a result of the modest amount of urbanization which occurred in the colonial export enclaves (see area bordered by railroads in Appendix 6), Africans got exposure to the remarkable gaps between their poor standards of living and European luxuries. Africans experienced overt racism and class-based discrimination in workplaces owned by foreign employers. Examples were the huge wage differentials paid to expatriate mine employees in Ghana, Nigeria and Zambia. In Zambia, for example, not only did Europeans have a separate union (Kalula, 1988), but Africans were also barred from the exclusive all-white work clubs.

British commerce coupled with the creation of administrative centers to facilitate the exploitation of Africans led to the growth of a few cities and towns where large numbers of Africans came face-to-face with the sharp contrasts between their chronic material poverty and the luxuries of European lifestyles within the commercial and administrative centers where they labored for low wages.[19] An important contribution of the rise of urbanization was the simultaneous birth of nationalism and political trade unionism as most Africans became convinced that the sole route to breaking out of poverty was ending colonial rule. That explains the coincidence in the emergence of both modern trade unionism and the independence movement in Africa in the 1930s and 1940s. A classic example, I have alluded to was the 1950 Positive Action in Ghana.[20]

Against a background of growing dissatisfaction with British rule, colonial minimum wage policies plus rising inflation led to a series of strikes in Ghana, including a strike by the employees of the meteorological services in Accra. British reprisals included firing the employees involved for engaging in "an illegal strike." That action provided the CPP and TUC leaders the opportunity to launch a campaign to rid the country of British domination (Jeffries, 1978: 55). Some of the conditions for ending the campaign included granting Ghana political autonomy in the form of dominion status. When the British refused their demands, the whole nation was plunged into a general strike-and-protest action led by the TUC and CPP leaders such as Pobee-Biney, Kobina Woode and Kwame Nkrumah.

The British, under the guise of preserving law and order, responded by invoking "a state of emergency" through which the army and police were deployed to keep the "peace," and TUC and CPP officials were jailed for subversion. TUC leaders who were not jailed were dismissed from their jobs without right of appeal. The British reaction in 1950 was important in several respects. First, by imposing a state of emergency and responding harshly by jailing the strike leaders, they set an example for subsequent Ghanaian governments to suppress unions. An illustration is that, similar measures, though on a smaller scale and with less dramatic effects, were adopted in 1961 and 1978 when the state was threatened by strikes. The point here is that the British elevated workers' strikes and protest actions to levels of national polit-

ical emergencies, which then permitted them to brutalize workers under the
pretext of protecting law, order and national securtiy.[21]
    The second point is that joint TUC-CPP action such as the 1950 Positive
Action may have confirmed and thus steeped the colonial administrators in the
belief that unions could be used as effective weapons by nationalists demanding independence. Thus, their hostility toward African unions became rationalized. As it were, the unions might have confirmed the suspicion that if left
uncontrolled, they could seriously threaten British hegemony! The CPP leaders may also have learned from these events that the might of labor when
thrown behind a political movement could yield several political benefits.
This may explain why after independence, the CPP took steps to ensure that
its political enemies were denied access to labor's political clout. This in
essence is the politically sensitive role of unions analyzed in the next section.
    In summary, I may observe that the British influenced the unions that
emerged in Ghana and elsewhere in Africa in three major ways. Firstly, political and economic repression associated with colonialism, secondly, the role
of the British colonial government as the dominant employer and thirdly, its
close ties to expatriate businesses, interacted to give birth simultaneously to a
nationalist struggle and a working-class movement led by unionists who rejected as false the dichotomy between economic unionism and the struggle for
independence in Africa. The fusion of these two movements and the momen-
tum they gained after World War II ultimately led to independence in sub-
Saharan Africa, beginning with Ghana in 1957. Next, I present highlights of
what I term the real British labor legacy, which directly contradicts the belief
that the British genuinely promoted free labor unions and impartial industrial
dispute settlement processes, as the ratification of Convention No. 84 on behalf of the Gold Coast required.[22]

4. 1. 6   The Labor Scene at Independence

The State of the Unions

    Several industrial relations commentators, including the ILO (1958) have
drawn attention to the weak and splintered state of the unions in Africa on the
eve of independence. The inability of these unions to protect their members
through collective bargaining is well documented (Jeffries, 1978; Gray, 1981;
Maitland-Jones, 1973). The weakness of African unions is better understood
in light of the fact that the employers they dealt with were often powerful
multinational companies and the colonial administration itself. Thus, it was
difficult for these financially and organizationally weak unions to match the
resources and power of employers.[23] Some data will illustrate their plight.
According to the ILO's survey of 1958, at the time of independence in Ghana,
out of more than 80 unions that were registered, 10 were officially defunct and
19 were virtually extinct. Nigeria's unions were in even worse shape.[24]
Maitland-Jones (1973: 142) reveals that even the grim statistics may not adequately reflect the weak nature of African unions. He argues that the data on

union membership often overestimated the strength of the unions by inflating their membership to make them appear stronger than they were.

The British, under the false pretense of promoting liberal unionization (but in effect creating splintered unions) in Ghana, for example, under the 1941 Ordinance, permitted five or more people to form separate labor organizations. This particular provision may account for the excessive number of weak unions which preceded independence and is referred to appropriately as the "mushrooming of unions" (Gray, 1981). Conversely, extremely cumbersome procedures for amalgamating unions, such as securing the approval of the Registrar of Trade Unions (who was British and an employee of the colonial administration), as required by the 1941 Ordinance (of the Gold Coast) thwarted union mergers and prevented them from pooling their resources. It is therefore correct to attribute the prevalence of weak labor organizations at the time of independence to deliberate British policies, laws and practices. Therefore, a situation emerged during the colonial period in which the evidence available clearly indicates that the British did not leave a legacy of resilient worker organizations based on institutionalized tripartism. This resulted from the desire of the British to avoid dealing with strong unions.

Colonial Collective Bargaining and Dispute Settlement

In the areas of collective bargaining and dispute settlement, the evidence available also does not support the view that the British wanted to encourage effective union roles. P. Obeng-Fosu (1991: 4 - 5) provides a valid description of the typical colonial labor situation in Ghana with respect to union registration and collective bargaining: "When the Labour Department was established in 1938, there was no provision for the registration of trade unions. Most . . . . grievances . . . . were settled by Chiefs . . . . under the supervision of colonial District Commissioners." Furthermore, he notes that "registration of trade unions under the 1941 Trades Union Ordinance did not confer bargaining rights on the trade unions. Negotiators would either be accepted or rejected by employers and joint negotiations were carried out in few establishments . . . . Strikes were illegal . . . ."[25]

Several union busting ploys used by the British included granting so-called "consultative," "provisional" or "probationary" status to African working-class organizations instead of full and legally recognized status as collective bargaining agents protected from unfair employer practices and retribution (ILO, 1958; Agyeman, 1980).[26] Since these organizations under colonial law were barred from striking and could only be involved in limited consultations over terms of employment, they were used by the British to subvert genuine trade unions. Thus, it would be accurate to assert that one of the three pillars for genuine tripartism — strong and representative labor unions — was missing from the colonial labor scene. In closing this discussion it might be appropriate to recall M. F. Lofchie's (1971: 10) views on the real nature of colonial rule in Africa:

Few today would feel it necessary to question the oppressive consequences of the colonial subordination on Africa, or debate the fact that it stifled African initiative and creativity in a wide range of areas of human endeavor — political and economic . . . .

The short duration of British laws and policies which permitted unions (from 1938 to 1957 in Ghana) could not have guaranteed the emergence of sound labor policies based on genuine tripartite relations (depicting mutual respect and interdependence among labor, government and private business). As P. S. Gray (1981: 117) has pointed out, the British government's preoccupation was the maintenance of law and order to ensure "the health of the colonial laissez-faire economy." The same author notes that to meet their economic missions to Africa, "the British were generally content to preside over an industrial relations system composed primarily of weak unions" (*Ibid.*).

A long-term effect of colonial labor policy in Ghana was that the CPP inherited from the British a labor situation in which unions were weak and dissipated their meager financial and other resources on excessive competition. These unions faced powerful and foreign employers who refused to bargain with them because the former were weak and also due to the fact that the law did not require employers to bargain with them. To compensate for these weaknesses, the TUC and CPP entered into an alliance which was sealed only one year after Independence, resulting in the creation of the "New Rationalized Union Structure," through the 1958 Industrial Relations Act (Tettegah, 1958; Cowan, 1960).[27] This statute, together with the policies of the first and subsequent Ghana governments, have granted and sustained the *de jure* and *de facto* monopoly the TUC has had over the entire Ghanaian labor movement. The TUC's monopoly has been a thorn in the relations between the Ghana government and the ILO since 1958 (see Chapter 3).

Ghana's lead in creating a relatively strong and well-endowed central labor organization was later replicated by Kenya in 1965, Zambia in 1971 and Nigeria in 1978. Today therefore, the relatively united labor fronts that exist in most ex-British colonies cannot be attributed to colonial policies that consciously promoted labor unity and trade union growth. The centralized labor structures we see are African responses to British practices which as demonstrated in this chapter denied Africans trade union rights. Current union systems with single central organizations and officially designated affiliates are the products of deliberately crafted policies and legislation by African political leaders such as Kwame Nkrumah, other nationalists and labor leaders who used the state's legislative powers and financial resources to forge single unions to replace the weak organizations that existed prior to independence. In the Ghanaian trade union situation, union leaders such as John Tettegah and Joe-Fio Meyer drafted the original relevant labor laws and used their influence in the ruling party — the CPP — to obtain its passage through Parliament.

4. 2   The Politically Sensitive Roles of Labor in Africa

The Geopolitical Location and Role of Unions in Developing Countries

Two concepts are useful in explaining the role of the state in labor relations in developing countries. These are the geopolitical location and role of unions and their productionist or consumptionist functions. These concepts were first applied to Africa by W. Friedland (1968) in referring to the politically and economically sensitive roles of organized labor. These roles may explain why several African governments, including those of Ghana and Nigeria, which have ratified Convention Nos. 87 and 98 are reluctant to recognize full union autonomy. According to Friedland, unions are harshly restricted because patterns of development and the location of industrial and administrative centers have led to situations in which union activities, especially strikes and other protests, are concentrated too close to the seats of government in Africa. The result is that governments perceive industrial actions as threats to their capacity to cling to power. This is particularly the case of governments that lack legitimacy or are weak and thus are in constant fear of being overthrown. Ghana's pre- and post-colonial labor situation yields overwhelming evidence in supporting Friedland's explanation of the origins of excessive state control of unions in Africa. As shown in this chapter, the situation in Nigeria and Zambia in recent years has proved to be not too different from that of Ghana.

Friedland (1968: 22) attributes tight labor control to governments' preference for trade unions' so-called positive social and industrial roles, called productionist functions. These are unions working for industrial harmony and worker discipline socializing workers into roles that enhance organizational efficiency, assisting workers to save their earnings for investment and using union dues to accumulate capital for business ventures. Opposed to the productionist roles are consumptionist or so-called socially costly activities such as unions advocating higher wages and other improved conditions of work such as vacation time, shielding workers from excessive discipline and striking to back their claims. The thesis of Friedland is that because African governments strongly prefer the former functions of unions — the so called socially useful functions — these governments clamp down hard on unions, especially national federations such as the TUC, ZCTU, NLC and COTU to circumvent their autonomy and channel their activities towards productionist roles.

I might observe that typically, most African governments operate on the assumption that workers' demands, especially for pay raises, would cause high rates of inflation, which would jeopardize their economic plans. In the late 1950s and 1960s African governments, especially the Ghana government with its various five- or seven-year plans, were concerned about how high labor costs could undermine the achievement of their planned economic growth targets. In the 1980s and 1990s, with the adoption of various versions of the World Bank and International Monetary Fund's economic programs emphasizing government cutbacks, the wage freeze has again emerged as a bone of contention between governments and labor unions (Panford, Forthcoming, Otobo, 1987). The extreme concerns of African governments to regulate the consumptionist roles of unions and to reduce the political threats unions pose are all reflected in labor codes which seek to virtually outlaw strikes, impose strict wage controls and confine union membership and activities to only unions approved by the state, as in Ghana, Kenya, Nigeria and Zambia. I will now apply an expanded version of Friedland's concepts with appropriate illustrations to describe and explain why contemporary African labor relations are often not in total harmony with the ILO standards African public authorities have voluntarily agreed to uphold.

4. 2. 1   The Direct Role of the State in Labor Relations

In Africa, because the state is the largest employer of unionized labor it has developed a direct stake in labor matters leading to industrial conflict having overt political implications. An example is that even if a strike is motivated solely by an economic claim, often it is against a publicly owned entity and hence could be perceived as a strike against the state itself. Because it is the largest employer, the state usually has difficulties distinguishing between pure economic strikes aimed at workers' occupational interests and those with political objectives. The task of distinguishing between economic and political strikes has remained difficult and has led to African governments' entanglement in laws and practices which bar workers from striking and from publicly displaying their discontent with working conditions, especially in the public sector. A common practice these governments have resorted to that has resulted in persistent violations of ILO norms is the creation of single-union systems.

Due to colonialism and other factors (to be discussed in Section 4.3), immediately upon gaining independence, several African countries, led by Ghana, imposed *de jure* centralized single-union structures on their labor movements. Since several labor practices and statutes associated with these centralized union organizations violate ILO principles on workers' rights, the Organization has sought in the last three decades to make countries such as Ghana amend their relevant laws and policies.[28] In light of the repeated efforts of the ILO and the chronic nature of the problems African members like Ghana have to contend with, a question that emerges is: why have these countries' problems persisted to the extent that they have become almost unsolvable? My position on these issues, as expressed elsewhere (Panford, 1988), is that a number of intricate factors (including the desire of the public authorities to retain their hegemony) have made it extremely difficult for the state to remain neutral in industrial relations and less willing to resist the urge to excessively intervene in internal union affairs, including the election of union officials,[29] and their financial affairs. The answer may also lie in the direct vested interests the state has acquired in African economies and in the outcomes of industrial relations. The complex role of the state in African economies may be appreciated by focusing on the broader socio-economic and political contexts of African societies. This section, therefore, analyzes how socio-political and economic trends in the independence era coupled with a legacy of colonialism have shaped the functions of the state in contemporary labor affairs.[30]

Chapter 1 dealt with the major debates which constitute the backdrop for studying the complex relations between the activities of organized labor and socio-economic development. One of the pertinent issues was the impact of industrial conflict on Africa's capacity to surmount underdevelopment. Iwuji (1979: 234 - 235) posed the problem thus: "Whether the process of collective bargaining is necessarily in conflict with the aspirations of a young independent country trying to consolidate its independence and reconstruct its economy, how free of government control trade unions should be?" He then hinted at the political and economic repercussions of autonomous trade union activities by asking further: "Whether the ideal of freedom of action for the trade union movement should be allowed at the expense of political stability and the national economy . . . ." (Ibid.). In examining the complex problems alluded to, caution is required because the problems identified may explain, but not necessarily justify, the repressive measures taken by the state in responding to the economic and political challenges union activities create. There is, therefore, the need to distinguish problems used as mere pretexts to suppress unions from the genuine technical problems developing countries confront in complying with ILO standards. (Section 4.3 describes these technical problems.) This distinction is also necessary to draw attention to the fact that even though most African nations face similar problems, they have, at times, varied their responses. For example, whereas in Ghana, the state intervened in internal TUC affairs barely a year after independence, in Nigeria, it took almost two decades for the state to impose a centralized structure.[31] The differences in timing may be attributed to the early adoption of socialist policies by the Nkrumah government, which led to the increased direct role of the state in labor relations. In Nigeria, the relatively *laissez-faire* policies of the first civilian federal administration were responsible for the delayed state direct intervention. Therefore, the factors presented here should be treated as constraints or catalysts that influenced the policies of African nations in managing the apparently conflicting needs of labor to freely pursue its interests and the state's need to keep order and industrial harmony to induce economic development;.

Immediately after gaining independence, the attention of Ghanaian labor and political leaders was focused on the weaknesses of the unions. A remarkable legacy of the British (as I have shown in the section on the role of colonialism above) was a situation in which the predominant unions were atomized and unrepresentative of the working class. Colonial policies had left the unions weak in all areas — finances, membership and leadership. A classic example was that until 1954, the TUC could not financially afford a full-time Secretary-General.[32] At the federation level, all attempts to voluntarily unify the two rival federations — the Ghana TUC and the Gold Coast TUC — failed.[33]   E. Iwuji (1979) describes a similar splintered union situation in Kenya before COTU was formed by a Presidential Declaration of 1965.[34] The Nigerian situation was worse. Union factionalism was fueled by ethnic, regional, religious and ideological rivalries which also thwarted voluntary efforts at unification.[35] In addition to the failure of African labor movements to internally negotiate solutions to the problems of excessive rivalry, the *de facto* accomplishment of labor unity by organized labor in western Europe, the United States and other countries influenced them to seek unification by relying on the state's legislative resources in the form of the Industrial Relations Actss of 1958 and 1965 in Ghana, Decree Nos. 31 and 22 of 1973 and 1978 in Nigeria, Industrial Relations Act, 1971 in Zambia and a Presidential Declaration of 1965 in Kenya (Tettegah, 1958; Cowan, 1960; Panford, 1988).

The influence of foreign-based labor organizations on the efforts of African unions to unite is best demonstrated in the case of the Ghana TUC. On his appointment as the first full-time Secretary-General of the Ghana TUC, Tettegah took a study tour of several countries' labor relations systems with special interest in the structure of their trade unions (Tettegah, 1958; Cowan, 1960). He was especially impressed by the accomplishments of the West German and Israeli unions, which established centralized labor unions enjoying cordial relations with political parties (Ananaba, 1979: 9). Partly to emulate foreign examples, the TUC leaders aligned themselves with the CPP, the party in power, with the objective of using state intervention to accomplish unity in order to overcome the problems associated with excessive union plurality.[36] The TUC leaders were concerned that too much union plurality (that is, several unions competing to organize a few workers) undermined their effectiveness at the bargaining table *vis-à-vis* the powerful transnational companies that operated in the country. With the exception of a few unionized workers such as the Sekondi-Takoradi-based Rail-Workers' Unions, most of the unions were largely unsuccessful as collective bargaining agents. As a result, the Ghana TUC faction within the labor movement became interested in creating a well organized and centralized national labor federation fully capable of protecting workers' economic, social and political interests in a newly-independent Ghana (Roberts, 1964: 50).

The Nkrumah-led CPP government also had a vested interest in the attainment of labor unity. As the largest employer, the government desired industrial peace to facilitate industrialization. The party's entire economic program was premised on the successful execution of its industrialization scheme. It, thus, sought to avert situations in which labor disunity led to an escalation of strikes caused by union organizing disputes. It also wanted to prevent uncoordinated bargaining from crippling the economy. In the party's view, these problems could be controlled by superimposing on workers a centralized labor structure with the TUC in charge of policy and coordinating union activities (Gray, 1981). A significant assumption here was that a divided labor movement would lead to a chaotic labor situation, which, in turn, would undermine collective bargaining. Thus, the Nkrumah regime may have been convinced by 1958 that labor unity, even if achieved through the merger of all unions into a single federation, was preferable to situations in which unity eluded workers. Labor unity was desired because of the anticipated payoff in the form of stable worker-management relations.

An underlying cause of the weak political status of African unions prior to independence, as explained in the preceding subchapter, was the failure of the British to institutionalize trade unionism. The absence of a socially accepted system of worker representation, the failure of the British to promote genuine collective bargaining and the relatively new experience with industrialization, have led to situations in which, even after over 30 years of self-government, several African nations are still grappling with the "teething problems" of industrialization and accompanying labor relations headaches.[37] In Ghana, for example, because of the absence of institutionalized collective bargaining, the TUC initiated government intervention in collective bargaining.[38] It, thus, vehemently protested against attempts by the National Liberation Council (NLC) to annul the powers conferred on the Labor Minister to extend collective agreements under the "Extension Powers" of the 1965 Industrial Relations Act (Hutchful, 1987: 224).[39]

Labor and government/ruling party alliances and *de facto* centralized labor organizations are not unique to Africa because several countries outside Africa have single or few labor federations, such as the Israeli and West German situations. Other examples are the *de facto* predominantly single, central labor confederations such as the British TUC, the American Federation of Labor and the Congress of Industrial Organization (the AFL-CIO), and the Canadian Labor Congress. But a number of post-independence political and economic conditions and developments may have facilitated the direct involvement of the state in the imposition of single unions and the creation official and legislated alliances with labor organizations. The ILO takes the position that the compulsory creation and maintenance of a national labor center, such as the Ghana TUC or the ZCTU, are in violation of its norms.

H. Bates (1970: 369) depicted the sensitive nature of unions in the politics and economies of developing countries when he noted that:

> Governments . . . insist that for the sake of rapid economic growth, strikes must be curtailed. The unions tend to organize the most important sectors of the economy. Strikes in any of these sectors do not merely reduce the output of that sector alone; because the economies are narrowly based, they tend to disrupt the economy as a whole. For these reasons, unions are asked to curtail strikes, for strikes would severely disrupt the attempts of governments to attain rapid economic development;.

The Physical Proximity of Unions to Governments

As noted already, in his explanation of government domination of unions in Africa, Friedland (1968) referred to their geopolitical location and economic functions. In his view, unions and their activities are perceived by African governments as capable of not only ruining their fragile economies and preventing their economic plans from coming to fruition, but they also saw in unions the immense capacity to cause their downfall by engaging in "subversive" activities such as general or politically motivated strikes. Therefore, in responding to Iwuji 's (1979) question about union activities, it may be observed that African governments have formulated their policies, laws and practices with the belief that unions' uninhibited actions can have both economic and politically disastrous consequences. Based on this perception, African governments seek to restrict unions, especially their strike activities, as Ghana's labor situation from 1958 to 1966 has proved.

The Imperatives of Accelerated Economic Growth?

Even before Ghana officially became a one-party state in 1964, the CPP and Kwame Nkrumah were committed to launching an economic program that required the state to mobilize massive amounts of capital from both domestic and foreign sources. At the center of this program were a number of five- or seven-year economic development plans. Although economic planning was not entirely new to Ghana, Nkrumah's development plans were unique in several respects.[40] His plans were more ambitious, often with economic growth targets of over five percent. Also, in their initial phases, the rate of investment was as high as 15 to 21 percent of the gross domestic product (Amin, 1973: 242). Such high targeted rates of investments may have been influenced by the policy prescriptions of development advisers including Arthur Lewis (Agyeman-Badu and Osei-Hwedie, 1982; Padmore, 1953).

The ambitious plans of the CPP were motivated by the desire on the part of the party to fulfill its promise to convert political power into improved material living conditions for all Ghanaians, but more especially, for workers. As G. Padmore (1953: 221) asserted, the CPP's development plans were attempts to fulfill economic and social promises it made during the nationalist struggle:

> Our entry into the Assembly in full strength will open up better opportunities to struggle for immediate self-government, asserts the C.P.P. manifesto. Whilst that struggle is proceeding, the C.P.P. will do all in its power to better the condition of the people of this country. It must be pointed out, however, that the implementation of this development programme can only be possible when self-government has been attained, and we are in full control of our own affairs.

Additionally and significantly, there was the prevailing view that Ghana, like most ex-colonial territories, lacked an entrepreneurial class and therefore could not industrialize without government finances:

> In Western society the . . . burden on state institutions was lightened considerably by the fact that the basic dynamism for economic transformation was supplied by an autonomous entrepreneurial class outside the state . . . . In Africa, where autonomous economic elites are lacking, the generation of economic growth is a state function. This means that embryonic political institutions have a twofold task to perform. They must be concerned with economic growth and with the alleviation of . . . human hardships (Lofchie, 1971: 5).

In order to meet the rising expectations which Nkrumah had stirred up during the independence struggle, he sought to implement a development plan based on rapid industrialization. Nkrumah and his advisers assumed that the quickest way for Ghana out of material poverty was to implement ambitious economic programs which, according to B. Callaway and E. Card (1971: 67), aimed at the:

> . . . actual restructuring of the inherited economic forms in which effective control would be gradually acquired through competition by the state against residual private enterprise. A mixed economy would exist for twenty or so years during which time the Ghana government would acquire control over the economy through effective competition with the foreign firms.

Therefore, from 1958 to 1966, a large number of factories were publicly funded to manufacture and assemble items from iron rods to shoes. The Seven-Year Plan of 1963 - 1970, for example, had the goal of capitalizing over 600 factories producing over 100 different items (Ewusi, 1976).

The Rapid Development of Social Infrastructure

In addition to investing in factories, the state undertook an expensive and rapid development of social infrastructure. Within the short span of a decade, services such as transportation, health, education and electricity were substantially increased, as shown by Callaway and Card (1971: 81):

> During the ten-year period, 1955 - 1965, Class I roads increased 46 percent and Class II roads increased 60 percent. Ghana had doubled its production of electricity before the opening of the Volta dam. The dam itself created the largest inland lake in the world (sic!). This lake was to become the center of a modern Ghanaian fishing industry and provide water for irrigation of extensive agricultural projects on the Accra plains. Tema Harbour, built at a cost of £27 million, is the largest artificial harbor in Africa.

According to these authors, expansion in the field of education was equally impressive. In 1964, 1.4 million students, or 18 percent of Ghana's population, were in school because enrollment in primary schools in that 10-year period shot up 200 percent. The labor relations implications of all the infrastructural and other developments are presented in the next sections.

The Wages of Rapid Industrialization and Economic Recovery

An ironic twist to Ghana's socialist program was that, although originally intended to sever what was perceived by Nkrumah and the CPP as the country's precarious links with western capitalism, because of the exhaustion of the country's foreign reserves (estimated at over £200 million), the government resorted to both deficit financing and heavy borrowing from western private and public sources — Britain, the United States and the World Bank.[41] For example, in 1962, the Kaiser Aluminum and Reynolds Metal Company raised $128 million and the U.S. and British governments, plus the World Bank, committed $98 million towards the construction of the Volta Dam in Ghana (Callaway and Card, 1971: 80). The perceived need for massive foreign capital served as an additional pressure for the CPP to maintain industrial peace and political stability. The government was particularly concerned about labor conflicts slowing down the pace of its industrialization and infrastructure programs. To attract the large doses of external finance the development plans required, the government saw the additional need to maintain a stable and favorable political climate — an atmosphere in which strikes or protest marches did not threaten foreign investments or political stability to the extent that investing in the country was perceived as too risky.[42] Hence, labor disputes between workers and project contractors became matters of National Assembly debates. During the debates on the 1965 Industrial Relations Acts, a parliamentarian, for example, asked the Minister of Labor to investigate a dispute between workers and the contractor for the Volta Dam.[43]

The result of the CPP's "jet-propelled" (Ewusi, 1984) industrialization and infrastructural program in the labor relations sphere was that the state increasingly became directly affected by labor-management relations and, therefore, developed a direct stake in labor activities, particularly wage claims through collective bargaining and strikes. Hence, the state could not retain any semblance of neutrality in relations between the TUC, its national unions and employers. After all, as the largest employer[44] of unionized labor, in the CPP leaders' view, the government could not sit on the fence and watch wages escalate to create high levels of inflation, which could substantially increase the cost of projects. In the government's view, that could aggravate the shortage of captial.[45]

The perceived need to control workers through unions as a means to maintain low wages became more imperative as the pace and the cost of projects increased and the country's foreign currency resources became depleted. In order to attract more foreign capital and extract greater amounts of domestic savings, the government was pressed into holding down wages further. The vicious cycle of financial problems may also have been compounded by the small percentage of total public expenditure that went into investments that produced quick returns. As noted, substantial investments went into social services with long periods of gestation such as primary and secondary education and road and bridge construction.[46] The government thus came under heavy pressure to tighten its budget.

The CPP government was able to keep wages low without incurring overt worker discontent (except the 1961 rail workers' strike) largely because of its alliance with the TUC, which allowed it to control virtually the entire working class. The alliance first became formal through the passage of the 1958 Industrial Relations Acts, which was later superseded by the 1965 Act. The 1958 Act led to a launching of a new phase of industrial relations, not only in Ghana, but also in several Anglophone sub-Saharan African nations. Within that alliance, the TUC statutorily and administratively was clearly assigned to police workers' activities, especially wage claims, strikes and other protest actions. With respect to its role in containing strikes, the TUC was helpful to the state because during the entire CPP era, the rates of strikes in the country were quite negligible. That may be attributed partially to the tight rein of the party over the entire Ghanaian body politic and the expanded social wage workers received in the form of free or subsidized services (see Section 5.1).

As a result, from 1961 to 1966, with the exception of a few cents increase in wages in 1962 (to pacify workers after the 1961 Sekondi-Takoradi rail workers' strike), the nominal wages paid to Ghanaian workers were kept constant, while inflation eroded their purchasing power (Ewusi, 1971: 43; Ananaba, 1979). Iwuji (1979: 222 - 223), described aptly the ripple effects of Kenya's wages and effectively elaborated on why African governments are extremely concerned about dampening the minimum wage:

> In Kenya, as in many developing countries, the minimum wage is in practice the effective or basic wage for most workers, especially unskilled workers. The Government's minimum wage rate (.i.e., its wage rate for unskilled labour) tends to act as the leader rate and to be copied by major private employers. Secondly, all other wage rates tend to take their cue from and to be closely linked to the minimum wage. Differentials for skilled labour, too, have been determined with reference to the minimum wage rate. Put differently, the minimum wage has become the reference point for higher wage and salary groups. Thus minimum wage not only dictates the pace and general level of other wage and salary rates but also greatly determines the wage and salary levels throughout the economy.[47]

In Africa, the minimum wage does not only act as the basic reference point for other wages, but also substantially affects national budgets. According to the PNDC's Secretary (Minister) for Finance and Economic Planning, the Ghana government spent approximately 75 percent of the national recurrent expenditure on wages and fringe benefits because public sector wage and salary bill jumped from five billion in 1984 to 11 billion cedis in 1985. In 1989, even after an IMF/World Bank -induced labor retrenchment, the government spent 48 percent of total noncapital expenditures on salaries and wages.[48]

In a major departure from the practices of the CPP, other Ghanaian and African governments have used confrontationary strategies including unilaterally imposed wage cuts or freezes as happened in Nigeria under General Buhari from 1982 to 1985 and under Ibrahim Babangida from 1986 until 1991 (D. Ghai, 1991: 154 - 156). In Ghana, from 1985 until 1993, when the PNDC's rule ended, there were periods of tension between the government and the TUC over the minimum wage and fringe benefits such as end of service (retirement) compensation. These disputes have not abated since the new J. J. Rawlings-led National Democratic Convention Party was sworn into office in January, 1993.

4. 2. 2   The Politics of Unions, Overcentralization and the Concentration of Industries in Ghana

In addition to the economic considerations that influenced the labor policies and laws adopted in Ghana, other factors — mostly political in nature — also reinforced the desire to control unions, especially the TUC. This point leads to what Friedland (1968) designated as the geopolitical functions of trade unions in Africa — the political repercussions of union actions. In most societies, ordinarily, labor-management conflicts, especially overt ones such as strikes, have the potential, for example, to disrupt the social order (by disturbing public peace, endangering the public's health and safety or by disrupting entire economies if a strike is national and prolonged). Strikes even have the potential to create public disaffection for a particular government when they get out of hand. However in, western industrialized communities, strikes have political implications only in the long run. They therefore do not create too much governmental concern in terms of political instability in the short term.

On the other hand, in contemporary Africa and in Ghana, in particular, because of the post-colonial political and economic trends I have described, labor disputes have assumed gigantic political significance. As under colonialism, they have acquired the status of national political crises. A good case in point is the 1980 strike/protest action of the 1,200 employees of the Ghana Industrial Holding Corporation (GIHOC, a state-owned company) who stormed the National Assembly demanding better wages and terms of employment. This strike illustrates how as an employer, the state, here represented by the National Assembly, become the victim of strikes and directly entangled in labor disputes.[49]

Two characteristics of African economic and administrative structures are largely responsible for the overt political ramifications of workers' job actions. These are the over-centralization of industry, infrastructure, commercial and administrative services and centers. Here, too, the British legacy has had a profound effect on labor policies. Ghana's situation adequately demonstrates the role of the British in creating the over-centralization of most commercial and public services. Due to British concerns to exploit the resources of colonial Ghana, the little infrastructural development that took place (mostly dealing with extractive businesses like mining and timber) was confined to only the southern region which was endowed with gold, bauxite, manganese and rich agricultural lands for cocoa and timber production. Hence, most of the road, rail and sea forms of transportation were located within this small region, as shown on the map in Appendix 6.

Because this region is relatively more developed and urbanized, it is referred to as "the Golden Triangle." This entire area is bordered on all sides by the country's rail system, as shown on the map. It is within this area that a high concentration of industry and other activities has occurred. Several of the urban areas found here are also the regional, district and local administrative headquarters: a seaport such as Sekondi-Takoradi in the west; Accra, the administrative and commercial capital in the center; and Kumasi, an important trading center to the north. The British created this "export enclave" for shipping raw materials and the minimum public administration necessary to oversee their commercial interests.

The Impact of the CPP's Industrial and Infrastructural Programs

The CPP's location of industries and social infrastructure mostly within the partially developed Golden Triangle as part of its accelerated economic development; program accentuated the centralized patterns of industrialization and public administration inherited from the British. Rapid concentration of several industries in the Golden Triangle, especially in urbanized centers such as Accra-Tema, Kumasi and Sekondi-Takoradi, led to a higher concentration of commercial and public services in this region. According to the Ghana Ministry of Industries, 43 out of 53 textile mills and 10 out of 11 pharmaceutical firms were all confined to this small area (Ewusi, 1976: 5), approximately less than a quarter of the country's total land area.

The concentration of population and economic activities in the Accra-Tema metropolitan area is even more dramatic. In this small, 18-mile radius area are virtually all the head offices of both Ghanaian and foreign-owned companies and 15 out of the 17 TUC national affiliates; the only artificial and deep water harbor, Tema; and the country's sole international airport, Accra Airport; plus the fact that Accra simultaneously serves as the national and Greater Accra regional capitals. Besides, all government ministries and foreign embassies are located in Accra. An interesting result of developments in the Accra-Tema area is that the construction of Tema Harbor, the rapid development of state-owned industrial estates, plus the fact that public administration is highly centralized, have all culminated in additional incentives which pull more businesses to the area. The Greater Accra region is deemed prime industrial location in Ghana because of its proximity to ministries responsible for processing the numerous documents that were required for foreign exchange and export and import trade. Thus, the highly bureaucratized system of public administration has also contributed to the high concentration of industrial or commercial activities in Ghana. Similar situations predominate in most other African countries, with the exceptions of Nigeria, Cote d'Ivoire (Ivory Coast) and Tanzania, which have separated their administrative from commercial capitals.

The over-clustering of both industry and administration has added immensely to the dense working-class population in the Accra-Tema region. Approximately 50 percent of Ghana's total population may be found within the Golden Triangle (Ewusi, 1984: 19). By having such large numbers of workers confined closely to the seat of the central government and the country's few industrial centers, governments of Ghana (without exceptions) have perceived worker protests, especially those involving demonstrations against public policies, as direct or potential threats to their power. The perceptions of politicians or their military counterparts become more critical during demonstrations which occur close to the Castle (the President's Office), the ministries or near the National Parliament, because they are more visible to the rulers, as was the case with the 1980 GIHOC strike.

Thus, a situation has evolved in Ghana in which the government's fear of strikes and other forms of expressed workers' dissatisfaction being used directly or exploited by political opponents to undermine their hegemony has been exacerbated by the public authorities also being the largest user of wage labor and, therefore, the target of strikes and other protests. For example, during the PNDC's reign, workers at the University of Ghana (Legon) who demonstrated against low wages carried placards that read "PNDC, your policies are now antiworker, so soon?", "Your new salaries have widened the gap more than ever, have you forgotten us" and "Jerry [referring to Rawlings, the PNDC's Chair] is this the power to the people you promised us?"[50] The political implications of such demonstrations and messages carried on the placards are better appreciated when one bears in mind that the PNDC relied on workers' support to gain legitimacy in the early and crucial years of 1981 to 1983. Like the Nkrumah/CPP government, the PNDC tied its political fate to improving the living and working conditions of workers.[51]

Workers' protest pose additional threats to governments because, with the exception of a few political or interest groups — such as the National Union of Ghanaian Students (NUGS) and the Association of Recognized Professional Bodies (lawyers, doctors and engineers) — unions are one of the few organizations which, within the one-party or military state, are able to not only articulate the discontent of workers, but also the general public's dissatisfaction with particular regimes. The advantage unions have over other groups (except the army) is the ability to back their claims with the withdrawal of their labor. As K. Ewusi (1984) indicated, and I have observed, because of unions' strategic roles in Africa, workers and their associations are uniquely qualified and able to articulate forcefully their economic and political concerns. Y. Agyeman-Badu and K. Osei-Hwedie (1982: 35 - 36) articulate Ghana's situation well:

> Once the masses are frustrated, they withdraw their support for the government. Over the years mass discontent with the government has appeared in several forms, including strikes, work stoppages and demonstrations by workers, students and market women . . . . Withdrawal of support for the government weakens its claim to legitimacy and sets the stage for a new round of power struggle among the political elite who feed on the economic frustration of the masses. The timing of most coups in Ghana indicates that it is not the level of frustration that signifies crisis of legitimacy to the competing elite. Rather, it is the elite's own perception of mass frustration that prompts them to change governments.

Ghai (1991: 155) adds that in Nigeria, the NLC is able to mobilize several other interest groups such as university teachers and students through a network of 42 Industrial Unions spread throughout the entire country. This capacity to quickly mobilize groups in opposition to government economic policies has become a source of concern to the Federal Nigerian Military authorities.

J. Kraus (1977: 1), in moving closer to why African governments are so concerned about restraining strikes, also observed that:

> In many African states, strikes are neither legitimate nor legal, but they are less easily curtailed than opposition political party activities, and thus repre-

sent one of the few avenues of implied or explicit mass intervention into the workings of increasingly elitist political regimes.

To complement Agyeman-Badu's, Osei-Hwedie's and Kraus' points about the politically sensitive nature of strikes, I will provide illustrations and an explanation of how that has occurred.

Several strikes in Ghana attained political significance. The most famous ones are the Sekondi-Takoradi (1961) strike which I have already referred to; the June to September, 1971, TUC strikes and workers' rallies to protest the policies of the PP government; and the 1978 public utility workers' strikes to force the SMC to hand over power to a new civilian administration. Although the NLC regime did not face a politically motivated strike, it sought to pre-empt such acts by making "incitement to strike" a capital offense (Hutchful, 1987). That was a first in Ghana's history. As noted by Kraus, strikes attain important political status during periods in which the one-party or military state, which was common in Africa, outlawed the political opposition, or in cases in which, such as in Ghana from 1957 to 1964 and from 1969 to 1972, the official opposition was emasculated. Bates (1970: 375) provides a valid elaboration on the conditions under which strikes became politically crucial in developing countries like Ghana and Zambia:

> A further reason for the refusal of governments to accord legitimacy to the demands of labor is the role of opposition parties. It is well known that political opposition is viewed as illegitimate in many developing nations, and it is a familiar argument that the imperative of rapid development makes the costs of political opposition intolerably high. It is frequently asserted that opposition parties can take advantage of the grievances created by the development policies and thereby threaten to undermine development programs. Whatever the validity of these arguments, they characterize the beliefs of many governing elites. As a result of these beliefs and as evidenced by Ghana, Tanzania, and Zambia, when trade union dissent is conjoined with the activities of opposition parties, the elites revert to coercion . . . .

The 1961 Rail Workers' Strike

Events surrounding the 1961 rail workers' strike in Sekondi-Takoradi paradoxically confirmed the CPP's suspicions that labor discontent might be exploited or fueled by opposition parties and thus support Bates' assessment of the politically sensitive nature of strikes in Ghana. S. Drake and L. Lacy's (1966) account of this 14-day strike shows why the Nkrumah government suspected the hand of the opposition and detained for six months without trial the strike leaders.[52] To the CPP, through their actions and speeches, the strikers assumed the role of "the unofficial opposition" when:

> By midweek practically every activity in the port was closed down. Municipal bus drivers had joined the strike, as had the city employees who collected garbage. Market women dispensed free food to the strikers at municipal bus garages and other strategic points. There was an air of excitement and pride throughout the city over the fact that they, the people of

Sekondi-Takoradi had brought business to a standstill, had stopped train service to all of Ghana and were displaying solidarity . . . . Morale was high.
The railway workers were heroes . . . . W. N. Grant, a prominent strike
leader told the crowd that if parliament did not give way to the demands of
the people, they would disband that body by force (*Ibid.*: 91 - 92).

Even if Grant exaggerated the ability of workers to overthrow the CPP,
the party interpreted his speech in conjunction with the strikers' activities as
tantamount to attempts to topple it from power. With the suspected or actual
role of the opposition, it was no wonder that Nkrumah treated this strike as
one of the most important political threats to his rule. Indeed, until his overthrow in 1966, this strike was considered the most crucial test of the legitimacy of Kwame Nkrumah and his CPP. As F. A. Botchway (1972) and Drake
and Lacy (1966) have asserted correctly, the strike was perceived as a direct
challenge to the CPP's claim to be one of the most representative mass political organizations in contemporary Africa. These were some of the reasons
why the party took extreme measures, including the invocation of a state of
emergency, when the strikers refused to call it off. A parallel situation
emerged in 1971 when the B. A. Bentum-led TUC attacked the PP government's policies and demanded their radical overhaul. In the case of the CPP,
when confronted with a challenge in the form of a strike, it resorted to manip-
ulating the TUC's leaders. Tettegah was removed as the Secretary-General
and, to facilitate tighter CPP control over organized labor, most of the head
offices of the national unions were relocated to Accra in 1962. In the case of
the anti-labor PP administration, on the other hand, it resorted to the ultimate
punitive measure in labor relations — the dissolution of the TUC via legislation.[53]

The issues raised in this section confirm the geopolitical and economic
significance of unions in contemporary Africa, which to a large extent influence policies and industrial relations practices in relation to the rights of
workers. One popular way in which union activities have been constricted by
the state is the *de jure* imposition of single, central labor bodies, through
which organized labor is closely monitored and policed by the state. As I
have shown, in both Nigeria and Ghana, when the state failed to use existing
labor codes to control the national labor organizations, the ultimate violation
of workers' rights — the dissolution of unions — was implemented. The
state's desire to control unions emanates from the fear that their wage claims
and strike activities, coupled with their articulation of working class or general
dissatisfaction with government policies, might undermine the governments'
capacity to retain power in politically unstable environments. This was especially the case in most African countries under one-party or military government in which the opposition was outlawed and the unions became one of the
few viable voices of discontent.

4. 3   Technical and Administrative Problems and the Application of ILO Standards in Africa

In addition to the problems of a colonial labor heritage and the geopolitical implications of union activities, other factors which may be linked to the continent's general economic and political malaise are also accountable for the failure to meet the ILO's membership requirements. These problems, which I designate as technical or administrative bottlenecks, are the subject matter of this section. They are the common administrative shortcomings which, in some situations, genuinely inhibited African countries' compliance with say, Article 19 of the Organization's Constitution, which requires members to submit Conventions and Recommendations adopted by the annual International Labor Conference (ILC) to the competent authority for examination. The competent national authority is the arm of government responsible for law-making or international treaties, such as the National Assembly or parliament within civilian or constitutional regimes.   In the case of Ghana, with the return to civilian or constitutional rule (in January, 1993), Parliament has become the appropriate competent authority. However, in military or one-party African states, there have been instances in which the Cabinet, the president or the military administration has acted as the authority competent to review and ratify ILO Conventions and Recommendations. Under military rule (from 1972 to 1979), the military government of the National Redemption Council, later the Supreme Military Council, was the competent authority for the examination of new ILO Recommendations and Conventions.

Article 22 of the ILO's Constitution imposes further obligations on members that ratify Conventions. Periodically, these members are required by the Governing Body, using its powers under this Article, to submit reports on the status of selected Conventions (see Appendx I for the texts of Articles 19 and 22 of the ILO's Constitution). Currently, countries such as Ghana and Nigeria that have ratified both Convention Nos. 87 and 98 are required by the Governing Body to report biannually on their labor policies, laws and practices *vis-à-vis* these Conventions (see Appendix 2 and 3 for copies of original report forms). The two-year reporting requirement was adopted by the Governing Body to allow the supervisory bodies of the ILO — the Committee of Experts, the Conference Committee on Standards and the International Labor Standards Department (which provides administrative services to these bodies which review national labor policies) adequate time to examine reports furnished by members.

Categories of Technical and Administrative Problems

Four categories of problems are identified as the major obstacles to Africa's full compliance with ILO standards. These are:

1.   Intradepartmental problems in the Labor Departments or Ministries in charge of international standards and domestic labor policies;
2.   The acute shortages of data/information, staff and other logistical input needed to fulfill complex ILO requirements;

3.   Problems of coordinating the activities of several public bureaucracies
     (interdepartmental problems); and
4.   The low levels of participation of Africans at Geneva-based conferences and
     activities.

These four categories may not exhaust the extensive range of problems that
afflict Africans at the ILO because my intent is to elaborate on only the com-
monly occurring ones. These problems were often the ones identified by
Africans as the most common and pressing. Some were discussed by African
participants at ILO fora such as Regional Conferences and seminars on ILO
standards.[54] These categories were also derived from my observation of
African participation at various ILO Governing Body meetings in 1985-1986
and the June 1986 International Labor Conference held in Geneva,
Switzerland.

4. 3. 1   Labor Administration: The Weak Link in African Compliance

As early as 1952, the ILO noted the pivotal role of labor administration in
Africa's compliance with the Organization's standards:

> In the less developed countries there are many prior problems which must be
> solved before programmes designed to improve labour conditions can be put
> into effect, and among these problems those of developing an effective ma-
> chinery for the administration of expanding . . . labour services inevitably
> assume a prominent place. In these circumstances, the organisation and
> functioning of national departments dealing with labour questions become
> increasingly important, and are bound to be a major preoccupation of the
> countries concerned . . . . (ILO, 1952: 63).[55]

In spite of this remark, labor departments in Africa have not undergone radical
organizational changes in terms of their structure, functions and jurisdiction
over international labor standards and national economic planning. Thus, in
over three decades of independence, a situation prevails in which the labor departments of most African states have not been equipped to meet effectively
ILO obligations.

An important problem most labor departments have to grapple with is the
bane of most African public bureaucracies — departmental or ministerial coordination problems. This problem has been exacerbated by long-distance
communication with the ILO and the respective countries' foreign missions or
embassies in Geneva.[56] These problems have been caused or compounded
further by the failure or inability of some African governments to be fully
committed to their international obligations. One high-level Ghanaian diplomat noted that the Nkrumah regime took its international obligations seriously
and most of the technical/administrative problems the country faces today
were nonexistent. Although labor departments are officially in charge of ILO
standards, participants in an ILO seminar on standards (ILO, 1985: 4) remarked that: "in many cases it was not within the competence of the Ministry

of Labor to propose modifications to legislation relevant to given Conventions."[57] In Ghana, for example up to 1993, two bodies — the PNDC representing the Executive section of Ghana government and the National Advisory Committee of Labor (NACL) — had to be persuaded before any action could be taken on ILO standards.

In performing duties connected with ILO standards, most African labor departments have been hampered by their low or "back seat" status within the hierarchy of public bureaucracies (Kalula, 1985, 1988). The low priority accorded labor departments is reflected in the small size of their budgets. For example, in 1987, the Ministry of Labor in Ghana was awarded one of the smallest budget: allocations.[58] Kalula made similar observations concerning Zambia's Ministry of Labor (1985). The low status of African labor departments can be attributed to several complex factors. Some of these are the failure of African countries to treat human resources as important strategic factors in solving development problems. Hence, the misperception that labor departments do not or cannot perform critical functions. This misperception is concretized by the descriptions given to some of these departments. In Ghana today, it is still referred to as the "labor card"[59] issuing department and in Sierra-Leone, the "thumb print cards" production department, referring to its role in issuing employment cards which required thumb printing as a form of identification.[60] These views reflect these departments' colonial heritage as organizations created to recruit and exploit African labor for European and other foreign interests. A similar view was expressed by the U.S. Department of Labor (1980: 6), when it described Ghana Labor Department's major original function as meeting "the recruiting needs of foreign employers."

Bearing in mind the immense economic problems, including the acute shortage of convertible currency African governments have to contend with, plus the misperceptions about the importance of labor administration, one cannot discount the role of the view that improving the performance of labor departments will divert resources from what are perceived to be more productive national endeavors. This is particularly the case in the implementation of ILO standards, which may require substantial foreign currency expenditure.[61]

Although the labor department in Ghana is explicitly recognized as responsible for all matters concerning the ILO and the technical representation of Ghana at ILO Conferences, it has had to contend with problems ranging from the lack of cooperation from other government departments or ministries to the lack of funds. Some of these Ministries are Trade, Industries, Justice and the Attorney General's Office, Foreign Affairs and the Office of the Government Statistician (the former Bureau of Statistics). The lack of cooperation may be attributed to the low interministerial priority assigned to the responsibilities of the Labor Department or the lack of adequate commitment on the part of the public authorities. The department typically has problems obtaining data and information from other departments, whose input is required to prepare ILO reports. This problem might be attributed to the lack of awareness of the implications of Ghana's membership in the ILO and the ratification of Conventions within most departments, with the exception of the Foreign Affairs Ministry. Foreign Affairs officials are knowledgeable about the ILO because of their extensive contacts with the Labor Department and other international organizations, including the UN and its agencies.

4. 3. 2   The Impact of Political Instability and a Declining Economy

Rapid changes in government, especially at the Cabinet level, and the deterioration of the Ghanaian economy have also had their toll on the Labor Department's capacity to meet the country's ILO obligations. At the national level, frequent changes in Labor Ministers have disrupted the development of long term labor policies. Since 1966, the country has not had consistent and long range labor policies. Because of the frequent turnover in governments, most governments had barely enough time "to get their feet wet" in labor matters before they were overthrown (see Section 2.2). An adverse outcome of the frequent changes in regimes is that the department has experienced a high turnover of Cabinet appointees. By 1989, although the PNDC had been in power for less than eight years, as many as seven ministers were appointed to the Labor Department. Each appointee, therefore, had an average term of a little over one year. In the Ministry of Finance and Economic Planning, on the other hand, a single PNDC Secretary has been at the helm since 1981.

In Ghana, disruptive reshuffling of Labor Secretaries by the PNDC regime posed problems, which in turn undermined the capacity of the Ministry of Labor to assist the government in meeting its ILO obligations. The rapid removal of Cabinet members constitutes a kind of brain drain that deprived the Labor Ministry of their knowledge, practical experience and insights into ILO and domestic labor issues. In addition, each new Cabinet member had to literally "learn the ropes" and barely had enough time to engage in meaningful long-term domestic labor policy planning, let alone adopt strategies to improve the country's record at the ILO. The crucial role of Cabinet experience in ensuring any country's full ILO participation was underscored by one veteran African employer representative. He noted that in spite of his over 10 years of experience in ILO activities, he still had a lot to learn about the Organization's intricate structure. One might only add to his observation that one requires to devote full time attention and effort to comprehend fully how the ILO operates.

A senior ILO official also remarked to me during my field work that in fulfilling members' obligations, a lot "hinged on the dynamism of the Labor Minister and other officials." This official supported his comments by pointing out that an effective Minister could be critical to a country ratifying Conventions or submitting good ILO reports and on time.[62] Most importantly, frequent changes in Cabinet appointments to the Labor Department has led to a situation in which within the short time they were in office, ministers were not able to mobilize the political and other organizational resources they needed to get the country to enhance its role at the ILO. This problem may have contributed to why, for example, Articles 19 and 22 reports to the ILO are delayed or at times neglected. According to the ILO, Ghana did not submit its first report for Convention No. 148, which was due in 1988, until June,

1992. With respect to Kenya, some instruments adopted as far back at 1978 were being processed through Parliament in 1992.[63]

Political instability in Africa has also aggravated the problems African members have to grapple with in meeting their ILO requirements. One of the problems of African nations at the ILO is fulfilling the Article 19 obligation to submit to the national competent authority instruments adopted by the International Labor Conference. Here, too abrupt and, at times, violent changes in government in countries such as Ghana and Nigeria have compounded existing problems. For example, the Ghana government once reported to the ILO that documents used to process instruments for submission to the competent authority had been lost because of a coup. Frequent changes in the competent authority has equally resulted in each new administration having to start all over again relations with the ILO. A resultant problem is that reports are delayed or not submitted because the political leaders (both civilian and military) are not familiar with or lack experience in dealing with the technical aspects of ILO requirements. In Nigeria, under the last civilian administration, the Senate (the majority of the members dealing with the ILO for the first time) repeatedly refused to submit documents used to review ILO instruments to the Organization from 1979 to 1981 on the grounds that they were "national secrets." This incident could, to some extent, be attributed to several factors, including the lack of experience in processing ILO documents and also possibly the majority of the Senators' (Parliamentarians) lack of knowledge about the ramifications of ILO membership under Article 19 (see Appendix 1 for the text of this Article).

The Frequent Staff Shortages

Other personnel problems have also plagued African labor departments. Typical is the lack of trained or experienced staff in charge of ILO matters. Although, compared to other African nations, Ghana's situation is relatively better (one of the most senior employees who work on standards has been at the department for 10 years),[64] the training given the staff in ILO standards is not adequate to allow them to perform their tasks effectively. Typically officers were trained in Geneva for about a week, and others for a few days in Arusha, Tanzania.[65] Currently, most African labor departments are experiencing chronic shortages of personnel competent in the technical aspects of ILO standards because of interdepartmental brain drain and the loss of personnel by the civil service to the private and parastatal sectors and international organizations.[66] In Ghana, for example, one of the few labor department officials with extensive ILO training (over two years at Geneva,) did not rejoin the department on his return home. He found employment with a state-owned company with better conditions of employment.

Unattractive civil service terms of employment may also be contributing to the shortage of staff in several African countries' labor departments. Being aware of this problem, employees of the Ghana Labor Department recently asked for "additional high level manpower recruitment and . . . development." They also urged the government to improve their conditions of service to enable the department to retain qualified employees (*Laborscope*, May 1989: 22).

Labor Departments' Nonpriority Status

The image of labor departments as "nonpriority" government organizations has also hurt them by making it difficult for them to attract highly qualified personnel. In Sierra Leone, for example, it is alleged that the Labor Department is "a dumping place" for public employees not needed in other departments ("Hard Labor," *West Africa*, June 19 - 25, 1989: 1007). Under such circumstances, it is difficult to attract competent staff. One Ghanaian Embassy official drew my attention to the fact that not until recently, in spite of the availability of several qualified Ghanaian legal experts, the Labor Department's personnel did not have legal background or training.

The inadequate provision of logistical support, ranging from local and convertible currencies, to printing and duplication materials, to other basic office supplies such as stationery, has also hampered the delivery of efficient services by the departments of labor in Africa. These shortages are often caused by the low budget: allocation given to labor departments and at times by general shortages due to the inability to import adequate supplies. In Ghana, for example, from the mid-1970s to the mid-1980s, transportation was a major problem because the department had only a few operating vehicles (*Laborscope*, May 1989: 22). The entire Inspection Division of the Department had only one vehicle in good working condition.[67]

One Sierra Leone government representative informed the 1987 International Labor Conference about how global economic problems undermined meeting basic ILO requirements:

> His Government was fully aware of its obligations under the ILO Constitution. Some years back, the ILO used to send the Government many copies of new instruments . . . adopted, and their submission to Parliament had therefore been a very easy matter. As a result of the world economic recession, that practice had been suspended and his Government has had to produce, in an improvised fashion, 150 copies of every instrument that had to be submitted. That partly explained why it had been unable to submit the instruments in question to the competent authorities.[68]

The above statement hints at the extent to which financial problems within the UN and its agencies, the ILO not excepted, have led to cutbacks in the material and technical services rendered to developing countries. The perennial logistical problems do not end African labor departments' woes. Budget problems and general economic decline have also adversely impacted on the more technical and substantive inputs required for efficient domestic labor administration and the fulfillment of ILO requirements.

Inadequate Data

E. Kalula (1988: 19 - 20) has identified a "multitude of problems," includ-ing the absence of useful or applicable data and information. What he calls the "back seat" role assigned labor departments, plus their meager financial and human resources, have culminated in the grossly insufficient collection, collation and reproduction of information and data for both local use and ILO purposes. Several years of independence in countries such as Ghana, Nigeria, Zambia and Kenya have not led to situations in which data collection and ap-plication are accorded priorities as government functions. Ghana's situation in especially the 1970s depicted the low priority status of data gathering. In Ghana, because of the failure to conduct the 10-year population census, re-searchers have had to depend on data collected almost 20 years ago through the 1970 Population Census. The moribund status of the state agency respon-sible for data collection (the Central Bureau of Statistics) from the mid-1970s to the early 1980s, also attests to the problem. In the field of labor, for exam-ple, annual department of labor reports were published sporadically. The Department released its reports for 1975 to 1990 in 1992.[69] One undesirable outcome of the lack of appropriate data was that in 1987, the ILO's Committee of Experts reported that from 1977 to 1987, it did not receive any information from the Ghana government on minimum wages. Delays in sub-mitting reports to the ILO may have been caused by several factors, including the *ad hoc* compilation, publishing and forwarding of data to the ILO in Geneva through the coordinated efforts of the Ministries of Labor and Foreign Affairs. The delays made it practically impossible for the ILO to assess Ghana's minimum wage situation in almost 10 years.

Two additional problems were also underscored by Kalula (1988: 20). Even when documents or data are available, they are not readily usable due to unsatisfactory collation and publication. Another important drawback is that most of the available materials are outdated:

> Materials. . . tend to be dated. Up-to-date material is difficult to find for var-ious reasons. Government departments take years to bring out annual re-ports, at certain times there has been a backlog of three years or more (*Ibid.*).[70]

The Absence of Unified Labor Codes

Currently, most African ILO members, including Ghana, lack what may be considered one essential block for establishing a completely effective labor administration system — a rationalized system of labor laws. E. Bello (1980: 96) has identified how the sheer volume and increasing complexity of con-temporary labor laws, coupled with the retention of redundant colonial labor statutes have culminated in inconsistent legislation. Besides, often these laws do not reflect genuine national labor needs. The plethora of the applicable in-dustrial relations statutes in Ghana illustrates Bello's views. As shown in Table II, the relevant industrial relations laws consist of an odd mixture of colonial legislation and an assortment of various acts and amendments made by different post-independence governments.

The confused state of labor laws in Ghana makes it difficult to use the relevant statutes as effective policy guidelines in dealing with ILO standards. The cumulative effect of modern laws being piled on top of unaltered colonial statutes is that the amount of work required to streamline existing laws has deterred most governments from undertaking such a task. Since 1966, two attempts at revamping the relevant statutes have been abandoned. First, the NLC failed to implement proposed amendments to the 1965 Industrial Relations Act (Hutchful, 1987). Instead, it passed Decree No. 157 of 1967, which further confused the status of trade union rights within the large Ghanaian public sector. Then there was the PNDC's proposed "Two-Year Labor Codification Program" of 1985 - 1986, officially aimed at rationalizing the country's labor laws. The government abandoned this program and later informed the ILO that attempts to convert the country's labor laws into a coherent system had been hampered by frequent changes in government.[71]

Table II
Relevant Ghanaian Industrial Relations Laws

1. Trade Unions Ordinance 1941 (Cap 91). Amended 1954.

2. Conspiracy and Protection of Property (Trade Disputes) Ordinance, 1941 (Cap 90).

3. Trade Disputes (Arbitration and Enquiry) Ordinance, 1941 (Cap 93).

4. Industrial Relations Act, 1965 (Act 299).

5. Labour Decree, 1967 (NLCD 157).

6. Labour Regulations, 1969 (LI 632).

7. Industrial Relations Act, 1965 (Act 299).

Source: Labor Department, Accra, Ghana, 1987.

A Haphazard Approach to the Ratification of Standards and Participation in ILO Affairs

My study of African problems at the ILO also showed that the ratification and submission of reports in spurts also contributed to African governments' problems. I am referring to situations in which Ghana, for example, ratified five separate Conventions on a single day in May, 1986. Nigeria, too, ratified Convention Nos. 87 and 98 simultaneously in 1960, immediately upon becoming independent. As much as the ILO desires, and indeed encourages, members to ratify more Conventions, in Ghana's case especially, the number ratified at once may have been excessive. The ILO's Regional Adviser for Africa on Standards may have had this in mind when in 1986 he advised that, in light of the ratifications, with the exception of Convention No. 144 dealing with tripartite consultations concerning ILO standards, he would not recommend that Ghana ratify any more Conventions in the near future. Ratifying several Conventions simultaneously leads to a situation in which the Labor Department is required to perform more work without additional resources. These extra burdens can lead to further deterioration in the department's situation in light of the acute shortage of logistical supports referred to in this chapter.

The final problem relates to several African ILO members not being able to participate in critical deliberations at the ILO. This problem, has the effect of not making it possible for African delegates to participate fully in the policy formulation, adoption and supervision of standards and other important ILO policies, programs and activities. It can also result in African delegates not being fully appreciative of the circumstances and critical factors that influenced some of the labor instruments they may have to incorporate into their domestic laws. These problems emerge in Geneva, where most of the Organization's activities occur. African participation is seriously weakened by the failure or inability of a country such as Sierra Leone to send any delegate to International Labor Conferences. There were no representatives of the government, the unions or the employers at the June, 1986 ILC. African delegations that manage to get to Geneva are often incomplete or too small to ensure full participation. They also face tremendous logistical problems related to traveling long distances from Africa — plane reservations, plus accommodation and transportation in Geneva. These delegates are often distracted by the amount of time and energy they spend resolving mundane problems during the few weeks they spend attending ILO meetings and conferences. At times, as a result of these problems, African delegates return home before the official closing of sessions.[72] That undermines African involvement at the ILO and deprives them of opportunities to bring to bear on deliberations and activities, the African point of view or concerns. The end result is that Africans often miss critical opportunities to make ILO standards, programs and activities reflect African interests or needs.

The problem of ineffective African involvement is complex because, it is tied to the general economic and political problems of Africa, especially the lack of adequate foreign exchange to fund complete delegations and/or to provide enough logistical support for delegates for Geneva-based activities. The problems have become so persistent and go beyond Africa that the ILO is considering funding Third World delegations to the annual International Labor Conference.[73] Under Article 18 of the ILO's Constitution, governments are required to fund workers' and employers' delegates.

In concluding this chapter, I wish to stress that it is difficult to determine the precise extent to which the problems I have alluded to and the lack of genuine commitment on the part of governments have undermined African participation at the ILO. This is the more so because of the economic crisis in most African countries today. Although with improved general economic conditions, some logistical bottlenecks could be removed (as depicted by the situation in Ghana from 1986 to 1992), that may have to be accompanied by African governments increasing their levels of commitment to enhance their participation by marshalling the necessary political will to improve their records at the ILO and their domestic labor relations and human resource utilization. In achieving these objectives, emphasis needs to be placed by governments on assigning priority status to labor departments and improving data collection and publishing on a consistent basis.

NOTES

1.   The point worth emphasizing is that, although since independence there have been fundamental changes in the labor laws and practices of the selected African countries, colonial laws and practices still constitute important sections of contemporary African labor laws and practices. As Table II shows, the new and at times radical labor laws adopted after independence have either been merged with or exist with colonial labor statutes called "ordinances." Hence in Ghana, the 1941 Trades Union Ordinance together with the Industrial Relations Act of 1965 are currently some of the most important industrial relations laws. Similarly in Nigeria, the 1938 Trades Union Ordinance is used to regulate the formation of unions (Otobo, 1987: 49). These two colonial legal remnants have not been repealed or modified.

2.   I wish to note that I do not attribute every contemporary African labor problem to the British because such a view is highly simplistic. My analysis seeks to explain their role and to debunk the erroneous view that they promoted voluntary unionism. Thus, I do not imply that colonial policies alone may justify the failure of African countries to comply with ILO standards or to create viable labor relations.

3.   See 1965 Presidential Declaration of Kenya leading to the founding of the Central Organization of Trade Unions; Decree No. 22 of 1978 creating the Nigerian Labor Congress; and the 1971 Industrial Relations Act, which launched the Zambian Congress of Trade Unions.

4.   Included in a number of ILO cases filed against the British was a 1951 complaint which accused the British of interfering in the internal affairs of Kenyan unions (Zeytinoglu, 1986: 59; Haas, 1970: 78 - 79).

5.   Walter Rodney (1982) provides one of the most succinct accounts of colonialism and its role in Africa's underdevelopment.

6.   Section 1 of the 1941 Trades Union Ordinance (the Gold Coast, now Ghana) specified that unions had to be registered to avoid dissolution:

1.   Every trade union shall be registered in accordance with the provisions of this Ordinance or be dissolved, within six months of the date —
    a.   of its formation, or
    b.   of any notification by the Registrar that he has refused under section 13 to register the trade union, or
    c.   of the determination of the appeal under section 13 where an appeal is entered against the refusal of the Registrar to register a trade union, or
    d.   of the commencement of this Ordinance, whichever is the later date.

2.   Every trade union which is not registered or dissolved within the period prescribed in the preceding subsection and every officer thereof shall be liable on summary conviction to a fine of £5 for every day that it remains unregistered after the expiration of such period.

7.   ILO, Committee of Freedom of Association Case Nos. 984 and 1189 against Kenya, 1985a.

8.   Section 3 (1) of the 1941 Ordinance that barred civil service unionization states:

. . . this Ordinance shall not apply to any combination of associations or persons in the service in the Gold Coast . . . and it shall be unlawful for any civil servant to be a member of a trade union.

See also, Section 11(1) of the same statute. According to the details of Case No. 25 of the Committee of Freedom of Association filed against the British colonial authorities by the World Federation of Trade Unions (WFTU) on behalf of Ghanaian workers, the broad definition of essential services by the British led to the exclusion of workers in nonessential sectors such as meteorological services from striking (ILO, 1985a).

9.   Ghana Labor Department, *Laborscope*, May 1989: 16; Obeng-Fosu 1991: 2 - 3.

10.   Even B. C. Roberts (1964) acknowledges the role of labor and political disturbances in the British Commonwealth territories as factors that influenced the creation of labor departments in Africa.

11.   The promulgation of the relevant colonial ordinances coincided with the adoption of so-called colonial "Welfare" and "Development" Acts. In Nigeria, the first of these Development Acts was the 1929 Colonial Development and Welfare Act passed by the British Labor Government (Otobo, 1987: 15).

12.   Information from the Research Department, Ghana TUC, March 1987.

13.   Tewson 1954: 317 - 318.

14.   Turkson (1976: 143). The foresight of Lunn and the TUC Secretary-General is borne by the fact that Britain is still a major trading partner of several former British African colonies, including Ghana and Nigeria.

15.   U.S. Department of Labor, 1980: 6.

16.   Kraus, 1979: 114. The public authorities in Ghana may have been following British precedent when the CPP used "party stalwarts" and state security agents (typically the Special Branch) to infiltrate the labor movement.

17.   Culled from Otobo (1987: 23).

18.   Economic and political pressure was used to exact political concessions, including a new constitution and elections leading to independence. These were implemented in 1951 and led to Ghana's independence at a pace which had hitherto not been imagined. See Austin (1964) for details of Ghana's decolonization process. Similar joint efforts occurred in Zambia, Kenya and Nigeria leading to independence.

19.   For details of the gross and racially motivated inequitable living and working conditions between Africans and Europeans under colonialism, see Rodney (1982).

20.   Austin, 1964. K. A. Ninsin and F. K. Drah (1987: 100 - 101) also explain how the dominance of the local economy by expatriate firms allied with the colonial administration contributed to nationalist agitation for independence in Nigeria.

21.   In Nigeria, at the Enugu coal mines, 21 striking workers were killed and another 51 seriously wounded by troops under British command (Otobo 1987: 30). Acknowledging this British legacy, however, does not justify similar repression of

workers by contemporary African governments. These kinds of developments and the repressive British responses were strong catalysts to independence movements in all of Anglophone Africa.

22.   ILO, 1958.

23.   A list of African unions' weaknesses includes lack of finances, unstable membership and a dearth of leadership and other organizational skills, especially within the ranks of blue-collar workers who were not permitted by British ordinances to recruit leaders from outside their trades. A classic effect was that, in Nigeria for example, it was common to find a single individual serving as the treasurer or secretary of three or more unions (Nwubueze, 1981).

24.   In 1940, five unions with a membership of 3,500 were registered. By 1942, 62 had been registered with 21,000 workers. The number of unions then shot to 80 seven years later, of which 30 were inactive. By 1965, close to 200 operated out of 332 registered (Maitland-Jones, 1973: 141 - 142).

25.   Otobo (1987: 30) confirms parallel developments in Nigeria where trade union rights to collective bargaining and strikes were virtually outlawed until the 1950s.

26.   The modern-day equivalents are workers' welfare associations, such as the Ghana National Association of Teachers (GNAT) and the Civil Servants' Association (GCSA), which do not have bargaining rights. These organizations enjoy only consultative status with their employers.

27.   Both Tettegah and Cowan were very active in the Ghana labor movement during the inception of the TUC.

28.   Some of the measures taken by the ILO are direct requests and unpublished comments sent to the Ghana government about its laws not being in total harmony with its standards and technical assistance missions to Ghana to assist the government to resolve domestic issues that result in violations of standards. One of the most recent missions was that of May 3 - 10, 1987, by the African Regional Adviser on Standards, who assisted the PNDC government to conduct a national tripartite seminar on international labor standards.

29.   According to researchers such as Gray (1981) and Jeffries (1978), who have studied internal Ghanaian union practices including elections, on the whole, the process of selecting national and TUC leaders has been fairly democratic, that is open and contested elections. However, there have been instances in which some Ghanaian governments — the CPP, the NLC and PP regimes — sought to interfere in the election of the Secretary-General of the TUC, largely because of the importance these governments attached to the position. In the case of the CPP, its Central Committee appointed the two Secretaries-General after 1962 and the NLC used its personal connections to get B. A. Bentum appointed to that post in 1966.

30.   This analysis is critical to formulating policies to rectify African violations of ILO standards because it deals with the major factors that have made it difficult for African ILO members to meet their obligations within the Organization.

31.   See Industrial Relations Act, 1958, of Ghana and Trade Unions Decree Nos. 31 and 22 of 1973 and 1978 of Nigeria.

32.   Tettegah became the first fully paid in 1954 with financial support from the CPP.

33.   The plight of Ghanaian unions became a public policy issue because trade unionists such as Tettegah and Joe-Fio Meyer, who were CPP Stalwarts (staunch members), lobbied successfully to get the Nkrumah government to assist them.

34.   See Republic of Kenya, *The Policy of Trade Union Organisation*, Government Printer, Nairobi, 1965; Amsden (1971).

35.   Ananaba, 1979; Nwubueze, 1975, 1981; U. J. Umoh, "Disunity in the Unions," *West Africa*, Oct. 7, 1985: 2100.

36.   At this point, it may be worth noting that the Adebo Commission, which was set up in Nigeria (1970 - 1971) to recommend solutions to the problems of unhealthy union competition, referred to the centralized TUC structure in Ghana as an appropriate model for Nigeria. This shows how Ghana TUC may have influenced the Nigerian labor situation.

37.   My point is that whereas the industrialized nations have had a much longer time to work out their labor relations problems, Africans have had little time to sort out their problems. The brief industrial experience in Africa has exacerbated the problems under discussion.

38.   According to Ako Adjei, the Nkrumah Minister who oversaw the adoption of the 1958 Industrial Relations Act of Ghana, John Tettegah and Joe-Fio Meyer (both TUC leaders) used their membership of the government and the party's influential Central Committee to persuade Nkrumah and other politicians about the usefulness of government intervention. Interviews held in Accra, Summer and Fall, 1991.

39.   This is an innovative way in which the TUC utilized its influence within the CPP to pass legislation favorable to workers. The "Extension Powers" authorize the Minister for Labor to apply to workers and employers collective bargaining terms adopted in a particular industry, but to which they may not have been original parties. From the workers' standpoint, this provision spread the benefits of collective agreements to workers who are not in a position to bargain with employers. See Sections 20 and 13(1) of the 1958 and 1965 Industrial Relations Acts, Ghana, respectively.

40.   One of the myths about Africa is that it was the socialist governments that introduced development planning to the continent after independence. Development planning was introduced in Ghana in the 1920s by the British Governor, Gordon Guggisberg (Ewusi, 1976; Turkson, 1976). In Nigeria, too, it was first introduced by the British colonial administration (Otobo, 1987).

41.   Nkrumah and his CPP borrowed capital from the West because of the Soviet failure to finance his development plans (Amin, 1973: 244). The CPP was in the middle of negotiations with the IMF and World Bank to reschedule Ghana's debts when Nkrumah was toppled (Hutchful, 1987).

42.   To the CPP and its labor allies, the way to industrial peace was legislation that centralized Ghanaian unions to facilitate the party's control over labor. The workers were rewarded with liberal benefits such as free or low cost education, health, housing and work place food services.

43.   Ghana National Assembly, 1965 Industrial Relations Bill, *Parliamentary Record of Proceedings* (1965) .

44.   Since independence, the state has employed between 50 and 70 percent of wage labor (Ewusi, 1984).

45.   One may detect here tensions between the CPP's pro-worker intentions and the state's role as the main financier of commercial ventures.

46.   According to S. Amin (1973: 242), from 1955 to 1962, only 7 to 14 percent of investments went into directly productive sectors such as factories for capital goods. This does not, however, imply that the 7 to 14 percent of the public expenditure was used in sectors which proved profitable. As I have argued (Panford, 1981), corruption, inefficient management and technical problems, plus foreign exchange shortages caused by substantial decline in commodity prices contributed to the problems of the Nkrumah and subsequent Ghanaian administrations. No government in Ghana has as yet been able to surmount these hurdles.

47.   The importance of the minimum wage is borne by the frequency with which it has been the source of friction between unions and African governments. In the 1980s, conflicts centering on minimum wages escalated largely because of the desire of the governments of Ghana and Nigeria to meet World Bank and IMF conditions for financial assistance. In Zambia, after a wave of strikes and public protests culminating in the loss of life, the government rescinded its IMF/World Bank-inspired policies on wage controls (ILO, *Social and Labor Bulletin,* 1985). In Nigeria since 1982, when the government imposed a wage freeze, there have been constant clashes between the police and various groups led by the NLC. The government resisted attempts to boost wages, arguing that wage increases had adverse macro-economic effects. As demonstrated in 1991, as soon as the head of state announced a new 250 naira wage, prices shot up (Otobo, 1987; Ghai, 1991; and N. Adio-Saka, "Confusion Over Interpretation of Minimum Wage: Defining Baseline," *West Africa,* Feb. 25 - March 3, 1991: 260; Panford, Forthcoming).

48.   Data/information compiled from "Ghana TUC Drops ERP Support," *African Business,* March 1986: 90; N. K. Bentsi-Enchill, "Ghana, Work for Idle Hands," *West Africa,* Jan. 27, 1986: 117, 197; "Salaries Cost Half of National Budget," *West Africa,* April 3 - 9, 1989.

49.   The high stakes are demonstrated by a recent industrial dispute in which the chief of police was summoned by the courts in Ghana in connection with the detention of 20 striking workers ("Court Orders IGP," *West Africa,* Nov. 4 - 10, 1991: 1859). In Nigeria, it is common for the head of state to personally intervene in labor disputes to avoid national strikes by the NLC and more recently, General I. Babangida had to clarify confusion over a new 250 naira minimum wage ("Defining Baseline," *West Africa*).

50.   "Workers Demonstrate at Legon," *West Africa,* March 31, 1986: 701.

51.   "Ghana TUC Drops ERP Support," *African Business,* March 1986: 90.

52.   The workers were given a presidential pardon by Nkrumah himself as a goodwill gesture towards labor.

53.   Similarly, in 1981, following a successful NLC-led general strike, the first of its kind since independence, the Federal Nigerian Civilian Government contemplated but abandoned dissolving the NLC, largely because of its political clout ("Nigeria: Strikes hit the national purse," *New African,* July 1981: 27; "Nigerian Labor Organizes Resistance to Plan for Splitting Union Control," *New African,* Dec. 1981: 22). In 1988, the government temporarily dissolved the NLC when it vehemently opposed the austerity dimensions of the nation's new economic program. A more recent similar phenomenon occurred with the passage of Zambia's 1990 Industrial Relations Act after leaders of ZCTU spearheaded the campaign to reinstate multiparty democracy and oust President Kaunda from power (Hamalengwa, 1992; ILO Committee for Freedom of Association, Case No. 1575 against Zambia; "Profile: Frederick Chiluba," "Taking off the Straight-jacket," *West Africa,* Feb. 24 - March 1, 1992: 319).

54.   Some of these regional conferences were held in Lagos, Nigeria (1960), Accra, Ghana (1969) and one of the most recent in Tunis, Tunisia (1983). See also ILO, 1985b and 1981.

55.   This observation supports my view that colonial labor policy is partly responsible for the inefficient labor relations systems in contemporary Africa. It also justifies the inclusion of a section on colonial labor policies in this study.

56.   Because Zambia does not have an embassy in Switzerland, it depends on the Zambian High Commission in London for communications with the ILO. This creates additional burdens for Zambian delegates.

57.   A glaring example of labor departments' lack of proper jurisdiction over ILO matters is found in Malawi, where the Foreign Affairs Ministry is responsible for all ILO affairs, including standards.

58.   "Government Expenditure Estimates," *West Africa*, Feb. 2, 1987: 236.

59.   Ghana, Department of Labor, *Laborscope*, May 1989.

60.   "Hard Labor," *West Africa*, June 19 - 25, 1989: 1007.

61.   They typically include air fare, hotel and other living costs for several delegates; postage and other correspondence for regular ILO meetings and the annual International Labor Conference in Geneva and paying member countries' annual assessments. The preparation of ILO reports entails substantial budgets for personnel and supplies such as stationery.

62.   It is worth drawing attention to the fact that until the PNDC appointed D. S. Boateng to the Labor Department, Ministers did not possess what may be termed a "labor background." Boateng was a former Principal of the Ghana Labor College, Accra.

63.   ILO, Committee of Experts, International Labor Conference, *General Report*, 1992; International Labor Conference, 79th Session, Geneva, *Provisional Record*, 1992.

64.   In explaining the failure of the Sierra Leone Government to furnish overdue reports, the government representative indicated that not only did the country lack human resources, but also suffered from a "break-down of organizational machinery." ILO, *Provisional Record*, 1992: 18. In the opinion of the ILO, "there is the danger that certain countries may find it difficult if not impossible to bring themselves up to date" (Committee of Experts, 1992: 47). Sierra Leone and to some extent Kenya fall in this category.

65.   Information from the Ghana Labor Department, Accra, 1987. I observed during my field work that on the average, labor department employees received a few days of training at the ILO's Head Office. Considering the complex nature of the ILO system, the average length of training is inadequate. In resolving this issue, however, one has to be reminded that the ILO has limited funds and training resources, and most African countries are also not in a position to allow their labor department employees to be absent from work over long periods because of staff shortages at home.

66.   An often neglected aspect of the African brain drain is the heavy loss of trained personnel to both governmental and non-governmental international organizations. This is particularly true in the cases of Ghana and Nigeria.

67.   ILO, International Labor Standards Department, Ghana, "Mission Report," May 3 - 10, 1987. Transportation improved in Ghana substantially after 1985 when the economy improved with the massive import of used vehicles by Ghanaians residing overseas.

68.   Third Item on the Agenda: Information and Reports on the Application of Conventions and Recommendations. Report of the Committee on the Application of Conventions and Recommendations, International Labor Conference, 73rd Session, 1987, *Provisional Record*.

69.   Although national data compilation was always a problem, beginning with the Nkrumah administration, some improvements occurred. However, the gains made were lost under the corrupt and incompetent NRC and SMC governments from 1972 to 1979. The country is yet to recover from these losses. See Republic of Ghana, Labor Department, *Annual Reports, 1975 - 1990*, Accra, 1992.

70.   The late release of Ghana labor reports dating back to 1975 attests to the problem of the data being outdated.

71.   The PNDC may have aborted plans to codify Ghana's labor laws for several reasons, including its major preoccupation with the implementation of the Economic Recovery Program, which it adopted in 1982.

72.   Africans cut short their stay in Geneva to reduce expenses involving the use of convertible currencies such as the British pound sterling, the U.S. dollar or the Swiss franc.

73.   ILO, International Labor Conference, Report of the Committee on the Application of Conventions and Recommendations, Part I, 1986: 7.

Chapter 5

The Influence of the ILO on African Workers' Rights and Labor Relations

5. 1   The Ghana Trade Union Congress: A Failed Promise?

This chapter is an analysis of the practical outcomes of Ghana's post-independence labor relations and a description and explanation of the role and influence of the International Labor Organization in the development of Ghanaian labor policies and worker rights practices. Another goal is to evaluate the relevance of the ILO's standards to Ghana's labor polices and practices and the constraints within which the ILO's standards supervisory system operates. In order to explain the full consequences of legislated union structures and post-independence labor union-state relations, I separate the short- from the long-term effects. The first half of this subchapter deals with the major short term gains the unions in Ghana made and the second part, the long run adverse effects of post-independence labor policies and practices on organized labor.

Financial Gains from Compulsory Labor Unity

The Ghana TUC, like most African government-sponsored labor federations, benefited substantially in the short run as a result of its close alliance with the CPP. The TUC was recognized as the sole representative of the working class. Its vitality from 1958 to 1966 was due largely to the opportunities created by the state to ensure its financial security. The success of the TUC was achieved through the imposition of checkoff for union dues; the 1959 and 1960 Amendments to the Industrial Relations Acts of 1958; guaranteed union membership and a large pool of workers from whom dues were collected; mandated "union shop" practices and the banning of all non-TUC-affiliated labor organizations. As a result, the TUC's revenue increased from a few thousand dollars in 1958 to over half a million by 1962 (Gray, 1980). The party also used its huge political muscle to support unions' collective bargaining activities especially after 1964 when the CPP became the sole political party. The party used the Labor Minister's "powers of extension" under the country's labor laws to extend to several workers the benefits of collective bargaining without requiring such workers to establish their rights to be represented by a union.[1] Recalcitrant employers were penalized by denying them import licenses and foreign exchange, which they needed to remain in business (Gray, 1981). One significant result was that the expatriate businesses that hitherto preferred weak house or company unions were made to bargain with the relatively strong unions formed after independence.

An Expanded Social Wage for Ghanaian Workers

The collective bargaining advantages extended to the TUC-affiliated unions were supplemented with one of the most elaborate welfare systems in Africa. From the 1960s to the mid-1970s, the country's social wage comprised state-subsidized or free services, from transportation of workers to free education from pre-school to university. From 1961 to 1971, 25 cents could buy a worker a hot lunch in a state-owned or subsidized canteen (cafeteria) or medical services, including a doctor's visit and prescriptions from a public clinic, hospital or health post. Workers in urban areas had access to state-provided low cost housing.[2]

State intervention in the form of a centralized union structure, with the TUC at the apex, in the short term reduced excessive tensions and rivalries within the labor movement.[3] From 1958 to 1971, union jurisdictional disputes were substantially reduced. Both the government and the TUC used the existing labor laws to encourage workers to resolve union organizing conflicts through a committee within the TUC. Besides enforcing labor unity, the CPP gave the TUC substantial material aid. An example is the donation of the TUC's head offices in Accra. That boosted the prestige of the Ghanaian labor federation, which is still recognized in Africa as one of the better endowed workers' organizations.[4]

The benefits the TUC and similar African labor federations reaped from government intervention and endorsement have not escaped the attention of industrial relations commentators. One author views the role of the state in imposing unity as a *sine qua non* condition for both labor solidarity and sound labor relations (Nwubueze, 1975, 1981). He, thus, viewed such actions as unproblematic. Even W. Ananaba (1979), a severe critic of African governments and trade union leaders, was convinced that the Federal Nigerian Military Government was justified in compelling labor federations to unite under the umbrella of the Nigerian Labor Congress in 1978.[5] In the view of Ananaba and others, labor gained at least one major advantage from Decree No. 22 and other similar statutes — it doused the excessive flames of unhealthy rivalry between labor leaders. R. O. Nwubueze (1981: 591 - 592) amplified Ananaba's point when he observed that:

The most important achievement of the military regime in this field . . . is the establishment of one Central Labour Organization in the country with reasonable funds from the government to enable it to establish its administrative infrastructure and acquire the strength and stability necessary for the leadership of its constituent unions. Thus, on the balance sheet, it can be concluded that the Nigerian unions gained much more than they lost as a result of increased intervention by the government in labor issues during the past twelve years.[6]

Nigeria represents the classic dilemmas caused by ethnic, religious, regional and ideological rivalries exacerbating intra- and inter-union tensions. A solution sought by the government was that Section 33 of Decree No. 31 of 1973 mandated that only unions that demonstrated regional balance in membership would be registered.

Several authors and practitioners have thus not only enthusiastically commended African governments for imposing labor unity, but have called for more intervention to ensure absolute unity where there are unions outside the single union federations. For example, A. Sackey argued that a basic problem confronting Ghanaian labor is that two workers' associations are not affiliated with the TUC:

> Closely related to the problem of an amorphous grouping of trades is the fragmentation of the labour movement in Ghana as a whole because of the prevalence of the situation in which the Ghana National Association of Teachers and the Civil Servants Association, two large organisations of workers, continue to stay out of the Ghana Trade Union Congress.[7]

The Price of State-imposed Labor Unity

Supporters of government-imposed unity have underestimated or ignored its costs. They fail to recognize that such intervention does not only violate ILO principles, especially the provisions of Convention Nos. 87 and 98 (which countries like Ghana and Nigeria have voluntarily undertaken to uphold), but also the pro-government interventionists neglect the long-term adverse effects of the policies they advocate. In Ghana, the long-term cost of depending on the state for both financial support and labor unity began to unfold in February, 1966, when the military's overthrow of Kwame Nkrumah led to the end of the social welfare experiment began after independence. The coup revealed the high risks involved in unions aligning themselves officially with political parties in a politically turbulent environment.[8] In Ghana and similarly in Nigeria, recent labor problems vindicate the ILO's view that compulsory unity has undesirable consequences for unions, particularly when labor unity is backed by partisan political alliances in countries that experience rapid changes in government.[9] The shortcomings of labor unity (from workers' standpoint) were remarkably revealed in Ghana from 1982 to 1985 when the TUC experienced the most acute internal leadership crisis in its history.[10] These crises which were resolved partly as a result of the ILO's intercession on behalf of the TUC bring into sharp focus the relevance of ILO principles and standards such as Convention Nos. 87 and 98.

The ILO recognizes the important role of the state in creating a legal framework for orderly labor-management relations. But it does not approve of the rigid types of government control and interference in union affairs as exemplified by the creation of state-endorsed single unions, as it has been in Ghana as a result of the Industrial Relations Actss of 1958 and 1965 and similar statutes in Nigeria, Kenya and Zambia. It also needs to be emphasized that the ILO fully recognizes that the essence of labor unions is labor unity. It, however, cautions against the attainment of unity at the cost of union autonomy. It subscribes to maintaining full union independence as a means to protecting workers' occupational interests. Available evidence supports the ILO's position that the state's imposition of labor unity *per se* does not provide unlimited benefits to unions and African societies. Some of the alleged social benefits inherent in state-sanctioned labor unity are labor solidarity and peaceful labor-employer relations which in turn would facilitate rapid industrialization and an end to underdevelopment.

African ILO members, especially the ratifiers of Convention Nos. 87 and 98 such as Ghana and Nigeria, have found themselves with almost intractable international labor and legal problems. These countries' problems at the ILO have become extremely difficult to resolve because as the Ghanaian situation since 1959 depicts, legislated union structures are difficult to change to meet ILO requirements. Hence in the case of Ghana, since 1959 and in Nigeria's since 1978, the ILO has repeatedly advised the two governments to amend the relevant labor laws. So far in spite of several efforts, both countries have not completely amended their laws. The relevant labor statutes have not been altered largely because these two governments could face a stern opposition from the labor movement for alleged union busting. Even some employers might oppose the abolition of the single-labor federation system on the grounds that it might lead to labor disunity and a chaotic labor situation.[11] The existence of the legislated single-union systems in all the selected African countries has created a policy dilemma for the various governments. Labor, its allies and most employers prefer to retain the TUC, the Nigerian Labor Congress, ZCTU and COTU as the solely permitted national labor federations. On the other hand, because of their membership of the ILO, the governments are often pressed to defend or modify their labor practices and policies which are not in full agreement with the Organization's norms.[12] These problems do not only place African ILO members in diplomatically uncomfortable positions, but also distract them from full participation in most ILO activities and programs.[13]

Legislated labor unity through the imposition of single trade unions has also undermined the role of trade unions as the guardians of workers' occupational interests and as the voice of workers on national policies. These two roles may at first appear unrelated, but both are critical to the legitimacy of workers' organizations as social institutions. The point is that unions are able to play their occupational roles when they have wider social acceptance. In other words, the more popular a union is, the more it can protect workers. My observation is that in Ghana, the alliance between the TUC and various governments has weakened its legitimacy and made it more difficult to improve workers' living and working conditions.

Two basic problems emanate from union-government alliances. Firstly, abrupt changes in government have aggravated leadership and other organizational problems of the TUC including the selection of appropriate strategies to employ to accomplish its goals. Secondly, as the crises of 1982 to 1985 showed, political alliances can fuel the flames of internal factions and leadership struggles. The problem of factionalism gets exacerbated because the leadership has to contend with a role conflict connected with their status as the "labor wing" or allies of ruling parties. The unions face the competing demands of workers for higher wages and government pressure to restrain workers from striking, demonstrating against policies workers see as anti-labor and from making wage claims. Ghana's labor scene on several occasions has exhibited these overt labor tensions emanating from the clash of workers' and governments' interests.

Between 1961 and 1966 and from 1972 to 1978, the TUC found itself in the position of being accused of not protecting Ghanaian workers. From the members' standpoint, the TUC's leaders were not militant enough in protecting workers and they risked being branded government puppets or having sold out to governments. J. K. Baiden, a former General Secretary of the Maritime and Dockworkers' Union (see Appendix 8 for list of TUC affiliates), at a press conference accused the A. M. Issifu-led TUC of being soft on wage demands because of its close alliance with the NRC/SMC headed by Col. I. K. Acheampong.[14] Baiden's press conference marked the beginning of an incipient dissension and leadership crises which virtually incapacitated the TUC from 1982 to 1985. Thus, in Ghana, the TUC's leadership has had to contend with a precarious situation, in which they had to walk a tight-rope between pressures from the governments they are aligned with and from rank-and-file demands, especially in periods of rapid inflation, to step up wage claims.[15] The leaders often find themselves in situations in which their actions cannot satisfy their two competing constituencies, governments versus workers. In such situations, for example, if the TUC tilts its functions towards meeting the needs of the government, it risks being stripped of its role as a *bona fide* workers' representative, as details of the TUC's problems will show.

The Ghana TUC has on two separate occasions been close to losing its legitimacy as the leading labor organization. During the eras of the CPP (from 1958 to 1966) and the NRC/SMC (between 1972 and 1978) it became the former's official labor auxiliary and one of the latter's staunchest political allies. Available evidence suggests that the TUC was not too successful in protecting workers' material living conditions in the long-term in spite of alliances it struck with the two regimes. As noted above, a benefit derived from the CPP was an expanded social wage. This gain diminished as a result of Nkrumah's overthrow and the corruption and incompetence of the NRC/SMC, which bankrupted the economy and led to a rapid decline in the quality and quantity of government-provided social services.[16] By 1981, due largely to the ineptitude and mismanagement of the country by the NRC/ SMC and President H. Limann's administration, broken down vehicles could not be repaired to transport government workers. There was also a marked deterioration in the country's health care, especially the state-owned sector. Most employees stopped using subsidized services either because they were unavailable or the quality fell sharply.

The TUC's credibility was questioned by workers because they were compelled to depend on their take-home wages, which were stripped of purchasing power by high rates of inflation. As Table III shows, by 1975 workers on fixed wages were hard hit by unbearable rates of inflation as high as 50 percent in a single year. Ghana's central labor organization's legitimacy was in doubt because throughout the reign of Nkrumah it refused to endorse strikes. It sought to use its close ties with the regime to tackle national labor problems amicably. Other factors outside the control of organized labor also explain why workers refrained from striking under the CPP, with the exception of the 1961 strike in the Sekondi-Takoradi area (see Appendix 6). These were the fear of reprisals from the government and the government's use of party labor activists to nip strikes in the planning stages (Drake and Lacy, 1966; Krause, 1979). Additionally, a cumbersome dispute resolution procedure made of conciliation and arbitration, the discretionary intervention of the Minister of Labor and a mandatory 28-day waiting period all combined to discourage strikes. Workers who struck illegally could be arrested.

Table III

Ghana: Consumer Price Indices
1967-1977

Year	All Items	Food
1967	84	78
1968	92	88
1969	96	95
1971	105	106
1972	115	119
1973	128	142
1974	163	185
1975	230	252
1976	352	414
1977	629	876

Base Year, 1970 = 100

Source: UN 1978 Statistical Year Book, New York, p. 692.

The virtual ban on strikes represents one of the numerous costs incurred by labor by entering into a formal alliance with the CPP. With regards to the relevance of the ILO's standards to Ghana, it could be said that the surrender of the strike weapon and the subsequent fall in workers' living conditions vindicate the Organization's strongly held view that labor unions should avoid strong and formal ties to political parties and governments.[17] Such alliances in the Ghanaian situation have culminated in the neglect of workers' interests and the diminished ability to protect workers on the part of unions. Besides the unions have grappled with serious factional problems that are outgrowths of the conflict of interest inherent in being the labor wings of political parties.[18] The labor situation in Ghana from 1958 to 1966 therefore illustrated the practical utility of the ILO's Convention Nos. 87 and 98, which seek to protect the autonomy of workers' associations.

The 1961 Strike and the Limits of Political Alliances

The 1961 strike by the rail workers of Sekondi-Takoradi was significant because it signified some workers' disapproval of the TUC- CPP alliance and signaled the limits of party control over the labor movement. From a policy standpoint, and bearing in mind the contentions of union control advocates (Mehta, 1957; Lewis , 1957; Schweinitz, 1959) and supporters of government imposed labor unity (Nwubueze, 1975, 1981; Van-Hear, 1988) that they create a peaceful industrial atmosphere, it may be said that the Sekondi-Takoradi strike taught a lesson that governmental controls in themselves are not adequate guarantees for industrial harmony. It is appropriate to restate Nwubueze's own views on more effective ways to manage industrial strife:

> It must be recognized that the right to strike is an essential part of the principle of free and voluntary collective bargaining. Since strikes result from various grievances arising from industrial life, the only way Governments can prevent their occurrence is to create a suitable industrial relations environment which minimizes friction between labour and management and provides a speedy and effective means of settling outstanding disputes.[19]

The Alliance with the CPP and the 1971 Dissolution of the TUC

The TUC has amply demonstrated its awareness of the exorbitant price it paid for aligning itself with the CPP:

> After the overthrow of the C.P.P. government in 1966, the TUC did not want to lose its independence again and in 1968 at a Conference at Tamale decided to remain non-aligned to any Government or opposition party. The TUC adopted a position of 'Positive Neutrality.' This position not withstanding, did not save the TUC from dissolution by the P.P. government of Dr. Busia during the Second Republic.[20]

The TUC's admission of the high cost of its close ties with the CPP supports the ILO's view that reliance on state power to insure labor unity is not in the long-term interests of workers.[21] As demonstrated in the Ghanaian situation, the Progress Party Government, made up of the remnants of the opposition to Nkrumah, used its majority in Parliament to dismantle the TUC (Gray, 1981: 54; Panford, 1988). That dissolution confirmed the adage that whatever government gives, government takes! Events surrounding the dissolution confirmed the ILO's admonition that in societies that experience abrupt changes in government it may not be in labor's long-term interest to be closely identified with particular regimes.

During the parliamentary debates that culminated in the abolition of the TUC, the K. A. Busia-led government offered the ostensible argument that some provisions of the 1965 Industrial Relations Acts violated ILO principles and Ghana's 1969 Constitution by designating the TUC as the solely recognized labor federation.[22] The government's apparent reason was that the TUC's status denied workers freedom of association. The unfolding of events connected to (and especially the timing of) the dissolution, however, revealed the actual intentions behind the PP's official reasons.

Firstly, the PP government comprised of fiercely anti-Nkrumah politicians who feared that the TUC could be used to revive the CPP. The actions of the PP government support this view. A few days prior to the dissolution, the government used its parliamentary majority (104 out of 140 members) to ban public displays of Nkrumah's photographs and all CPP insignia. Apparently, the PP was haunted by the fear of Nkrumah's return from exile in Guinea. Secondly, materials available from the ILO contradict the government's claim that it was acting upon the recommendations of the ILO. Documents I examined at the ILO show that it was physically impossible at that time (that is, in 1971) for the government to have received in Accra the Organization's recommendations from Geneva before rushing the dissolution through Parliament in less than 24 hours.[23] The speed with which the dissolution was sent through the legislature and the anti-TUC pronouncements made by government representatives indicated the real motives of the administration, which was to dismantle instantly an organization it had failed to coopt or to coerce. It is also of interest to note that on no occasion did the government allude to ILO provisions during the dissolution proceedings in Parliament. It also did not specify that it was acting on the advice of the Organization. The only mention of the ILO was from the opposition (in Parliament), which was concerned about the representation of workers at the ILO after the liquidation of the TUC.

Other significant events related to the dismemberment of the TUC show that the PP acted to penalize the Bentum-led federation for persistently opposing the regime's policies including the devaluation of the currency. Beginning in June, 1971, when the nation's budget was announced by the PP, TUC leaders, led by the then Secretary-General, B. A. Bentum, organized massive workers' rallies all over the country, called on workers to reject the government's budget: and demanded a complete overhaul of the national economic agenda. The government responded by attacking the TUC and its leaders. By September, 1971, when the TUC was dissolved, the labor leaders and the PP had traded personal and acrimonious attacks. As happened in 1961, there was a serious conflict between workers and the government of Ghana. This time, however, the TUC led the workers. Faced with what the PP regime considered an unacceptable political challenge, it resorted to banning the TUC (Gray, 1981; Jeffries, 1978).[24]

The TUC after the 1971 Dissolution

Although the direct and immediate effects of the dissolution could not be discerned (because the NRC, led by Acheampong, restored the TUC through NRC Decree No. 22 of February, 1972), there have been recent indications of the high cost of the restoration. Both the TUC and the entire country's labor relations have been adversely affected. The serious TUC internal problems from 1982 to 1985 can be traced to it. These problems eroded the stature of the TUC in Africa and on the international labor scene and disrupted the country's labor relations because the PNDC could not implement a planned Two-Year Labor Codification Program of 1982 - 1983. Besides, the PNDC had to wrestle with the country's damaged reputation within the international labor community.[25]

The Leadership Turmoils of 1982-1985

I will now shift my focus to the damages sustained by the TUC. The crises of 1982 to 1985 diverted the entire labor movement's attention from trade union concerns such as collective bargaining. They also marked a watershed period in the country because the TUC's legitimacy was substantially weakened. For the first time, TUC leaders became direct targets of at times violent protests by factions within the labor movement. The sudden resignation of Issifu as the Secretary-General in February, 1982[26] as a result of workers' demands for his ouster, and the fact that the police intervened and surrounded the TUC's building in Accra with armored personnel carriers, indicate the seriousness of these internal feuds. The factions were formed along ideological lines with some demanding a radicalization of the TUC through the expulsion of all leaders including the then Executive Board.

The deep-seated nature of the tensions within the TUC became obvious when the resignation of Issifu did not restore peace. Instead in April, 1982, under the banner of a new radical coalition of workers and their allies outside the unions — the Association of Local Unions (ALU), workers from Accra and Tema forcibly occupied the TUC building and ejected the remaining leaders. It was alleged as part of the complaints against the Ghana government in Case No. 1135 (filed at the ILO) that some TUC officials were assaulted during the take over. The crises were resolved in 1985 partly as a result of the persistent encouragement of the PNDC by the ILO to ensure that normalcy returned to the TUC. In its deliberations, the ILO's Committee of Freedom of Association repeatedly pointed out to the PNDC its obligations as a member of the Organization and a ratifier of Convention Nos. 87 and 98 to create national conditions in which all workers organizations and their officials could

pursue legitimate trade union activities in full freedom without fear of intimidation.[27]

The crises were finally resolved when elections were conducted to elect
leaders of the TUC. Some incumbents were returned to their posts together
with some new leaders. One Ghanaian labor commentator summed up the
causes of the crises:

> The mass militant action of April 29, 1982, which resulted in the overthrow
> of the old leadership of the Ghana TUC can be said to have been the culmi-
> nating point of long years of struggle against bankrupt trade union leaders
> who . . . were accused of . . . . being insensitive to the needs of workers . . . .
> E. K. Aboagye of the TUC describes the situation as follows: "The old lead-
> ers did not genuinely represent and seek to advance the interests of work-
> ers."[28]

The internal struggles within the TUC, as shown in Sackey's description,
centered on the allegation that TUC leaders had reneged on protecting workers. For example, in spite of job losses due to plant closings, it was alleged
that the TUC did not alleviate the plight of workers. These closures could be
attributed to several causes including the ineptitude and corruption of the
NRC/SMC which the TUC supported, a world recession in the 1980s, structural constraints on the Ghanaian economy and the adoption of an IMF/World
Bank -style economic program by the PNDC.

In addition to the immediate causes cited, the turmoil the TUC encountered can be linked to its restoration by Col. Acheampong. One early sign of
an impending disastrous leadership contest was Baiden's press conference of
1978, in which he openly accused the Issifu-led TUC of being soft on wage
demands. Because the NRC reinstated the TUC, by 1978, in spite of visible
declines in Ghanaian living conditions, the TUC remained the foremost ally of
Col. Acheampong. Once again, the TUC aligned itself with a particular government. The only difference this time was that the NRC/SMC by 1978 -
1979 had not only become authoritarian but totally inept in managing the
Ghanaian economy:

> The military Junta led by Col. I. K. Acheampong which overthrew the
> Progress Party government led by Busia in January 1972, restored the TUC
> to its former position, after its dissolution in 1971. The NRC and the SMC
> governments enjoyed the unflinching support of the labour movement and a
> rapport was established between the government and the TUC right from the
> beginning.[29]

The TUC and the NRC/SMC traded favors. Issifu was appointed by the
NRC to policy-making bodies such as the Manpower Planning and the Prices
and Incomes Boards. Also for the first time, a TUC leader became a "Special
Advisor" to the Head of State, a position the Catholic Archbishop (Kojo
Amissah) declined. While TUC officials were declaring their unconditional
support for the NRC, the TUC's own Research Department acknowledged that
"this was also the period in which workers' purchasing power was eroded

fast."[30] This was particularly the case in the mid-1970s, when the economy showed clear signs of deterioration:

> The year 1975 . . . proved to be a critical turning point, and by 1977, the economic disorder was unprecedented. The credit extended to the state by banks had skyrocketed from 17 million cedis in 1973 to 781 million cedis in 1977 . . . . production had dropped, shortages were recorded in essential commodities, inflation soared and smuggling was rampant. Hoarding and profiteering, as means of survival, had reached such heights that the term Kalabule . . . . was coined to denote economic malpratices. Corruption was everywhere . . . . because of the skyrocketing cost of locally produced food, working people were unable to afford staple foods . . . . The crisis was by no means abstract. The estimated cost of a meal for five was fifteen cedis at a time when the minimum wage was four cedis.[31]

According to D. Pellow and N. Charzan (1986: 59) Ghana has not recovered from the catastrophic economic legacy of the Acheampong-led NRC/SMC because:

> The reformist promise of the second military government was systematically squandered by an incompetent and self-serving leader. His government was characterized by mismanagement and riddled by corruption. The Border Guard was at the center of the nation's smuggling, and state distribution agencies were responsible for shortages. During the era, private fortunes were amassed at the same time as the country was becoming impoverished.

Despite the institutional and economic decay that became associated with the NRC/SMC, the Issifu-led TUC never distanced itself from that regime. While public discontent grew, the labor movement continued its support for all government policies, including the infamous "Union Government" (Unigov) concept and referendum.[32] The unpopularity of the NRC/SMC was demonstrated by groups such as students, professional bodies and the Protestant and Catholic Churches, which vehemently opposed the government for being inept and corrupt. They resoundedly rejected Unigov, a nonpartisan government proposed by Acheampong as a result of severe pressure from opponents to hand over to a civilian/constitutional government. Opponents of Unigov rejected it on the grounds that it was a ploy by Acheampong to cling to power. As the pressure intensified, the regime agreed to hold a referendum on the concept over which it launched a desperate and often violent campaign to win.

During the campaign, the TUC used its resources including an extensive network in the form of regional and district offices to support the NRC/SMC. It publicly committed the country's entire organized labor to support the regime. As it were, it cast its fate with a regime that grew unpopular daily. Because the referendum was rigged, its true outcome could never be determined.[33] However, the SMC's claim to have won proved a pyrrhic victory, as demand for the regime to resign increased. Simultaneously, groups of public utility workers in various regional capitals such as Kumasi, Accra, Tamale and Koforidua without the endorsement of the TUC, embarked on strikes or "work to rule" or "go slow," as they were called. Fearing that the whole regime might be toppled because of Acheampong's unpopularity, the deputy head of state, Gen. Frederick Akuffo, replaced Acheampong through a palace coup in 1978. That led to a chain of events which unraveled the consequences of the TUC tying its fortune to that of Acheampong and the NRC/SMC.

On June 4, 1979, the Akuffo-led SMC was toppled by junior military officers who declared their intent to clean up the military and other social institutions. The cleaning exercise was suspended in September 1979 when a new civilian regime was installed. The suspension proved temporary because on December 31, 1981, Flt. Lt. J. Rawlings returned to power as head of state and declared a "Holy War" aimed at purging the society of corruption. The declaration of the resumption of the war on corruption (both political and economic) may have been interpreted by disaffected factions in the labor movement as a signal to rid it of leaders like Issifu and others who in their view had been unresponsive to the needs of workers. The point worth emphasizing is that the birth of the PNDC and its initial revolutionary fervor may have served as catalysts to attempts within and outside the TUC to voice frustrations with the TUC leadership. It was some of these workers who took over the TUC's building in Accra and sparked the 1982 - 1985 crises, which were resolved partly as a result of the intervention of the ILO.

By throwing its full support behind a regime as unpopular as the NRC/SMC, the TUC squandered its legitimacy as a workers' representative within the Ghanaian body politic. The public perception was that it was not to be trusted to express the *bona fide* demands of workers and to protect genuine national interests. As it were, the basis of the existence of the TUC began to be questioned by both workers and political activists outside the TUC (Yeebo, 1991; Adu-Amankwah, 1990; Panford, 1988). Thus, since the 1978 referendum and the fall of the NRC/SMC, the TUC has struggled to repair its tarnished image and also been left with little or no public sympathy and support. Hence in the 1982 - 1985 crises when the TUC leadership was attacked, few if any, social groups came to its defense. Most Ghanaians must have had the attitude that the TUC "got what it deserved" or it had outlived its usefulness to the society.[34]

The 1982 - 1985 labor crises taught one basic moral: labor's alliance with the CPP and the NRC/SMC proved that close alignment with particular regimes, especially corrupt and bankrupt ones such as the NRC/SMC, could have disastrous consequences for workers and the TUC as an institution. A point worth reiterating is that since, realistically, most governments are capable of inflicting severe sanctions on the TUC, the latter is not always expected to oppose all governments and all policies. But the TUC, in its institutional interests, should have averted not only aligning itself with a corrupt and unpopular regime (such as the NRC/SMC) but should also not have become a leading advocate of policies that hurt workers and devastated the economy. Admittedly, some students and progressive professionals such as university professors, medical doctors and lawyers were harassed and some even killed due to police brutality, but their organizations gained increased social stature for defending the national interest. Also significantly, unlike the TUC, they did not grapple with serious internal crises after the collapse of the Acheampong government.

The leadership crises I have described underscore the typical conflict of interest problems that emanate from trade union and political party or government alliances under circumstances in which workers are hurt by public policies. Therefore, Ghanaian labor relations has depicted a situation in which because of overt involvement in highly partisan politics, the TUC has found it extremely difficult to manage a number of complex role conflicts,. Besides detracting it from normal trade union functions, including collective bargaining, managing its conflict of interest problems has dissipated its resources and diminished its stature as the legitimate conduit for workers' grievances and concerns over national policies. From 1975 to 1979, the TUC ceased articulating the economic and social needs of Ghanaian workers because it became too closely identified with a regime that was notorious for bankrupting the nation's economy.

Thus, by collaborating with a regime as unpopular as Acheampong's, the TUC lost an opportunity to retain and enhance its legitimacy as the champion of workers' causes. It could have used its enhanced role to buttress its collective bargaining functions after the fall of the NRC/SMC. Instead, as K. A. Ninsin and F. K. Drah (1987) correctly pointed out, it failed to step into the void in the body politic created by the NRC/SMC's ban on competitive politics and representative government. By endorsing Union Government and other unpopular policies of the NRC/SMC, it contributed to the violent suppression of dissenting opinions. One may also correctly conjecture that if the TUC had played a different role, the country could have avoided wasting resources, both political and economic, on the fraudulent referendum of 1978.

This section may be concluded by observing that post-independence labor policies in Ghana have not only failed to conform completely to ILO principles, but in addition, have not yielded the alleged fruits in the form of labor peace, rapid industrialization and solutions to the nation's economic problems that the advocates of labor control argued in the 1950s and 1960s the country would reap. The society not only lost an important political pressure group during the reign of the NRC/SMC, but also the TUC had severe problems protecting workers' (its most important constituents) material living conditions. Therefore, past TUC strategies, including official alignment with specific regimes, have not allowed it to utilize its potentials to fulfill the promise to protect Ghanaian workers. From the society's standpoint, in spite of the relatively successful state control of unions through the TUC, the evidence presented in this book does not show that past labor policies which digressed from the recommendations of the ILO accomplished their professed goals. Past policy failures draw attention to the critical need to adopt new strategies incorporating ILO standards for the management of the country's labor affairs.

5. 2   The Impact of the ILO on African Labor Legislation and Practices

The ILO's Influence on Ghanaian Labor Legislation and Industrial Relations

This section deals with the complicated task of gauging the extent to which the ILO is able to make Ghanaian and other African member states' laws and practices conform to its principles and Conventions on workers' rights. Of particular interest is the success or failure of the Organization to secure from members annulments of or amendments to labor statutes and policies which contradict its standards. In addition, I will demonstrate how the ILO has attempted to shape labor practices that constitute flagrant violations of workers' rights such as the dissolution of trade unions; the arrest and detention of trade unionists, the seizure of union accounts and the invasion of their premises. Ghana's labor statutes and practices are assessed followed by the examination of the Nigerian, Zambian and Kenyan situations.

The ILO has been relatively successful in getting the Government of Ghana to modify the relevant labor laws to partially meet workers' rights in Convention Nos. 87 and 98, which the country has ratified. In 1965, the Kwame Nkrumah administration amended the 1958 Industrial Relations Acts in response to recommendations made by the ILO. Beginning in 1959, a year after Ghana ratified Convention No. 98, the ILO's Committee of Experts persistently drew the government's attention to how the 1958 Industrial Relations Act was not in agreement with the Organization's principles. As the then Labor Minister stated in Parliament, the country adopted the 1965 Industrial Relations Act to meet ILO standards.[35] In the government's own words, the decision to ratify Convention No. 87 led to the annulment of the 1958 Act. Thus the passage of the 1965 Act was immediately followed by the ratification of Convention No. 87 by the Ghana government. This is an example of how the desire (on the part of the public authorities) to ratify and meet ILO standards led to a change in Ghana's labor statutes. Ananaba (1979: 12) explains how the ILO was able to influence the Ghana government to annul the 1958 Act:

> Constant reports of violation of trade union rights in Ghana forced the ICFTU to file a complaint with the ILO in June 1962 against the Ghana Government. This complaint was investigated by the special Committee of Freedom of Association which upheld most of the points raised by the ICFTU. Consequently, the Ghana Government . . . . amended some sections of the Industrial Relations Act of 1958. Another reason for amending the Act was the Government's anxiety to ensure that the Ghana TUC was free from criticism, and that the TUC developed an organisational model which would be followed by other trade unions in Africa.

As mentioned in Chapter 3, in the case of Ghana, the ILO has not been totally successful in making the government expunge from the relevant statutes the monopoly status of the TUC, compulsory trade union membership and the absence of provisions permitting the right of all unions to affiliate locally and internationally. Evidence of the lack of complete success on the part of the Organization is that since 1969, the Committee of Experts' recommendations that the 1965 Act be amended to comply fully with international trade union rights have not attained their intended effects. Instead, from 1982 to 1983 under a proposed "Two-Year Labor Codification Program" and again since April, 1990, the Ghana government's response has been that the National Advisory Committee on Labor (NACL) has been deliberating changes to the 1965 Act.[36] Although the 1965 Act has not been amended to meet ILO standards one can discern from the proceedings of the NACL, including the submissions to it by the TUC, some influence of the ILO on the amendments that may be made to the 1965 Act in future. Proposed changes in the statutes reflect the comments of the ILO's Committee of Experts and attempts by members of the NACL to implement the recommended changes via proposed legislation. Several examples will support my observation.

In explaining proposed amendments to the 1965 Act, the NACL explicitly acknowledged that its review of the Act resulted from "ILO queries and comments" and the contention that "provisions of the 1965 Act conflict with some provisions of Convention Nos. 87 and 98."[37] Furthermore, the NACL mentioned that because of Ghana's ratification of Convention No. 151, Labor Relations (Public Service) in May, 1986, "it became imperative for the 1965 Act to be amended" to permit public employees such as nurses, teachers and civil servants to bargain with the government to determine conditions of employment.[38] The Ghana TUC has, in addition, urged the NACL to propose to the government the inclusion of the right to international affiliation in future amendments to the 1965 Act. This is one of several changes endorsed by the ILO. I may therefore state correctly that although all changes proposed by the ILO have not been implemented, recent policy deliberations by the NACL reflect concerns raised by the ILO dating as far back as 1959 when Ghana ratified Convention No. 98.

5. 2. 1   The Labor Statutes of Other African Countries

In the other countries selected for this study, the ILO's record has been mixed. In Nigeria, Trades Union Decree No. 22 of 1978 stifled trade union freedoms when it compelled four existing labor federations to join the Nigerian Labor Congress. Since then, comments by the ILO's Committee of Experts and the International Labor Conference Committee on the Application of Conventions and Recommendations have not led to the Nigerian authorities modifying the basic labor laws. However, as shown in Case No. 1530 of 1990 against the Nigerian government, the annulment in 1990 of Decree No. 35 of December 1989 could be attributed to the influence of the ILO. This case was initiated at the ILO by the International Confederation of Free Trade Unions and their International Secretariats against the Federal Nigerian Military Government for violating Article 5 of Convention No. 87, which Nigeria has ratified.[39]

The unions that filed Case No. 1530 against Nigeria alleged that Decree No. 35 grossly violated ILO Conventions and the Constitution of the Organization because it virtually banned international trade union affiliation by Nigerian unions. They also alleged that Section 2 of the said decree led to some Nigerian Labor Congress unions severing their ties with international trade unions. First, the government urged the Committee for Freedom of Association to close the case because of its intent to repeal that decree. Then on April 26, 1991, the government informed the ILO of the repeal of the decree and the passage of the necessary amendments to Nigerian labor laws. The ILO requested copies of the relevant instruments to permit a closure of the case. That was followed by an announcement of the repeal by the Nigerian public authorities. Thus although it took two years to get the ban on international affiliation lifted, through ILO intervention, the freedom of all Nigerian trade unions to "interact freely with their counter parts in other parts of the world" was restored.[40]

In the case of Zambia, although it has not ratified the two Conventions dealt with, recent legislative events point to the capacity of the ILO to make the government repeal laws considered by Zambian trade unions to be in violation of basic ILO principles. As a result of the promulgation of Industrial Relations Act, 1990 (No. 36) which came into force on January 23, 1991, Case No. 1575 was filed against the Kenneth Kaunda administration.[41] Some of the key complaints were that the new industrial relations act which superseded that of 1971 was too restrictive and allowed interference in internal union affairs by public officials. It was also alleged that the act was motivated by the desire of the outgoing Kaunda government to dismember the Zambian Congress of Trade Unions and its affiliates. Due to a combination of the intervention of the ILO and the change in government (from the Kaunda-led United National Independence Party to the Frederick Chiluba-led Movement for Multiparty Democracy) the new administration, in a communication dated May 7, 1993, informed the ILO of the following. A tripartite labor advisory group reviewed the 1990 Act and drafted another one using guidelines provided by the ILO. The new draft was submitted to Parliament in March, 1993 which was sent to the President for his action. The new Zambian government indicated that "the recommendations of the Committee (of Freedom of Association) have been extremely helpful to the amendment of the Industrial Relations Act."[42] Therefore, it might be observed that even in the situation of Zambia, which has not ratified Convention No. 87 or 98, the intervention of the ILO, aided by a change in government, led to measures to repeal the 1990 Act that seriously undermined workers' rights. As shown in the statements of the new Zambian regime, the ILO's suggestions proved helpful in the restoration of ZCTU and trade union freedoms.

5. 2. 2   ILO Standards and African Labor Practices

Since from a trade union standpoint, the real value of Convention Nos. 87 and 98 lies in the degree to which they shape actual labor policies and their outcomes, I will now shift my focus towards the impact of the ILO on key labor practices in Ghana and other countries chosen for this book. With respect to Ghana, as it is in the situation of labor statutes, the ILO has had a mix of both successes and failures. I wish, however, to state that it is difficult to pin point the precise influence of the ILO. As the Ghanaian situation I will describe shows, several factors (some local, others of international nature) interacted in a complex fashion to influence the industrial relations practices of post-independence Africa. Three Ghanaian episodes are presented in the attempt to depict the role and influence of the ILO.

The first Ghanaian incident involved the ultimate violation of trade union and human rights — the killing of striking gold miners in 1969 under the NLC administration (Kraus, 1979).[43] Because the deaths of the workers were not reported in the form of a complaint at the ILO, they were not investigated by the Committee of Freedom of Association or any ILO organ. The absence of a reprimand of the Ghana government points to a major weakness inherent in the ILO. (These weaknesses are analyzed in the next section.) Another significant and blatant violation of ILO norms occurred again under the rule of the NLC. Because of its anti-labor posture, and World Bank and International Monetary Fund policies to reduce public sector labor expenditures, the government dismissed *en masse* over 2,000 workers of the state-owned Cargo Handling Company (Hutchful, 1987). This time, a complaint was launched at the ILO in the form of Case No. 578 of 1969 against the government. But before the ILO could render a decision, the case was withdrawn by the complainants because of the emergence of a new administration and its desire to project an image of respect for workers and trade union rights. The new government of the PP could also have been motivated by the fact that Ghana was host to the ILO's Third African Regional Conference. Under these circumstances, the new administration quickly reinstated all the fired workers and the dispute was settled amicably. At the Accra Conference, the Prime Minister explained the role of the ILO in the resolution of the problems that led to Case No. 578 against Ghana:

> Permit me to mention one example of the practical ways in which my Government is trying to express its adherence to the enlightened principles for which the ILO stands. Some of you may have heard that the Ghana labour movement had lodged a complaint against the Government for violating some of those principles in a matter of a labour dispute at Tema Harbour. Notwithstanding the legal rights of the Government, we have proposed a solution that will make it quite clear that we respect the right of workers not to be arbitrarily treated. The proposals of my Government have just this morning been accepted by the leaders of the labour movement who have recognised them to be generous proposals. We made them as our small contribution towards the recognition of the rights of workers to be respected and treated with dignity.[44]

The influence of the ILO in Case No. 578 stems from the fact that even though the case was withdrawn, the filing of the complaint and the occurrence of a major ILO activity (the Third African Regional Conference) coinciding with a change in government played a role in the peaceful resolution of the complaints. As the Prime Minister admitted, the absence of an acceptable resolution could easily have led to an explosive labor situation. Hence, it might be inferred correctly from Case No. 578 that the ILO's standards supervisory system, which hinges on the adjudication of complaints in regards to violations of trade union rights, in this case proved useful to the workers involved. The ILO ensured some measure of accountability on the part of the Ghanaian national authorities.

The most recent case against the Ghana government for violating workers' rights was filed jointly by the Ghana TUC, the Organization of African Trade Union Unity and other international trade unions. The complaints alleged that the PNDC violated Convention Nos. 87 and 98 by freezing the assets of the TUC and failing to ensure the safety of TUC leaders who were attacked by disaffected workers.[45] This case, No. 1135, dragged on from 1982 to 1985 when it was resolved by the TUC electing new leaders. Case No. 1135 depicts the relative effectiveness of the ILO's standards supervisory system. The intervention of the Organization and its persistent remarks on governmental responsibility for insuring the safety of trade unionists and the protection of union premises contributed significantly to the PNDC allowing the TUC to resume its functions as the country's central labor federation. The role of the ILO and other international labor organizations in preventing the demise of the TUC can be inferred from Zaya Yeebo (1991: 91), a PNDC operative's acknowledgment that ". . . wild but justifiable protests from international labour organizations, who were already criticizing the PNDC . . . ." engendered the restoration of the TUC. As it were from the horse's own mouth, the protest and the anticipated increased protest by international organizations spearheaded by the ILO deterred the Ghana government from dissolving the country's labor federation. Hence, my assessment that in Case No. 1135, the ILO was instrumental in insuring the survival of the TUC and its 17 national affiliates.[46]

On the other hand, with respect to Kenya, in Case No. 1189 dealing with complaints emanating from the government's dissolution of the Association of Civil Servants, the ILO was less successful in attempts to restore the trade union rights of the workers affected.[47] In spite of repeated appeals, the government refused to restore the union, which it stripped of collective bargaining rights. The practical implication was that it became illegal for members of this union to bargain with employers and they could be severely penalized for striking. Thus, Case No. 1189 represents one of the instances in which the ILO was not able to use its supervisory system and pressure from the international labor community to prevent labor practices which denied workers rights enshrined in Convention Nos. 87 and 98 and in the ILO's Constitution.

In terms of curtailing practices such as the arrest and detention of workers' leaders for trade union activities in Nigeria, the ILO's success rate is high. In the summer of 1986, when 25 trade unionists were arrested, the ILO's Director General was able to use his "good offices" to secure their release. The 25 workers, all belonging to the Nigerian Labor Congress, were detained for planning protests against the Federal Government's imposition of one of the most austere economic policies. During the June, 1986 International Labor Conference, the Director General (of the ILO) met the Nigerian Minister of Labor to discuss the release of the workers. The Director General emphasized the need to resolve the conflict peacefully and the rights of workers to protest in an orderly fashion against public policies that impinged upon them. Partly as a result of this dialogue, the release of the detained trade unionists was announced at the International Labor Conference and in less than two weeks, the affected leaders resumed their trade union activities.[48]

Based on the cases and situations of violation of trade union rights in Africa, it might be observed that the ILO's partial successes in restoring trade union organizations and in protecting workers from extreme violations of their rights result from three basic methods. First, it seeks to encourage governments to adopt labor laws that are in agreement with the provisions of its standards and in cases where the laws do not match these standards, to amend them. Second, the ILO performs this function by offering technical assistance in the form of model labor laws or by proposing specific amendments to existing national labor laws. For example, the Organization could make available to members an adviser to assist in the modification of relevant laws and third, when the public authorities flagrantly violate workers' rights through the expulsion, exile, arrest or detention of workers or the dissolution of their unions, through the adverse publicity and diplomatic embarrassment generated by the proceedings of the Committee of Freedom of Association and the open discussion at the International Labor Conference and the published reports of the Committee of Experts and the Governing Body, African member states are subtly pressed to amend their labor laws and practices. The ILO encourages desired governmental responses and behaviors by providing relatively effective avenues for dialogue. The Organization acts as one last resort for governments and workers to have their conflicts resolved when all national mechanisms have failed or been exhausted.

The relative success of the ILO can be attributed to two factors. The first is its emphasis on tripartism. By permitting workers to file complaints which are adjudicated by representatives of workers, employers and governments, public policies, laws and labor practices which would not be subject to adjudication by local courts are evaluated in terms of their compliance with international labor standards. An additional benefit from workers' rights standpoint is that by having three workers on the Committee of Freedom of Association (out of a total of nine), workers are given opportunities to participate in protecting themselves. Because the workers on the Committee deal with cases from outside their countries, fear of reprisals from governments does not deter them. Second, during my field work, my respondents (including those representing African governments that were alleged to have violated ILO standards) were unanimous in their declaration of the fairness of the ILO in resolving cases. The perceived fairness of especially the Committee of Freedom of Association from the African standpoint, has in the view of the continent's participants, contributed to the relatively effective role and hence significant influence of the Organization in the four countries selected for this study. It may be said correctly that even though the 1965 Industrial Relations Acts of

Ghana and similar statutes in Kenya, Nigeria and Zambia do not totally meet the standards espoused by the ILO, it has been quite effective in deterring the most blatant violations of workers' rights in these countries. A brief comparison of African trade union situations with, say, those of Asia and Latin America would confirm my point. In my review of trade union rights I observed that instances of torture and the murder of workers and trade unionists were rare phenomena in post-independence Africa compared to other developing regions of the world. The contributions of the ILO to African workers' rights are better appreciated when one factors into the analysis of its role the severe constraints it faces. These constraints, what I refer to as the "delimitations" in the ILO system, are discussed in the final section of this chapter.

5. 3   Delimitations of the ILO's Workers' Rights Supervisory System

Sovereign Nations and the Enforcement of ILO Standards

Like any other international body, the ILO faces a set of problems which prevents it from translating its ideals of workers' rights into the daily realities of industrial relations, especially in Africa and in other developing regions.[49] The problems of the ILO for convenience may be classified into two types.[50] These are factors internal to it, such as its composition of independent sovereign nations, and external constraints, including the impact of the global economy and international financial institutions including the World Bank and the International Monetary Fund (IMF). I will focus mainly on issues relating to the makeup and the internal processes of the ILO. The roles of external agencies such as the World Bank and IMF are raised in the conclusion of this book.

One major delimiting factor the Organization has had to confront is the fact that it is composed of nations that, because they are sovereign, can refuse to meet their ILO membership obligations. That has prevented the Organization from fully ensuring the worldwide protection of workers. Despite the relative success of tripartism at the ILO, it has contended with the effectiveness of its supervisory system hinging on what Ghebali (1989: 229) referred to as "the cooperation of those directly subject to supervision, .i.e., governments." This phenomenon has in turn given rise to what E. B. Haas (1964: 135) designated as "a law without force doctrine." That referred to ILO member states being independent, retaining their membership of the Organization voluntarily and wielding the ultimate authority to make national laws and policies to meet ILO guidelines. The Organization, as in the case of most human rights organizations, does not have coercive resources to compel compliance by members. As indicated by most of my respondents, it grapples with an unusually difficult paradox: the need to be extremely tactful in nudging countries to comply with standards so as not to antagonize them to withdraw (from the Organization) or to denounce Conventions they have ratified. Between 1960 and the 1980s, the Organization experienced the withdrawal of countries, including South Africa, Vietnam, China and Poland, largely because of criticisms for failing to meet ILO standards. Officials of the ILO especially those of the International Labor Standards Department, are extremely sensitive about the withdrawal of nations because of their justified apprehension that countries that withdrew fell completely outside the influence of the ILO and became free to subject workers to tighter restrictions.

Because of the constitutional right of members to withdraw from the ILO (after a two-year notice) and also the right not to be liable for Conventions properly denounced, the Organization as a whole, but more especially, employees of the standards supervisory organs, have to deal delicately with members by finding the most appropriate diplomatic techniques to get them to modify their laws or polices. This perplexing reality makes it difficult for the Organization to achieve its ideal of universal free trade unionism. Closely related to the inability to enforce total compliance is the Organization's dependence on moral pressure, in the belief that public exposure of violations can influence the behavior of governments. Hence, a major condition for the effectiveness of the ILO is that governments, subjected to the subtle pressure and diplomatic embarrassment emanating from public proceedings such as the hearings of the Governing Body and the deliberations of the Conference Committee for the Application of Conventions and Recommendations, would not violate ILO principles and standards (Samson, 1979: 6 - 7). Thus, it might be observed that the success of the ILO hinges largely on the expectation that most countries will abide by its norms to avoid being branded as international outlaws and soil their international image. This assumption comes into play when a particular government is concerned about or susceptible to international diplomatic embarrassment.

The Role Strains of Persuasion and Criticism

The ILO experiences a great deal of role strain in the attempt to balance its mediation or conciliation roles with that of adjudicating cases brought to the Committee of Freedom of Association.[51] This refers to the organizational tensions that arise out of officials and members criticizing governments and in other instances mediating labor conflicts by bringing the labor relations partners together. The Committee of Experts, and officials such as the Director General and the Heads of the International Labor Standards and the Freedom of Association Branch, perceived as crucial the use of their "good offices" as mediators to resolve thorny labor problems amicably. They emphasized the creation of opportunities for dialogue between labor and governments as an essential ILO activity. These officials also went to great lengths to show that the bodies of the Organization, including the Committee of Freedom of Association, were not "courts of law" and therefore acted with the sole purpose of engendering atmospheres in which governments will be inclined to improve workers' rights conditions.[52] However, because these bodies often adjudicate situations, laws and cases, they create environments which are similar to those of law courts.[53] Thus there has emerged within the ILO two apparently contradictory modes of operation — one with a thrust towards persuasion and the other towards criticism or subtle diplomatic pressure to solicit desired changes from governments. Officials the standards supervisory bodies have had to grapple with applying an admixture of these contradictory modes of operation (Haas, 1964: 127), which could have contributed to undermining their effectiveness.

The Limits of Long-distance Supervision

Another constraint inherent in the ILO's supervisory system is the use of periodic or requested reports furnished by member states as primary sources to document prevailing workers' rights situations. Typically the Organization, in the case of Convention Nos. 87 and 98, requires countries such as Ghana and Nigeria, which are ratifiers, to complete reports every other year on the status of workers' rights to freedom of association and to collective bargaining (see Appendices 2 and 3 for copies of report forms used by the ILO). In cases of alleged violations of workers' rights, the Organization informs the government involved about the allegations and asks for responses. This long-distance correspondence between, say, the Ghana government and the ILO would constitute the basis for adjudicating the case or situation involved. Although in cases that involve hearings, oral responses and testimonies might be used, often the complex task of ascertaining actual labor practices and the outcomes of laws and policies depends on documents forwarded by governments. In a limited number of cases, efforts are made to overcome the limitations posed by long-distance correspondence through on the spot investigations or missions by representatives of the ILO. Although such steps are useful, their short duration (on the average five working days) does not permit the realization of maximum benefits of such on the spot visits to countries. Their short duration and the possibilities of obstructions by governments may not allow a realistic assessment of trade union conditions.

Another handicap suffered by the ILO because it depends on long-distance correspondence was recently acknowledged by the Organization. The Committee of Experts devoted substantial portions of its 1992 reports submitted to the International Labor Conference to "delaying tactics" employed by members to scuttle its review of their laws and practices (Committee of Experts, 1992). It remarked that most countries did not meet deadlines for submitting reports and, therefore, it was unable to evaluate their labor laws and practices. Even when reports were submitted, several were "incomplete" and did not enable it to reach proper conclusions regarding the application of the Conventions concerned (*Ibid.*: 37). That was especially the case of countries, including Sierra Leone, which according to the Committee has not submitted reports that were due over two years. The delays and incomplete reports allow uncooperating governments to prevent the ILO from reviewing their laws, policies and practices which are not in agreement with the Organization's norms and therefore escape its supervision. As in the case of Malawi, with respect to Case No. 1638, by not providing the information requested by the Committee of Freedom of Association through "delaying tactics," the government is able to prolong the detention of the affected trade unionists.[54] In this and similar situations, the ILO's goal of preventing governments from detaining trade unionists for engaging in *bona fide* trade union activities is at least temporarily not accomplished. As it were, the Malawian government was able to detain the affected workers by providing partial or no responses to the queries of the ILO.

The Shortcomings of Tripartism in Africa

With respect to the effectiveness of ILO in Africa, a severe limitation arising out of the structure of the Organization is the inoperation of full tripartism in the supervision of international labor standards. The significance of tripartism was highlighted by a senior ILO employee who remarked, "Tripartism, on which the whole Organization hinged and on which it relied for the supervision of standards, especially those on workers' rights was as good as workers made it."[55] That official added that since the ILO derived its resilience from the participation of workers, whenever workers' representatives became lax in performing their roles, governments could not be held accountable for not meeting the ILO's standards. That meant the ILO's supervision of workers' rights could only be effective if workers were vigilant and active in protecting themselves. One method through which the ILO has sought to routinize the input of workers is the provision that both workers and employers' representatives should be permitted by governments to submit "comments" on reports sent to the ILO. Although this provision exists, the majority of African trade unions do not submit such comments. The absence of comments could have led to government reports to the ILO not reflecting actual workers' conditions in Africa, and hence blunting the effectiveness of the ILO's supervision.

The Absence of Rule of Law

The absence of rule of law, which is a vital link in the infrasructure for protecting workers/human rights, has also contributed to undermining the effectiveness of the ILO in Africa. My review of the Organization's supervisory system showed that it placed a great deal of emphasis on the efficacy of independent judiciaries that granted workers and other citizens protection from violations of trade union and civil liberties. In Africa, however, one finds that conditions are not totally conducive to the rule of law as assumed by the ILO. Although the role of the judiciary in the protection of Ghanaian workers has not been explored in-depth, my examination of the country's labor relations unearthed a scant use of the law courts to protect workers.[56] The ILO's Committee of Experts (1992: 386 - 389) alluded to this situation when it stated that it "considers it significant that . . . only one civil servant out" of 568 dismissed civil servants "sought to bring action before the courts." That observation was indicative of the low rates of litigation in not only Ghana, but the rest of Africa, especially in protecting workers.[57]

As both the Committee of Experts remarked (1992: 387) and several African trade unionists agreed: "The problems often encountered in remedial procedures — such as the costs, difficulties with burden of proof, the fear . . . . of exposure to reprisals — may effectively deter" workers from relying on the courts. The virtual absence of litigation to protect workers may point to the enormous nature of these obstacles. One might also add that formal or court litigation is still not popular in Africa. That may explain why Ghana, Nigeria, Kenya and Zambia each has less than four cases filed with the ILO's Committee of Freedom of Association. An additional phenomenon exacerbating the scant use of formal litigation is the absence of an independent judiciary. The reluctance of the Busia administration to accept the verdict of the Sallah case may be one of several symptoms of the fact that throughout their history African courts have never exercised genuine autonomy and, therefore, have been unwilling or incapable of defending both workers' and human rights.

The Irony of "Doing More With Less"

Similar to the experience of its constituent African members, since the 1980s, the ILO has had to struggle with a shortage of funds which has led to severe bottlenecks in the form of inadequate personnel and hence a diminished organizational capacity to assist developing countries to meet its standards. As E. Kalula (1985) has pointed out, the ILO, like all other UN Agencies, is feeling the pinch of limited funds because worldwide recessions have contributed to several member states defaulting on their annual membership assessments. Some of the hardest hit members are the nonoil producing countries in Africa, whose export revenues have continued to decline. As a result of diminishing resources, the ILO has not been able to provide adequate technical assistance to African members to improve both their workers' rights and economic conditions. In 1986, for example, all the 18 English-speaking members of the ILO competed for two fellowships offered by the ILO for training in international labor standards. At the same time, all the 50 African nations had to rely on the services of only two regional advisors for standards. The situation was worse in 1984 when they had a single advisor.[58]

While the size of personnel at the ILO has shrunk, the volume of work done by the various (ILO) bodies, especially the Committee of Freedom of Association and the Committee of Experts, has grown with increases in membership in the Organization and the case load. With respect to Africa, since 1986 four countries have joined the Anglophone nations, increasing their number from 18 to 22. The number of cases dealt with by the Committee of Freedom of Association stood at 1,710 in April, 1993, compared to 1,322 in 1985.[59] The net effect of all these changes is that the Organization is experiencing growth in work load without a commensurate increase in resources, leading to its inability to closely monitor workers' rights in all member countries. Even though by 1986 (due to growth in membership), staff at the ILO in charge of standards examined on the average three Conventions for each member state, the pressure on the staff is mounting as more countries join the organization. The limitations I have presented and others not included in this study have made it more difficult for the ILO to translate its ideals of trade union rights into actual trade union situations.

NOTES

1.   See Sections 20 and 13(1) of the 1958 and 1965 Industrial Relations Acts, Ghana and Section 3.2 of this book.

2.   For a description of the dramatic expansion in social infrastructure such as health and education, see Lofchie (1971) and Hansen and Ninsin (1989).

3.   Although the ILO emphasizes the desirability of workers' unity, it underscores the adverse impact of government-imposed unity. Some of the negative consequences identified by the ILO are presented in the latter part of this chapter.

4.   African trade unionists I met during my field work were impressed by the organizational resources of the Ghana TUC. Several of my respondents referred to its stature and emphasized its resilience as an institution in a relatively turbulent political environment. The TUC has proven to be one of the few Nkrumah institutions that have endured.

5.   Trades Union Decree No. 22 of 1978 compelled 71 national unions to affiliate with 42 industrial unions, which were grouped under the Nigerian Labor Congress. In Kenya, COTU was formed as a result of a "1965 Presidential Declaration" after inter-union hostilities led to the killing and wounding of some workers.

6.   For similar views, see Van Hear, 1988; "Trade Unions," *Financial Times*, Feb. 14, 1977, signed A. H.; U. J. Umoh, "Disunity in the Unions," *West Africa*, Oct. 7, 1985: 2100.

7.   A. Sackey, "Working for Recognition,"*West Africa*, May 30, 1983: 1295.

8.   In Nigeria, with the return to a civilian regime in 1979 and, hence, a change in the political climate, the new government contemplated dissolving the NLC after the first successful general strike ("Nigerian Labor Organizes Resistance to Plan for Splitting Union Control," *New African*, Dec. 1981: 22).

9.   ILO, 1983a: 61 - 62.

10.   Like most labor groups, the Ghana TUC had previously experienced mild leadership succession problems, but the crises of 1982 to 1985 proved the most debilitating because they undermined its functions and threatened its survival.

11.   At the 1986 International Labor Conference in Geneva, Switzerland, I observed Nigerian workers, employers and government representative's vehement defense of the status of the Nigerian Labor Congress as the sole labor federation.

12.   More recently in Ghana, nonTUC affiliated labor associations, such as the Ghana Registered Nurses' Association (GRNA), the Ghana National Association of Teachers (GNAT) and the Ghana Civil Servants' Association (GCSA) have petitioned the government to amend sections of the labor statutes to permit them to be recognized as trade unions authorized to collectively bargain with employers. Currently, under the 1965 Industrial Relations Act, only TUC members are certified as collective bargaining agents.

13.   My point is that African members are not able to utilize opportunities for securing technical assistance to improve labor administration and their economies.

14.   J. K. Baiden, "Press Conference," Ghana News Agency, Accra, September 6, 1978.

15.   An illustration of this predicament is that a commentator denounced the TUC for narrowing "its scope of objectivity so much that the general public had come to believe the TUC's only function was to demand wage and salary increases, not taking cognizance of national economic constraints" "TUC Denounced," *West Africa*, January 7, 1985: 38.

16.   Ray (1986) and Pellow and Chazan (1986) provide details of the corrupt nature of the NRC/ SMC regime.

17.   ILO, 1983a; 1985a.

18.   The Ghana TUC admitted this problem in its correspondence of 1987. Ghana TUC, Research Department, Accra, March 1987.

19.   Nwubueze, 1981: 591. B. C. Roberts (1964) expressed similar views about the need to create efficient dispute resolution mechanisms. The antithesis of this view is T. M. Yesufu's (1968) position that all industrial conflict is inherently dysfunctional and should therefore be outlawed.

20.   Ghana TUC, Research Department, March 1987. This statement also indicates the TUC's awareness of its dissolution in 1971 being a consequence of alignment with the CPP.

21.   The TUC acknowledged again the high price of political alliances when at its Fourth Quadrennial Congress of 1992 it amended its constitution to bar officials from involvement in partisan politics.

22.   Industrial Relations Amendment Act, 383 of 1971, Ghana Parliamentary Debates, *Official Reports*, Industrial Relations (Amendment) Bill, Sept. 9, 1971: columns 1531 - 1650, and Sept. 10, 1971: columns 1651 - 1668.

23.   *Ibid.* The dates on the relevant ILO documents indicate that they could not have reached the government before the adoption of the amendments to the 1965 Industrial Relations Act.

24.   Events leading to attempts — first by the Federal Nigerian Civilian Administration in 1981 and second by the military regime's 1988 "temporary suspension" of the Nigerian Labor Congress — are similar to circumstances that led to the dissolution of the Ghana TUC ("NLC Executive Dissolved," *West Africa*, March 7, 1988: 399; "Restructuring NLC," *West Africa*, Sept. 26 - Oct. 2, 1988: 1807; "Nigeria: Strikes Hit the National Purse," *New African*, July 1981: 27; "Nigerian Labor Organizes Resistance to Plan for Splitting Union Control," *New African*, Dec., 1981: 22). In Nigeria, these "contemplated" and "temporary" dissolutions were catalyzed by the NLC's leading of the first post-independence national general strike and protests by workers against the military's austere economic policies. The threats posed by the unions are borne by decrees mandating severe penalties, including life imprisonment, for striking in the public utility sector (Otobo, 1987).

25.   As a result of Case No. 1135 of the ILO's Freedom of Association Committee, which was filed against the Ghana government, the PNDC administration found itself for four years in the diplomatically perplexing situation of having to defend its labor and human rights policies and practices because one of the allegations was that TUC officials could not pursue *bona fide* union activities as a result of their lives being in danger. It was also alleged that TUC assets and accounts had been frozen by the public authorities. For details of this case, see ILO, 1985a.

26.   *Ghana News,* Ghana Embassy, Washington, DC, 1982: 12.

27.   Representatives of African trade unions and governments indicated to me in Geneva (1985 - 1986) that without the intercession of the ILO, the TUC may not have been restored. This was confirmed by Z. Yeebo's (1991: 91) assertion that ". . . wild but justifiable protests from international labour organizations . . . ." prevented certain PNDC members from installing their handpicked TUC Secretary-General during the crises.

28. A. Sackey, "Working for Recognition," *West Africa*, May 30, 1983: 1294.

29. Ghana TUC, March 1987, response to Questionnaire. See Appendix 5.

30. TUC Research Department (1987).

31. Pellow and Charzan (1986: 58). See also Table III for the steep rise in inflation at that time.

32. Because of possible reprisals from the NRC/SMC, one did not expect the TUC to denounce all government policies, but an objective assessment of the conditions of workers and the economy could have led to the TUC distancing itself from the government or remaining silent. Also, like the Catholic Archbishop, Issifu could have declined the appointment as Advisor to the Head of State.

33. The government declared itself the winner after the Electoral Commissioner, Justice I. K. Abban, and his assistant, H. Meizah, were forced to flee when armed thugs hired by the government stormed the Office of the Electoral Commissioner in Accra on the day of the referendum.

34. Several Ghanaian workers' representatives have candidly admitted the institutional problems the TUC faced because of the support it gave to Acheampong. (Information from interviews and in-depth discussions with TUC representatives with this author in Geneva, Switzerland, 1985 - 1986 and in Ghana, Summer and Fall, 1991.)

35. Ghana National Assembly, 1965 Industrial Relations Bill., *Parliamentary Record of Proceedings*.

36. The NACL is a tripartite body of representatives of labor, employers and government that advises the government on local and international labor matters.

37. Information from the Ghana Labor Department, Accra, August 1993.

38. *Ibid.* Under current Ghanaian laws, these employees are excluded from collective bargaining because their associations — the GCSA, GRNA, GNAT — are not certified collective bargaining agents. They are thus prohibited from bargaining and striking.

39. See Appendix 2 for the text of Convention No. 87 and ILO, Governing Body, ILO: Geneva, May - June, 1991; 73 - 76.

40. Statement by Paschal Bafyau, President of the Nigerian Labor Congress welcoming the repeal of Decree No. 35 of 1989 ("Ban Lifted," *West Africa*, August 19 - 25, 1991: 1380 - 1381).

41. See ILO, Case No. 1575, 284th Report of the Committee of Freedom of Association, 1992.

42. Information received from the ILO's Washington, DC Branch Office, June 11, 1993.

43. The killing of the strikers was an atypical incident in Ghana. It, however, revealed the extent to which the military government that replaced the Nkrumah government was anti-labor and the extremes to which it went to insure absolute labor control.

44. ILO, 1970b: 41.

45. For details of Case No. 1135 see ILO, 1985a.

46. African participants at the ILO's 1986 International Labor Conference held in Geneva, Switzerland were emphatic about the role of the ILO in safeguarding trade union rights in Ghana during the 1982 - 1985 TUC turmoils.

47. See ILO, 1985a, for a summary of Case No. 1189 against the Kenyan government.

48. Other factors, such as internal pressure mounted by trade unions and their allies — students and university professors — plus additional protests by the London-based Commonwealth Trade Union Secretariat, combined with the role of the ILO to result in the release of the 25 leaders.

49.   For discussions of the general problems of international organizations, see Haas (1964, 1970) and Ghebali (1989).

50.   My classification is an adaptation of Haas' (1964: 129) typology of the problems of the ILO.

51.   See Haas (1964) for tensions emanating from these apparently contradictory functions.

52.   Interviews at the ILO, Geneva, 1985 and 1986.

53.   Several African delegates informed me during my field work that the ILO operated like a court of law.

54.   Case No. 1638, Malawi (ILO, 1993: 145 - 160).

55.   Information from the ILO, International Labor Standards Department, Geneva, 1986.

56.   For the role of the judiciary in Africa, see K. A. Mingst, "Judicial Systems of sub-Saharan Africa: An Analysis of Neglect," *African Studies Review, 31*(1), 1988: 135 - 148.

57.   According to the Ghana government's information to the ILO, there have been as few as three court cases involving the rights of workers. Some of these were *Sallah vs. Attorney-General* of 1970 (the famous "No Court, No Court" case, the outcome of which the then Prime Minister, K. A. Busia, strenuously objected to because it called for reinstating the plaintiff) and the second, *Owusu-Afriyie vs. State Hotels*, 1977 (ILO, Committee of Experts, 1992: 386).

58.   Communication from the International Labor Standards Department, ILO, Geneva, 1986.

59.   Data from the ILO's Geneva and Washington, DC Offices, April 19, 1993.

Chapter 6

Sound Labor Policies Towards Sustainable Development in Africa

6. 1 Policy Prescriptions for Workers' Rights and Labor Administration

A consensus from participants in ILO seminars and other activities dealing with international labor standards and labor relations is the urgent need to develop policies and administrative practices to assist African member states to overcome development problems and, at the same time, meet international labor norms. Underlying this need is the awareness that past labor policies have not solved problems, such as the violation of ILO standards, and failed to meet national development objectives.[1] Using the recommendations of the various participants and considering the issues raised in Section 4.3 of this book, I will present in this section prescriptions for laying the foundations for alternative labor policies. These alternative polices may be considered sound because they focus on major labor problems that need to be tackled. They are laws and practices which are aimed at simultaneously enhancing the capacity of a country such as Ghana to surmount complex labor relations and development problems, meeting the needs of all the industrial relations parties, especially workers and conforming to ILO guidelines for labor laws, policies and practices.

The Goals of Labor Policies

I will begin my policy recommendations by reiterating a key erroneous assumption of past and current failed policies (see Chapter 1 for the rest of these assumptions). The policies of the countries reviewed in this book have largely been motivated by the incorrect view that governments can unilaterally manage all development problems. Closely associated with this is the notion that all labor problems will disappear if trade unions were controlled by the state. As I have already emphasized, the practical implications of such assumptions are enormous. As H. Bates (1970: 373) pointed out, other factors, including the policies of the state with respect to agriculture and exports, the availability and cost of credit, and the rates of savings and inflation (and I will mention the quality of industrial organization or management and a long list of other factors) impinge on both the rate of industrialization and economic development;. In addition, as G. Mutahaba (1982) has noted, in spite of the spate of development planning, manpower planning or effective human resource use has not featured as a strategic factor in African economies. Partly due to the erroneous view that labor control will guarantee accelerated industrial growth, labor relations was not accorded a high status in resolving Africa's problem of lack of development. All this has created an urgency to start formulating for Ghana and the rest of Africa new labor policies based on the benefits of rationalized labor relations premised on the existence of autonomous labor organizations and rooted in a principle of mutual benefits to the society and workers.

ILO Conventions treated in this book are considered *bona fide* guidelines for managing effectively Africa's labor relations because after all, workers and their families are also part of the society and should therefore be beneficiaries of development policies. Here, the ILO's position that highly economistic development strategies have not successfully alleviated poverty in Africa becomes relevant (ILO, 1987). The ILO urges a reorientation of development plans towards social aims such as meeting the basic needs of all the members of society.[2] Similar views were expressed by Rawlings, the former chair of the PNDC and the current head of state of Ghana when in 1986 he announced that his government considered the basic needs of all Ghanaians and their dignity as national priorities.[3]

In terms of satisfying ILO requirements emanating from the ratification of Convention Nos. 87 and 98, a policy dilemma alluded to in previous chapters is the prevalence of legislated single-union systems all over Africa. The policy challenge posed by these trade union structures is developing the capacity and the political will to formulate new labor laws to permit full freedom of association for the affected trade unions without incurring the excesses of splintered trade unionism. That may be avoided by establishing objective or democratic criteria for designating the most representative unions for the purposes of obtaining labor's input into domestic and international labor policymaking. The ILO does not discourage the designation of unions as the *de facto* majority if the process used is fair and does not permanently permit government-approved unions to monopolize trade union representation at national and international levels.[4] It is important to point out that in seeking to protect the rights of minority unions (that is, those outside the state-sponsored unions) the Organization has no intention of encouraging chaotic labor relations. It places a lot of premium on the essence of trade unionism, which it considers to be solidarity among workers. Since, as demonstrated in Section 5.1, compulsory trade union unity has not solved all of Africa's labor problems, the ILO endorses laws and practices aimed at facilitating negotiated solutions to workers' organizing problems.[5]

In most English-speaking African nations, no objective basis exists for registering and granting unions collective bargaining agency. In Ghana, for example, beginning with the 1941 Trade Union Ordinance (passed by the British Colonial authorities), the Chief Labor Officer, who is the civil service head of the Department of Labor, has been designated as the Registrar of Trade Unions. He is solely in charge of union recognition and certification for collective bargaining. The ILO urged the government to change the process for recognizing unions in Ghana because in its view, the laws are not explicit on the criteria the Chief Labor Officer uses. The Organization expressed the concern that since he is an employee of the state he might be susceptible to undue excessive government influence in his duties as the registrar. In addition, under current laws, all trade union applications for recognition have to be submitted through the TUC in its capacity as the sole central trade union organization.

The solution proposed by the ILO is that an autonomous officer may be appointed as the Registrar of Unions and the sections of the relevant statute empowering the TUC to apply for certificates for unions should be annulled. Since 1990, the NACL with the approval of the TUC has recommended amendments to Ghana's 1965 Industrial Relations Acts which are in agreement with the proposals of the ILO.[6] A major concern of the ILO is the passage of laws and the adoption of policies to reduce governments being tempted to interfere in what it deems internal union matters. E. Iwuji (1979), in his evaluation of Kenyan labor practices, explained the advantages of creating an autonomous Office of the Registrar of Unions separate from that of the Chief Labor Officer. He mentioned the following. First, through this separation, there may be fewer opportunities for government interference in union matters. A goal here is to decrease the rate of violations of ILO standards in Africa. Second, labor administration will become efficient via an enhanced form of division of labor. The Chief Labor Officer will be free to focus exclusively on his conciliation and arbitration duties and in assisting the government to formulate appropriate labor policies. That may contribute to the speedy resolution of industrial disputes and the creation of a peaceful industrial atmosphere. As R. O. Nwubueze (1981) has noted, the creation of effective dispute settlement mechanisms may be more useful in resolving labor-management conflicts than the rigid control of unions. The implementation of both Iwuji and Nwubueze's suggestions, however, will have to be preceded by African governments' willingness to change their current labor laws and practices.

The Dilemmas of Free Riders and Compulsory Trade Unionism

From the trade unions' standpoint a dilemma that will need to be resolved if African labor laws were changed to permit full freedom of association is that of compulsory union membership and mandated checkoff of union dues. The unions will have to contend with "free riders," that is, employees who benefit from unions but are not members and do not pay dues. The difficulty stems from the need of unions to be financially solvent by collecting dues (to pay for benefits) and the ILO's urging that all workers should join unions only on voluntary basis. The temporary dissolution of the Ghana TUC (from September, 1971 to January, 1972) proved what could happen if the provisions of Ghanaian labor laws insuring compulsory unionization were annulled. The TUC could not pay the salaries of officials and rent owed to landlords because as part of its dismemberment, the Progress Party government abolished the checkoff system (Gray, 1981). Instead of union dues being deducted at source automatically, employers could only collect dues on behalf of unions if they had written authorization from workers. W. Ananaba (1979: 169) cited a union security arrangement which was voluntarily negotiated and met the ILO's requirements. This agreement provides a welcome relief to the paradox of workers' rights to freedom of association and trade unions' need for financial stability:

> Upon written instruction from the employee, the employer undertakes to deduct union dues monthly from the employee's salary and pay such amount to the union . . . . Employees shall have the right to voluntarily join or refrain from joining the union. Employees who choose not to join the union and are covered by the terms of this contract, shall be required to pay, as a condition for enjoying the provisions of this agreement, a monthly service fee to the union for the purposes of aiding the union in connection with its legal obligations and responsibilities as the agent of the employees in the bargaining unit. The aforesaid fee shall . . . . in no case exceed the membership dues paid by those who voluntarily choose to join the union.

This agreement may serve as a model for other unions and employers. It also attests to the ability of both employees and management to negotiate union security agreements without state interference.

Labor Administration and the Role of Labor Departments

The next set of policy recommendations deals with the role of labor administration and especially the functions of labor departments or ministries to ensure that African ILO members meet their constitutional and ratification obligations. Another concern is the extent to which these departments meet the challenges of modern nationhood. These departments are important in two respects. First, typically they are responsible for coordinating domestic labor affairs and second, they are in charge of preparing member states' reports to the ILO. Since the low prestige accorded labor departments in Africa is identified as one of several problems hampering their effectiveness, some effort needs to be devoted to altering the public authorities' perceptions of their role.[7] Each African government needs to be encouraged to demonstrate its commitment to turning their labor administration into "important and integral arm of government which functions in a very vital capacity."[8] Governments could demonstrate such commitment in several ways. Some of these are presented.

The first is to increase budget: allocations to enable labor departments to meet logistical needs, which typically are stationary supplies, printing equipment, human resources/personnel and transportation. These are especially crucial to data/information collection and publication. The staff of Ghana's Labor Department underscored the importance of budgets when they observed that:

> ... the Department can only provide adequate services when the necessary logistical support and appropriate technological base are available. The Department thus expects increases in budgetary allocations in succeeding years. It is high time, for instance, that the statistical data on employment and unemployment, vacancies declared by employers, number of strikes and affected industries, causes of strikes, number of workers and hours lost, etc., were computerized. The Department thus needs computers to function in a more scientific manner, as indeed the Sector PNDC Secretary observed in an address to the staff. [9]

Overcoming this logistical hurdle is of course closely linked to improvements in Africa's economy. As a Sierra Leonean Minister of Labor indicated, his department "like other departments, has had to grapple with severe economic problems, some of which are certainly beyond the control of any one government."[10] As much as all the problems of any African nation cannot be completely attributed to external causes solely, the minister's point is still pertinent. One has to acknowledge the role deteriorating African economies has played in reducing the capacity of African governments to finance the activities of labor departments.

In addition to adequate funding, African governments, but more especially the Ghana government, have to provide stability in cabinet appointments to labor departments. In light of the adverse consequences of frequent and disruptive cabinet reshuffles (a subject of Section 4.3), appointments should permit Ministers of Labor adequate time "to learn the ropes" of their jobs and, more importantly, to marshal adequate financial and political support to back the department's work at home and at the ILO. There is also the need to appoint to labor ministries (as happens to prestigious departments such as defense, industry, economic planning and finance) appointees with relevant training, background or experience in the complexities of industrial relations as ministers. Well-qualified ministers may facilitate the policy formulation and implementation of sound labor policies to meet local needs and ILO standards. One therefore advocates the appointment of ministers who are technically competent in labor matters. The Ghana government is thus encouraged to maintain a tradition it has started by appointing D. S. Boateng as the PNDC's Minister of labor. He was one of the first ministers to have had a labor background. E. Bello (1980: 108) underscored the role of qualified personnel:

> Machinery for the supervision of conditions of employment is indispensable to the implementation of labour legislation and of governmental labour policy. Labour legislation is meaningless unless it is enforced by a body of officials adequately qualified to keep a close watch on events at places of work and to ensure compliance with the law. Their duties include keeping the law

as it now stands under constant review and the discussion of proposals for change.

The Role of Labor Codification

The absence of streamlined, up-to-date and practically functional labor codes is one of the weakest links in labor administration throughout Africa. Ghana's admixture of colonial labor laws (called "Ordinances") and post-independence statutes (see Table II) typifies the African situation. Currently, the laws inherited under colonial rule are mostly dysfunctional and those enacted since independence do not meet modern-day challenges. Also, as demonstrated elsewhere in this book, most of them contradict ILO standards. In the case of Ghana, therefore, it is strongly recommended that the new National Democratic Convention administration should revive the plan made in 1983 to codify the country's labor laws.[11] This has become necessary to make the relevant laws meet the provisions of the 1992 Constitution with regards to freedom of association. The consolidation of varying sources of laws will permit the Labor Department to play a more useful role by furnishing clear cut and practical guidelines which will enable it to advise the key labor relations actors — labor, private employers and government — more effectively. An important by-product of a methodologically executed codification exercise is that it might result in the annulment of statutes that are redundant and continue to be sources of embarrassment to African nations at the ILO.

In Section 4.1 my thesis was that the British did not establish the foundations for developing effective labor administration in Africa. One of the consequences of British colonial labor policies is that labor departments in Africa have largely confined their services to union registration and industrial dispute adjustment without undertaking conspicuous roles in national development planning. Hence, although a great deal of rhetoric is made about "human resources being the most important national resource," labor administration and labor departments have never been treated as central to the success of any single national economic plan. The solution to this neglect is the overhaul of labor administrative agencies with the objective of turning them into organizations capable of rendering technical services to national policy-making, ranging from IMF - and World Bank - inspired economic restructuring to home-grown solutions to the continent's socio-economic ills. In connection with capacity building, emphasis must be placed on enhancing the role of workers and their organizations in the policy formulation of public policy. Innovative measures to decrease and manage overt labor conflicts in order to ensure higher productivity while meeting labor's needs and ILO requirements should be deployed (some of these are described below). Therefore, labor policies should be designed with the intent to convert labor departments into integral parts of labor administration systems which are centered on the well-being of all members of society, including workers, and not only the recruitment needs of domestic and expatriate employers or protecting the capacity of a particular government to remain in power.

Meeting Ghana's Obligations at the ILO

In order to accomplish the objectives stated in the introduction of this book, I will now deal with how Ghana can improve the fulfillment of its ILO obligations. The recommended improvements derive from the administrative and technical problems presented in Section 4.3, my field observations and suggestions made by participants of various ILO fora convened to evaluate these problems.[12] The major issues identified by these sources were the creation of appropriate labor administrative structures and labor departments being assigned proper jurisdiction over international labor issues. These structures should reflect the commitment of countries such as Ghana, Kenya, Nigeria and Zambia to meet ILO obligations on a consistent basis. That meant abandoning the *ad hoc* basis on which ILO affairs were handled. That is especially relevant to the situations of Ghana and Nigeria in respect to Convention Nos. 87 and 98. It is equally important that labor administrators work towards concretely justifying the additional political clout and other resources allocated to them. They may, for example, decrease the level of industrial conflict through expedient resolution mechanisms, and improve productivity, working conditions and the on-time publication of national labor data and information. Another priority area could be filling the huge policy void alluded to by Mutahaba (1982) — the failure to incorporate into African economic planning the strategic importance of human resources. As Iwuji (1979) has asserted, labor administrators have to embark on a new mission which goes beyond the traditional function of issuing labor (or employment) cards and mediating disputes. In order to attain these objectives, labor outfits have to be molded into agencies with a pro-active policy orientation ready and equipped to play key roles in national development. Here the capacity of labor departments to insure closer contacts among governments, labor and private employers in order to facilitate and institutionalize national consultations becomes very crucial (*Ibid.*: 236).

The Efficient Preparation of ILO Reports

In the international arena, the following policies are prescribed with the objective of managing effectively Ghana and other countries' membership of the ILO. In Ghana's situation, to speed up the processing and submission of reports to the ILO, it is urged that the several "bureaucratic layers" involved should be slashed. In the past, the Chief Labor Officer had to route reports to the PNDC government through three senior Labor Ministry officials. In order to decrease the delays caused by such routing, the Chief Labor Officer should be authorized to report directly to the Minister of Labor, who in turn would submit the relevant documents to Parliament. Upon approval of documents, the Chief should transmit them to the ILO. These measures might help to avert the late submission of reports to the ILO.

As an additional step to safeguard the prompt delivery of reports to the ILO, it is recommended that a single senior labor officer, say, an Assistant or Deputy Chief Labor Officer, should be charged with overseeing ILO reports and other activities in the Labor Department or Ministry. Such an appointment may lead to increased specialization in ILO affairs and promote an efficient coordination of Ghana's involvement at the ILO. The qualifications of the appointee may include being well versed in ILO standards and the legal and policy implications of Ghana's membership in the ILO and the ratification of conventions. If the individual lacks the requisite training, assistance may be sought through the ILO's technical cooperation programs. Since it is anticipated that she or he will become the key resource person on all ILO matters, this individual should be made a delegate to all ILO activities, especially the yearly International Labor Conference held in Geneva. She or he may be assigned the role of a technical advisor to the government delegation. Also, experienced officials in charge of ILO affairs should be encouraged to expand the pool of trained officers by training other employees. Such competent personnel can engage in mutually beneficial exchange of experience with their counterparts from other African countries.[13]   A high-ranking Ghanaian diplomat in Geneva supported the creation of a position he designated as an "ILO Affairs Officer" similar to the Foreign Affairs Ministry's "country or desk officers." This is a laudable proposition that needs to be investigated and adopted if feasible within the Labor Department.

During my field work in Geneva (from 1985 to 1986) I observed that the Canadians played prominent roles within the ILO. E. A. Landy (1970: 587) attributed Canada's success to the establishment of a separate division within the Labor Ministry that was solely responsible for international labor relations. Through the ILO's technical cooperation programs or bi-lateral arrangements, Ghana and other African governments might study this special unit to determine which features might be suitably applied to their domestic situations. There is the need, however, to strongly caution against the "wholesale" transplantation of the Canadian system. Key emphasis must be placed on creatively borrowing aspects of this foreign system to meet national needs, especially taking into consideration Africa's meager financial resources.

In order to make officials in charge of ILO activities efficient, they need to be supplied with basic ILO documents such as a current constitution, list of conventions ratified by each country, texts of conventions and report forms with schedules of reports due for submission, and manual of procedures used by the ILO to assess members' compliance with standards. It is equally important that such documents are organized to permit easy access and on-time delivery of reports, including those sent to the ILO in Geneva. The Labor Ministry of Ghana is to be commended for taking the first step towards fulfilling this need through the creation of a library that houses ILO documents.

As part of the strategy to insure on-time submission of ILO reports, African nations need to make efforts to surmount the tendency to submit them in large batches. Instead, as soon as single reports are ready, they should be forwarded to the ILO. Such a measure in combination with the others I have referred to will contribute to reducing the huge backlog of overdue reports. In the Ghanaian and Nigerian cases, some reports are two years late. In other African nations, such as Sierra Leone, the situation borders on never been able to catch up on late reports due to excessive tardiness.[14]   The appointment of full time "ILO desk officers" or similar officials may resolve most of the technical and administrative problems African ILO members face if such appointees are properly authorized to coordinate ILO related matters and oversee the timely submission of reports, and are able to design efficient work methods to overcome reports being prepared sporadically. Crucial to their effectiveness is the efficient coordination of the roles of several different government department and agencies whose input may be required. Some of these are the Justice Ministry or Attorney General's Office, and the Ministries of Trade and Industry, Finance and Economic Development, and Foreign Affairs. One of the biggest tasks could be educating officials of these public agencies about the international legal implications of Ghana's membership of the ILO.

The implementation and the realization of the benefits I attribute to the policy prescriptions outlined above are premised on certain conditions. I have already alluded to some — the desire of African governments to make the political and material commitments required plus a change in attitude towards labor administration and its role in development. Another is demonstrating a good faith intent to negotiate with both workers and employers the contents of national policies that impinge upon labor. That will depend on the extent to which governments are willing to accept workers and their organizations as legitimate components of society and appreciating their actual and potential contributions to socio-economic development. The success of such an approach will flow out of the use of negotiated solutions to labor problems as the norm and not the exception.[15] At this juncture, it may be appropriate to cite examples of labor policy blunders and practices which African governments should strive not to repeat.

As I have already shown, past policies have been based on the assumption that workers are "strike happy" and are incapable of using negotiations to resolve conflicts at the workplace and in the society. Hence although the National Redemption Council had cordial relations with the Ghanaian trade unions, the Prices and Incomes Board (PIB) it established excluded trade unionists or workers from the seven-person board (Kusi and Gyimah-Boakye, 1991: 32). The PIB (until it became defunct) oversaw prices and wages in the country. The TUC tried unsuccessfully to get the board reconstituted. Similarly, towards the end of its reign, the PNDC undermined the spirit of tripartism and established labor relations patterns through which workers' interests were integrated into national policies. A PNDC policy which the Ghanaian unions perceived as anti-labor was the launching of the "Private Sector Advisory Group," whose leadership and membership excluded workers and trade unions. Its functions as laid out by the PNDC Minister for Finance included advising the government on labor matters.[16] The unions expressed their disapproval by caustically stating ".... we wish to remind the Government .... that our national labour laws have been constructively shaped to have their grounding from ILO Conventions .... In attempts to weaken the labour laws and trade unions, the PNDC .... has sought .... to deregulate .. .. such labor practices."[17] The unions' spokesperson added that the government's neglect of established tripartite practices does not only deny workers' fairness, but could also potentially lead to a chaotic labor scene by reducing workers' input into national policy-making. Another PNDC tendency which should not be emulated is the frequent postponement of the deliberations of labor advisory bodies such as the Salaries and Wages Rationalization Committee and Tripartite Committee on Wages and Salaries.[18] The latter, for example, did not meet for close to a year after its last meeting. The exclusion of workers from labor policy-making groups and their not functioning as expected because of the lack of cooperation from the government could be interpreted by workers that the government was pro-capital or management and anti-labor. Such perceptions might have fueled the tense relations between organized labor and the PNDC.[19]

Nigeria has had its share of labor policy blunders. The country created its first Tripartite Minimum Wage Committee in 1991 and the first minimum wage determined by it was undermined by the Ibrahim Babangida-led government when it announced another version (of the minimum wage). According to N. Adio-Saka, "The Government itself seemed confused and it took over a week to diffuse the tension."[20] The chaos that resulted was reflected in a threatened strike by workers and confusion over the validity of existing collective bargaining agreements. Above all, "even the Federal Civil Service Commission, which works out . . . salary increments, was not sure of itself and sought further clarification from the Presidency" (*Ibid.*).

Last but not the least of inappropriate contemporary African labor practices is the habit of not implementing the recommendations of government-initiated probes allegedly aimed at improving the conditions of work in the public sector. In connection with this problem, one Nigerian observed that in his country "although the Udoji Report . . . . was a comprehensive one; it was confined to a dustbin with only the . . . . aspects dealing with salary adjustments adequately looked into."[21] The problems of Nigeria pale in comparison with Ghana's 19 civil service reform commissions.[22] Although the failure to implement the policies recommended could be partially attributed to political instability and the two countries' fiscal crises, one significant result is that it might be interpreted by workers as resulting from lack of good faith on the part of governments. Such commissions could also be perceived as ploys used by governments to detract from real changes needed in labor policies, administration and conditions of employment.

The policy errors cited above could be viewed as the result of the neglect by the public authorities of both the actual and potential benefits of worker input into national development. Such practices neglect the notion that unions can function (when accorded the right kind of legitimacy) as effective avenues for managing potentially disruptive labor situations. Because of their large membership (in Ghana, the TUC has approximately half a million members and the Nigerian Labor Congress, four million), they are in positions to mobilize substantial segments of the population behind policies which are deemed to be in the national interest. Events in Ghana, Zambia and Nigeria attest to the contributions of unions.

P. S. Gray (1981: 201) provided an apt description of the role of unions in Africa, which until the late 1980s and early 1990s was marked by the predominance of the one-party or military state:

> Under military rule, the unions may fill the void left by the proscription of
> parties. They are among the few remaining groups which have the potential
> to induce members' participation in modern sector economic activity . . . .
> This potential is essential to the development effort. The unions regulate po-
> litical demands and translate them into concrete policy recommendations.
> Furthermore, they have made the urban wage worker a part of the debate on
> national priorities and have served as a channel through which the nation ar-
> ticulates its hopes.

In Ghana, although the TUC decided to retain its neutrality in the 1992 presidential and parliamentary elections, it contributed to the public discussions on
the political future of the country. On several occasions, it added its voice to
demands for a return to civilian rule with an elected Parliament and
President.[23] One might appropriately remark that unlike its anti-social posture during the Acheampong era, the TUC joined groups that called for an
elected government. In the Zambian situation, the trade unions led by the
Zambian Congress of Trade Unions, did not only add their voices and put their
weight behind pressure groups that advocated an end to one-party domination
by the United National Independence Party (UNIP), but its leader, Frederick
Chiluba, spearheaded a political coalition (the Movement for Multiparty
Democracy) that successfully ousted UNIP through the ballot box. That was
a remarkable accomplishment, since few governments have been dislodged
from power using the electoral process in Africa. H. Hamalengwa (1992)
concluded in his study of Zambia that by fiercely preserving their autonomy,
Zambian unions made positive contributions to the survival of a fragile
democracy.[24] More recently, the Nigerian Labor Congress (NLC) too has
demonstrated that it would not remain aloof from the on-going struggles to
end military rule. Since the mid 1980s the unions, led by the Nigerian Labor
Congress, have been active in demands for a just and democratic Nigeria
through the creation of economic policies and political institutions and processes including but not limited to free presidential elections. In June, 1993,
when the Babangida-led military authorities unilaterally voided presidential
elections, the unions joined human rights and other groups to press for full
civilian rule. That pressure may have accounted for the military handing over
to an interim government in August, 1993.

A legitimate question that could be raised in light of the policies recom
mended in this book is: Do countries such as Ghana, Kenya, Nigeria and
Zambia have the capacity or potential to implement them? The available evidence indicates that Ghana and the other countries have the capacity or the
potential to develop the requisite organizational infrastructure to create rationalized labor relations systems, incorporating workers' participation, with the
needs of society for law and order and those of management to operate in a
peaceful industrial atmosphere. Examples exist within and outside Ghana.
On a positive note, various Ghana governments have taken measures in the
past to promote tripartism and to facilitate government-worker consultations.
As far back as 1958 (a year after Ghana's independence), the country's first
post-independence industrial relations act laid the foundations for tripartism

through the establishment of the National Advisory Committee of Labor (NACL). Currently under Section 35 of the Industrial Relations Act, the NACL serves as a medium for consultations among organized labor, employers and the government in making certain domestic PNDClabor policies and for ratifying ILO Conventions.[25] In addition to the NACL, there are National Tripartite Wage Committees which, provided with the right operating conditions, could advise the government on wage policies. Also since independence, as a means to secure labor's input into the management of the public sector, TUC representatives have been included in the management boards of public enterprises. Other means of resolving thorny workplace problems encouraged in Ghana in the early to mid-1980s were "Workers' Durbars," at which management and workers openly discussed issues (Obeng-Fosu, 1991).[26] The PNDC might also have used these durbars to mobilize workers behind its revolutionary aims before it turned to structural adjustment policies at the behest of the World Bank and IMF (Panford, forthcoming).

With proper education, training (especially sensitivity training in the problems of workers' participation and consultations) and increased determination, the measures alluded to in this chapter and similar ones can be made useful mechanisms for reaping the advantages of sound labor relations in Africa.[27] These vehicles can be useful "sounding boards" for testing innovative and or controversial labor policies prior to full implementation. That may lead to public policies being accorded greater legitimacy as Bates (1970: 373) has sought to demonstrate:

> When labor participates in consultative bodies and other such forums, its demands tend to become more responsible; in addition, by having unions participate in the making of development policies, the government can ensure a higher level of union consent for government programs.

Thus, although labor consultations and participation may be difficult and often time-consuming (especially in the initial stages), they will in the long run prove beneficial to all the parties involved and to society because they will allow workers to vent their disagreements in constructive ways, which might decrease the rate of excessively disruptive labor conflicts.

The history of workers' protests in Ghana indicates concretely the adverse consequences of the failure to consult workers and their organizations on national economic development;. Both the strike-*cum*-protest actions of 1961 against the CPP and in 1971 against the PP can be attributed to the neglect of the two regimes to confer with workers who were to bear the cost of development projects via payroll deductions. By striking, the workers, as it were, rejected the notion that they could be forced to pay for development programs without participation! Recently, under the erstwhile PNDC, the hazards of not involving workers in setting the country's economic agenda were revealed by the tensions that fueled the mutually suspicious TUC-PNDC relations. The hostilities centered on the appropriateness of the PNDC's Economic Recovery Program and its impact on workers.

There is additional evidence to support the view that unions under the right conditions could play multiple socially constructive roles, admittedly some in their own interests. In Ghana, the Private Road and Transport Union of the TUC was instrumental in the outstanding success of the switch from left- to right-hand driving in 1974. It featured prominently in the public education program that made the switch successful. The resources of this and other unions can similarly be mobilized for other public causes such as literacy, civil rights and voter registration campaigns.

Examples from Kenya and Zambia also demonstrate the benefits of using negotiations to resolve perplexing labor and national economic problems. The Zambian government's decision to permit ZCTU to join negotiations with the IMF in 1983 helped to diffuse a potentially dangerous situation caused by the IMF's demand that wage raises be limited to 10 percent (Lungu, 1986: 400).[28] In Kenya, on three separate occasions in 1963, 1970 and 1971, through tripartite efforts, agreements were reached to suspend strikes. Employers and the state reciprocated with job creation (Iwuji , 1979: 230 - 231). In all the instances I have alluded to, a key to the success of tripartitism was sincerity on the part of the public authorities. Genuine consultations helped to avoid national crises because the state did not use its muscle to coerce workers. Another factor noted by Iwuji was the strength of COTU. This is one of the several societal benefits of viable labor organizations in Africa. Zimbabwe's Labor Minister has explained how strong unions could facilitate industrialization and economic development; through collective bargaining:. In referring to the role of collective bargaining, he noted that it provided a more stable form of labor relations by permitting mutually useful exchange of information and a discussion of problems which could generate empathy for each industrial relations actor's position (ILO, 1988: 3).

In concluding this section, it may be appropriate to recall a statement made by Ghana's Minister of Labor to Parliament before Convention No. 87 was ratified in 1965:

> As a Member-State of the International Labour Organisation, Ghana respects the solemn obligation of the Organisation to further among the nations of the world programmes which will achieve the effective recognition of the right of collective bargaining, the co-operation of management and labor in the continuous improvement of productive efficiency, and the collaboration of workers and employers in the preparation and application of social and economic measures.[29]

The ideals the minister expressed could be accomplished if public policies, especially those on labor, have the aim of meeting the genuine needs of all members of society not excluding workers and their families. Their realization, however, must be preceded by a cautious and realistic approach girded by an appreciation of the complex nuances of labor-management relations and a sincere and lasting commitment to nurture tripartism using whenever possible the policy guidelines contained in ILO Conventions.

The ILO (1987: 54) has succinctly articulated the advantages inherent in tapping not only the physical labor of workers but also their political support in especially the African context:

> . . . government efforts and resources are not enough to meet the multiple exigencies of accelerated development, especially in countries with a narrow fiscal base and a fragile public administration, development must be supported and supplemented by harnessing . . . as effectively as possible, the efforts, knowledge and resources of the various non-government groups within the national community. The active participation of organised labour in the process of national development is thus immensely valuable . . . .

I wish to draw attention to one additional factor that could enhance the attainment of the policy goals outlined in this chapter. Ghanaian and other African trade unionists I interacted with were not only interested in the occupational concerns of workers but also exhibited a great deal of enthusiasm and support for national development. For instance, the TUC responded to my questions about the priorities of labor by stating that they included maintaining "industrial harmony" and "ensuring national development" (see Appendix 5, Ghana TUC Questionnaire).[30] Thus, the only missing ingredients for the successful implementation of the policies advocated for in this book were sincerity and consistency on the part of African governments to resort to voluntarily negotiated solutions to all labor issues and national economic problems. Government strategies will work if they go beyond sheer tokenism or ploys to deflect attention from serious national socio-economic ills. If a country such as Ghana succeeds in using genuine tripartism, based on respect for workers and other civil liberties, to peacefully resolve thorny labor problems, then as Iwuji (1979) asserted, society as a whole would gain because such participatory approaches could be extended to other social groups and activities. Besides, the dire conditions of Africa today make even more imperative the efficient use of all labor/human resources.

6. 2   Africa and the ILO: A Summing Up

Due to the scope of this study, some issues that might impinge on the topic selected may not have been raised or treated extensively. Bearing this in mind and in light of the complicated issues surrounding the chosen subject and the further questions it may have raised, the following issues may be investigated further to complement the research and findings of this book. In the Introduction to this book, I analyzed the controversy that hung over the role of labor in Africa. One solution, social science methodology permitting, is to conduct more empirical individual country analyses to gauge the full extent to which trade union freedoms affect African economies or the rate of industrialization. Hence, in addition to this study which has focused largely on Ghana, similar studies might be conducted on other African countries. As one of several important conditions for assessing the actual role of unions, the systematic documentation of the noncollective bargaining functions (that is, the broader social roles) of unions in Africa has to be initiated. Because this area is relatively neglected, the true contributions of unions to society may have been underestimated. This neglect was acknowledged by the International Industrial Relations Association's (IIRA) First African Regional Congress held in 1989: "There is a need in the development of African countries for a fresh interpretation of the role of workers and their organizations in economic decision-making and policy development at the national level."[31]

There are several activities and projects undertaken single-handedly or jointly by unions that have not been considered in the evaluation of the social benefits of unions. A summary description of such activities from Ghana, Kenya and Nigeria is as follows.[32] The Ghana TUC, together with the Friedrich-Ebert Foundation of Germany, the African-American Labor Center (of the American Federation of Labor and the Congress of Industrial Organization) and the State Insurance Corporation (of Ghana) constructed a total of 136 housing units for workers in Takoradi and Kumasi (Arthiabah, 1985: 21). Similarly, the Kenyan unions, led by the Civil Servants' Association, have contributed to alleviate housing shortages by operating a successful cooperative housing scheme.[33]

Ghanaian unions have additionally been involved in vocational education and adult literacy programs. Examples are the Sewing School based in Takoradi that trains workers and their dependents in sewing, catering, home economics and child care. In Cape Coast (in the Central Region) the TUC runs the famous Secretarial School, which has graduated several hundreds of clerically trained school leavers. Besides, there is the well-known Labour College, which trains workers in "the techniques and struggle for economic and social justice . . . . Literacy . . . . and trade union organizing" (Ibid.). Currently, the TUC is negotiating with various universities in Ghana to establish an industrial and labor relations certificate program to assure university-type of training for trade unionists and other labor relations practitioners.[34] A more recent trade union activity that should not go unnoticed is that while trade liberalization and privatization whittle away the scanty industrial base of Ghana, the unions have mounted a "Buy Made in Ghana" campaign to preserve jobs and industries.[35] Nigerian unions have also embarked on several educational programs as their contribution to national development. In 1990, as a follow-up to the Constitution of the Nigerian Labor Congress that required the Congress to invest at least 10 percent of its revenues in education, the unions proposed to spend 50 million naira on a five-year education and training program to upgrade workers' skills in languages, literacy, health and safety, as well as productivity.[36] The last activities plus similar programs which go beyond the narrow occupational interests of unions might be used in conjunction with the findings of this study to acquire a deeper appreciation for the role of unions in Ghana and the rest of Africa to shed more light on whether unions make positive contributions or are liabilities to their societies.

Two issues emerge in connection with the role of the ILO as areas for further investigation. The first that needs to be monitored in future is the apparent tension in the Organization between the implementation of worker's/human rights standards and technical cooperation which centers on technical or economic efficiency. For example, in 1987, during a mission to Ghana, one ILO official recorded violations of ILO standards involving a project funded through the Organization.[37] The Organization needs to resolve this role conflict to insure that the completion of technical projects does not undermine its workers' and human rights objectives. This need has become more pressing as a result of the perceived need to accelerate the so-called revitalization of African economies under the aegis of the IMF and World Bank

The second ILO-related issue deals with the critical conditions that have to be met to permit the flourishing of workers' or human rights in Africa. For purposes of brevity, a few conditions will be listed. Prominent among those that have to be investigated are how the absence of popular, well-respected and enforced constitutions; an independent judiciary; pro-workers' rights and civil rights activist groups; and a truly autonomous and virile press has led to the prevalence of restrictions on trade union rights and other liberties in Africa.[38] Closely connected to those issues is the assumption by the ILO that all members will abide by the rule of law. As is evident through the dissolution of unions and the arrest of trade unionists, this assumption may not be applicable to all African countries. The historical, socio-legal and economic conditions that have acted as deterrents to the rule of law (that is, laws that are just and protect human rights) and how those conditions can be eradicated need to be studied further.

6. 3   Concluding Observations

I have identified the contentious views about the role of labor and also shown that labor policies were based on certain unproven assumptions about the impact of unions on Africa's capacity to resolve the immense socio-economic problems of the continent. Most of these policy assumptions, as I pointed out, did not reflect the actual situation in the countries studied in this book. The significance of these erroneous assumptions lay in the tremendous influence they exerted over post-independence labor policies, laws and their practical outcomes as demonstrated in the case of Ghana. In conducting this study, I examined two ILO Conventions, Nos. 87 and 98 (which seek to confer on workers rights to free trade unionism) in the attempt to assess the extent to which they were applied within African labor practices using Ghana as a special case study. The Ghanaian materials used in this study were supplemented with others from Kenya, Nigeria and Zambia.

The following are some of my key conclusions and observations. There was no conclusive evidence that granting workers the right to form unions of their own choice to protect them through collective bargaining and other trade union activities diminished the capacity of the countries I studied to tackle development problems. As I demonstrated with the case of Ghana, although since 1958 the state has relatively dominated the trade unions via legislation coupled with cooptation and coercive tactics, the country has not reaped the fruits that the advocates of state control of unions professed. On the contrary, as shown in Chapters 2 and 5 of this book, Ghanaian and other African societies still face the perennial economic, social and political problems they inherited at the end of formal colonialism. As illustrated in Chapter 5, from 1975 to 1985, when the Ghanaian economy was in a free fall, inflation wiped out workers' real incomes and livng conditions deteriorated dramatically. From workers' standpoint, not only did they suffer a degradation of living and working conditions, but also their unions, led by the TUC, failed to realize their potentials to protect them and to act as advocates of economic and political programs to reverse the social decay of the mid-1970s and 1980s. Finally but not the least, it might be pointed out that although the Ghanaian and other states were relatively successful in curtailing trade union rights, these countries did not escape political instability:

> African states, despite their anti-trade union and anti-human rights posture, are still very much undeveloped and disunited, with no indication of the direly needed common bond emerging. Even with the repression of unions they remain very unstable and show no indications that a better society is emerging.[39]

Thus, at least in the case of Ghana, post-independence conditions appear not to confirm the presumption that restrictions on unions could accelerate industrialization and economic growth, and insure political stability. The policies that focused almost exclusively on labor control failed because as I have argued, they rejected a fundamental economic truism — that there are several factors of production and labor is only one of them. In examining the numerous factors that undermined successful industrialization, I emphasized the role of the state, particularly the extent to which abrupt and often violent changes in government made the adoption of consistent economic strategies not possible. They led to the abandonment of ongoing policies and development projects resulting in the wastage of scarce resources. In the labor sphere, as I pointed out, the high levels of political instability undermined the crafting of long-range labor and human resource development and utilization. In addition, I drew attention to a common phenomenon in Africa: paying lip service to human resources as "the most important resource," without consistent efforts by governments to integrate labor-management relations into national development plans.

An additional thrust of this book was that Ghana has not only failed to implement a viable labor policy, but also past and existing laws and practices have led to several international relations problems because they do not meet ILO standards. As a prelude to finding practical solutions to the problems alluded to (both domestic and international), I first explained how colonial labor and economic policies and the geopolitical roles of unions constrained Ghana's capacity to fashion policies to meet genuine national needs and the country's commitments at the ILO. Central to the technical/administrative obstacles that I evaluated was the country's worsening economy. That was partially attributed to the decline in the value of the country's exported raw materials and agricultural produce. The economic burdens of nonoil producing/exporting nations such as Ghana, Kenya and Zambia have been made heavier by the skyrocketing prices of imported oil. I wish however, to reiterate that all these obstacles might explain, but not justify, the severe restrictions some governments placed on unions. Hence, for example, the inhumane colonial labor policies and the violation of workers' rights cannot be accepted as rationales for the violation of ILO norms by post-independence African regimes. The obstacles presented were analyzed to furnish a complete understanding of the total contexts — historical, legal, social, economic and political — in which trade unions and workers' rights have evolved and the circumstances under which African governments have attempted to apply ILO standards.

Based on my assessment of the problems common in the selected countries, I recommended some policies with the purpose of laying the foundations for future rationalized (what is also called sound) labor polices and relations. One essential ingredient of these policies is insuring that future strategies focus less on the hegemonic interests of particular regimes (both military and civilian types) and paying increased attention to the mutual benefits of workers, society and employers. These new policies are expected to be grounded in relevant ILO standards which may be used as ideals that these countries must strive for and practical guidelines that are attainable. The policy prescriptions of this book were based on the assumption that the ideals contained in ILO standards and my stated policy goals could be combined to provide a vision of labor policies which in the future would inspire progressive African governments to marshal the political will necessary to change the course of labor relations, especially relations between workers and governments. Thus I am presuming that equipped with the proper vision, some African governments would seek keep to develop the political will to change their labor policies. The absence of political will is one of the biggest challenges in the field of workers'/human rights.

The ILO's standards and technical cooperation programs could be of practical value to African member states, especially in times of economic and political crises, because they do not only offer hope, but in some instances have proven usefulness in assisting to defuse the tensions that emanated from attempts to overcome underdevelopment. Admittedly, as shown in this study and by other authors,[40] the ILO has not been very successful in getting African states to radically overhaul their labor laws and policies. But it has scored some partial successes in making some governments including those of Ghana in 1965, Zambia in 1992 - 1993 and Nigeria in 1991 to expunge from their statutes provisions that violated workers' rights. I wish, however, to affirm that the Organization's influence was more visible, almost dramatic, in assisting the release of detained trade unionists.

One outstanding event illustrates the influence of the ILO. In the summer of 1986, 25 Nigerian trade unionists were detained by the federal authorities for planning to demonstrate in support of students who protested the austere economic polices of the government. As soon as the ILO was informed of the arrests, the Director General (of the ILO) consulted with Nigeria's Labor Minister who was in Geneva for the annual International Labor Conference.

Before the end of the Conference, the ILO announced the release of the 25 worker leaders and their resumption of trade union duties. In this case, the ILO's role was relatively conspicuous. However, the Organization's most valuable contributions to workers' rights in Africa may be more imperceptible. As one African labor unionist attending a meeting in Geneva in 1986 put it, "Honestly, I would not have been a trade union leader if I were not assured by the ILO that as long as I pursued genuine trade union activities, I will be protected." This statement was confirmed by African government representatives, who admitted that had it not been for the ILO, some governments would have arrested more trade unionists and abolished unions more arbitrarily.

The consensus among several African trade unionists was that even if the ILO were not always able to ensure direct and immediate alterations in their counries' labor laws and policies, in subtle and indirect ways, it offered workers and their leaders protection against more blatant abuses of their civil and trade union rights by governments. Besides the ideals the ILO espoused, I observed that it had accumulated tremendous experience in the implementation of labor policies, an experience that if applied judiciously by African governments could assist in reducing some of their labor and development pains. Various bodies of the ILO could be used to resolve through negotiations and dialogue the inevitable complex labor conflicts that emerge out of attempts to convert underdeveloped economies into developed ones in an era of fierce competition for increasingly shrinking and expensive material resources. Through its emphasis on workers' rights, the ILO could assist African member states to add to solutions to their economic problems a human dimension without which full development could not be accomplished.

NOTES

1. In Ghana since 1990, when the National Advisory Committee on Labor (NACL) was reconstituted, much of its deliberations have centered on amending the country's 1965 Industrial Relations Act to meet the provisions of Convention No. 87 of the ILO. The NACL is a tripartite group responsible for advising the Ghana Government on domestic and international labor issues.

2. ILO, Report of the Director General, Sixth African Regional Conference, Tunis, Oct. 1983, "Social Aspects of Development in Africa," ILO: Geneva, 1983.

3. N. K. Bentsi-Enchill, "Workers and the PNDC," *West Africa*, Jan. 26, 1987: 152, 153.

4. ILO, 1983a, 1985a.

5. I am referring to the 1982 to 1985 crises that paralyzed the Ghana TUC and with respect to the Nigerian Labor Congress, chronic fiscal crisis which it faces in spite of the legislatively backed affiliation of 42 industrial unions. Most of these 42 unions persistently refuse to remit to the Nigerian national federation funds from the checkoff of union dues.

6.   During a NACL meeting, which I observed in 1991, one of the agenda items was an amendment to the 1965 Industrial Relations Act (field work, Accra, Summer and Fall, 1991).

7.   E. Kalula (1985) addresses what he calls the "back seat" status of African labor departments.

8.   Statement by Sierra Leone Minister of Labor "Hard Labor," *West Africa*, June 19 - 25, 1989: 1007.

9.   Ghana Labor Department, *Laborscope*, May 1989: 21.

10.   "Hard Labor," *West Africa*.

11.   Upon the recommendations of the National Advisory Committee on Labor, the PNDC proposed to undertake a Two-Year Labor Codific ation Program (1982 - 1983). This proposal was not implemented largely because of the chaotic labor situation that resulted from the 1982 - 1985 TUC leadership crises. Another factor that contributed to the abandonment of the codification plan was the government's preoccupation with IMF and World Bank conditionalities, which typically included labor retrenchment.

12.   Some of these are "The National Tripartite Seminar on International Labor Standards," Accra, Ghana, May 1987; "The Fifth African Regional Seminar on National and International Labor Standards," Lusaka, Zambia, Sept. 23 - Oct. 2, 1985.

13.   Here, I wish to emphasize that African nations can maximize the benefits of the limited technical assistance they receive from the ILO and other international agencies through the mutual exchange of personnel for training instead of almost always resorting to expatriate "expert advisors."

14.   ILO Committee of Experts Reports to the International Labor Conference, 1990, 1991, 1992 and 1993.

15.   A further premise is that the public authorities will recognize that different segments of society have different interests which may be reconciled peacefully.

16.   Kwesi Botchwey, "Growth Potential," *West Africa*, July 8 - 14, 1991: 1119.

17.   K. Opare-Ababio, Address to the Third Public Services Workers' Union's Quadrennial Conference, Winneba, Ghana, September 3, 1991: 5.

18.   *West Africa*, May 24 - 30, 1993: 874.

19.   For how IMF and World Bank conditionalities contributed to the worsening of Ghana's labor climate, see Panford, Forthcoming.

20.   N. Adio-Saka, "Defining Baseline: Confusion over Interpretation of Minimum Wage," *West Africa*, Feb. 25 - March 3, 1991: 260.

21.   P. Idowu, "Responding to Realities: Search for Efficient Civil Service in West Africa," *West Africa*, March 9 - 15, 1992: 414.

22.   *Ibid.*

23.   See, TUC, Paper to the National Commission for Democracy, "The Role of Workers in the Search and Realization of Functional Democracy," No date. Obtained from the Research Department, Ghana TUC, Accra, March 1987.

24.   The ZCTU was one of the few African labor organizations that escaped being incorporated within the one-party state.

25.   According to the Ghana Labor Department, upon the recommendations of the NACL, the government ratified five Conventions in May, 1986. Other practical uses of such a body were discussed in Section 5.1.

26.   Similar arrangements exist in Nigeria and Zambia (ILO, *Key Issues in the Promotion of Sound Labor Relations in Africa*, ILO: Geneva, 1991: 28 - 29).

27.   The Management Development Institute (a state-owned management consulting agency) in the mid-1980s offered training and advisory services in labor negotiations to workers and managers. These services could be indicative of growing

awareness in Ghana of the importance of negotiations in resolving labor and other conflicts ("Labor Management," *West Africa*, Nov. 10, 1986: 2379).

28.   An explosive situation emerged in Senegal in 1993 when IMF policies led to a proposed 15 percent reduction in public sector wages. Actions taken by the unions included a 48-hour strike that "seriously disturbed transportation in Dakar," the capital. The strikes were suspended when the Senegalese head of state entered into negotiations with the unions ("Economic Recovery Programme Suspended," *West Africa*, September 27 - October 3, 1993: 1720).

29.   Ghana National Assembly, Parliamentary Debates, "Government Motions: International Labor Organization, Convention No. 87," May 21, 1965: Column 206.

30.   See also Ghana TUC, 1958 Constitution, Accra, 1958. One of the aims of the TUC according to this constitution was nation building.

31.   T. Fashoyin, Summary of Public Policy Implications of Discussions of the First IIRA African Regional Congress," Lagos, Nigeria, November 9-11, 1988, cited in International Industrial Relations Association (IIRA), *Bulletin* No. 26, August 1989: 4.

32.   These activities represent some of the documented noncollective bargaining activities of unions in my selected countries and do not necessarily exhaust the broad spectrum of social, political and economic endeavors of all unions.

33.   Information from the ILO, Geneva, July, 1985.

34.   Information from the Ghana TUC and the Ghana Labor Department, Accra, August, 1993. Other activities are the building of a Nurses' Hostel funded by the Enrolled and Community Health Nurses of Ghana and the General Certificate of Education (GCE) Classes sponsored by the Ghana National Association of Teachers (GNAT) to upgrade the qualifications of teachers (*The Teachers*, Newsletter of the GNAT, April - June, 1990, No. 2: 9).

35.   "May Day Celebrations," *West Africa*, May 17 - 23, 1993: 831. For a discussion of Ghana's World Bank- and IMF-instigated de-industrialization, see Panford, Forthcoming; Sawyerr, 1990.

36.   *West Africa*, October 8 - 14, 1990: 2625.

37.   ILO, Regional Adviser on Standards, *Report on Mission to Ghana*, May, 1987.

38.   Senior level trade unionists from 15 African countries who participated in an Advanced Leadership Training Seminar (New Strategies in Defense of Workers Rights in Africa, African-American Labor Center (AFL-CIO), Washington, DC, September 8, 1993) delineated other factors such as the regime type, and the willingness of the judiciary to challenge labor statutes and governmental practices that are unconstitutional or violate ILO norms. They stressed how the fear of retaliation by the public authorities may undercut the emergence of human rights. Another issue they touched on was the role of legal education/training in Africa and the inheritance and retention of colonial legal systems.

39.   Okunade, 1989: 67.

40.   See Samson (1979) and Galenson (1981).

Appendix 1

Texts of Articles 19 and 22 of the ILO's 1988 Constitution

Conventions and Recommendations Decisions of the Conference

Article 19

1. When the Conference has decided on the adoption of proposals with regard to an item on the agenda, it will rest with the Conference to determine whether these proposals should take the form: *(a)* of an international Convention, or *(b)* of a Recommendation to meet circumstances where the subject, or aspect of it, dealt with is not considered suitable or appropriate at that time for a Convention.

Vote required

2. In either case a majority of two-thirds of the votes cast by the delegates present shall be necessary on the final vote for the adoption of the Convention or Recommendation, as the case may be, by the Conference.

Modifications for special local conditions

3. In framing any Convention or Recommendation of general application the Conference shall have due regard to those countries in which climatic conditions, the imperfect development of industrial organisation, or other special circumstances make the industrial conditions substantially different and shall suggest the modifications, if any, which it considers may be required to meet the case of such countries.

Authentic texts

4. Two copies of the Convention or Recommendation shall be authenticated by the signatures of the President of the Conference and of the Director-General. Of these copies one shall be deposited in the archives of the International Labour Office and the other with the Secretary-General of the United Nations.

The Director-General will communicate a certificate copy of the Convention or Recommendation to each of the Members.

Obligations of Members in respect of Conventions

5. In the case of a Convention —
   (a) the Convention will be communicated to all Members for ratification;
   (b) each of the Members undertakes that it will, within the period of one year at most from the closing of the session of the Conference, or if it is impossible owing to exceptional circumstances to do so within the period of one year, then at the earliest practicable moment and in no case later than 18 months after the closing of the session of the Conference, bring the Convention before the authority or authorities within whose competence the matter lies, for the enactment of legislation or other action;
   (c) the Members shall inform the Director-General of the International Labour Office of the measures taken in accordance with this article to bring the Convention before the said competent authority or authorities, with particulars of the authority or authorities regarded as competent, and of the action taken by them;
   (d) if the Member obtains the consent of the authority or authorities within whose competence the matter lies, it will communicate the formal ratification of the Convention to the Director-General and will take such action as may be necessary to make effective the provisions of such Convention;
   (e) if the Member does not obtain the consent of the authority or authorities within whose competence the matter lies, no further obligation shall rest upon the Member except that it shall report to the Director-General of the International Labour Office, at appropriate intervals as requested by the Governing Body, the position of its law and practice in regard to the matters dealt with in the Convention, showing the extent to which effect has been given, or is proposed to be given, to any of the provisions of the Convention by legislation, administrative action, collective agreement or otherwise and stating the difficulties which prevent or delay the ratification of such Convention.

Obligations of Members in respect of Recommendations

6. In the case of a Recommendation —

(a) the Recommendation will be communicated to all Members for their consideration with a view to effect being given to it by national legislation or otherwise;

(b) each of the Members undertakes that it will, within a period of one year at most from the closing of the session of the Conference, or if it is impossible owing to exceptional circumstances to do so within the period of one year, then at the earliest practicable moment and in no case later than 18 months after the closing of the Conference, bring the Recommendation before the authority or authorities within whose competence the matter lies for the enactment of legislation or other action;

(c) the Members shall inform the Director-General of the International Labour Office of the measures taken in accordance with this article to bring the Recommendation before the said competent authority or authorities with particulars of the authority or authorities regarded as competent, and of the action taken by them;

(d) apart from bringing the Recommendation before the said competent authority or authorities, no further obligation shall rest upon the Members, except that they shall report to the Director-General of the International Labour Office, at appropriate intervals as requested by the Governing Body, the position of the law and practice in their country in regard to the matters dealt with in the Recommendation, showing the extent to which effect has been given, or is proposed to be given, to the provisions of the Recommendation and such modifications of these provisions as it has been found or may be found necessary to make in adopting or applying them.

Obligations of federal States

7. In the case of a federal State, the following provisions shall apply:

(a) in respect of Conventions and Recommendations which the federal government regards as appropriate under its constitutional system for federal action, the obligations of the federal State shall be the same as those of Members which are not federal States;

(b) in respect of Conventions and Recommendations which the federal government regards as appropriate under its constitutional system, in whole or in part, for action by the constituent states, provinces, or cantons rather than for federal action, the federal government shall —

   (i)   make, in accordance with its Constitution and the Constitutions of the states, provinces or cantons concerned, effective arrangements for the reference of such Conventions and Recommendations not later than 18 months from the closing of the session of the Conference to the appropriate federal, state, provincial or cantonal authorities for the enactment of legislation or other action;

   (ii) arrange, subject to the concurrence of the state, provincial or cantonal governments concerned, for periodical consultations between the federal and the state, provincial or cantonal authorities with a view to promoting within the federal State co-ordinated action to give effect to the provisions of such Conventions and Recommendations;

   (iii) inform the Director-General of the International Labour Office of the measures taken in accordance with this article to bring such Conventions and Recommendations before the appropriate federal, state, provincial or cantonal authorities with particulars of the authorities regarded as appropriate and of the action taken by them;

   (iv) in respect of each such Convention which it has not ratified, report to the Director-General of the International Labour Office, at appropriate intervals as requested by the Governing Body, the position of the law and practice of the federation and its constituent states, provinces or cantons in regard to the Convention, showing the extent to which effect has been given, or is proposed to be given, to any of the provisions of the Convention by legislation, administrative action, collective agreement, or otherwise;

(v)   in respect of each such Recommendation, report to the Director-General of the International Labour Office, at appropriate intervals as requested by the Governing Body, the position of the law and practice of the federation and its constituent states, provinces or cantons in regard to the Recommendation, showing the extent to which effect has been given, or is proposed to be given, to the provisions of the Recommendation and such modifications of these provisions as have been found or may be found necessary in adopting or applying them.

Effect of Conventions and Recommendations on more favourable existing provisions

8. In no case shall the adoption of any Convention or Recommendation by the Conference, or the ratification of any Convention by any Member, be deemed to affect any law, award, custom or agreement which ensures more favourable conditions to the workers concerned than those provided for in the Convention or Recommendation.

Annual reports on ratified Conventions

Article 22

Each of the Members agrees to make an annual report to the International Labour Office on the Measures which it has taken to give effect to the provisions of Conventions to which it is a party. These reports shall be made in such form and shall contain such particulars as the Governing Body may request.

Source: "Text of the Constitution," *The Constitution of the International Labour Organisation*, 1988, International Labour Organisation, pp. 13 - 16, 17.

Appendix 2

Text of ILO Convention No. 87 and Report Form

Appl. 22.87

87. Freedom of Association and Protection of the Right to Organise, 1948

INTERNATIONAL LABOUR OFFICE

REPORT FORM

FOR THE

FREEDOM OF ASSOCIATION AND PROTECTION OF THE RIGHT TO ORGANISE CONVENTION, 1948 (NO. 87)

The present report form is for the use of countries which have ratified the Convention. It has been approved by the Governing Body of the International Labour Office, in accordance with article 22 of the ILO Constitution, which reads as follows: "Each of the Members agrees to make an annual report to the International Labour Office on the measures which it has taken to give effect to the provisions of Conventions to which it is a party. These reports shall be made in such a form and shall contain such particulars as the Governing Body may request."

GENEVA
1990

PRACTICAL GUIDANCE FOR DRAWING UP REPORTS

First reports

If this is your Government's first report following the entry into force of the Convention in your country, full information should be given on each of the provisions of the Convention and on each of the questions set out in the report form.

Subsequent reports
In subsequent reports, information need normally be given on the following points:
(a) any new legislative or other measures affecting the application of the Convention;
(b) replies to the questions in the report form on the practical application of the Convention (for example, statistics, results of inspections, judicial or administrative decisions) and on the communication of copies of the report to the representative organisations of employers and workers and on any observations received from these organisations;
(c) **replies to comments by supervisory bodies**: the report must contain replies to any comments regarding the application of the Convention in your country which may have been addressed to your Government by the Committee of Experts or by the Conference Committee on the Application of Conventions and Recommendations.

Article 22 of the Constitution of the ILO

Report for the period... to ....
made by the Government of..

on the

FREEDOM OF ASSOCIATION AND PROTECTION OF THE RIGHT TO ORGANISE CONVENTION, 1948

ratification of which was registered on . . . .

I.   Please indicate whether effect is given to the Articles of the
     Convention —
     (a) by customary law or practice, or
     (b) by legislation.

     In the first alternative, please indicate how effect is given to the
     Articles of the Convention.

     In the second alternative, please give a list of the constitutional and
     legislative provisions or administrative or other regulations which
     give effect to the Articles of the Convention. Where this has not
     already been done please forward copies of these various provisions,
     etc., to the International Labour Office with this report.

II. Please give any available information concerning the customary law,
     practice, legislative provisions and regulations and any other
     measures the effect of which is to ensure the application of each of the
     following Articles of the Convention. In addition, please provide any
     indication specifically requested below under individual Articles.

          If, in your country, ratification of the Convention gives the force
          of national law to its provisions please indicate, in addition to the
          constitutional texts from which this effect is derived, any
          measures which may have been taken to give effect to those
          provisions of the Convention which may require the intervention
          of the national authorities to ensure their application.

          If the Committee of Experts or the Conference Committee on the
          Application of Conventions and Recommendations has requested
          additional information or has made an observation on the
          measures adopted to apply the Convention, please supply the
          information asked for or indicate the action taken by your
          Government to settle the points in question.

Article 1

Each Member of the International Labour Organisation for which this
Convention is in force undertakes to give effect to the following provisions.

Article 2

Workers and employers, without distinction whatsoever, shall have the
right to establish and subject, only to the organisation concerned, to join
organisations of their own choosing without previous authorisation.

Please state what substantive or formal conditions, if any, must be fulfilled by workers' and employers' organisations when they are being established.

Please specify whether there exist any special legal provisions regarding the establishment of organisations by certain categories of workers (other than members of the armed forces and the police) and, in particular, by public officials an d employees of publicly owned undertakings.

If so, please indicate <u>under each of the Articles of the Convention</u> what are the special legal provisions which apply as regards the establishment, functioning and dissolution of such organisations.

Article 3

1. Workers' and employers' organisations shall have the right to draw up their constitutions and rules, to elect their representatives in full freedom, to organise their administration and activities and to formulate their programmes.

2. The public authorities shall refrain from any interference which would restrict this right or impede the lawful exercise thereof.

Please state the conditions, if any, governing the constitutions of such organisations or the objects which they may legally pursue.

Article 4

Workers' and employers' organisations shall not be liable to be dissolved or suspended by administrative authority.

Please state the legal provisions, if any, which relate to the suspension or dissolution of workers' and employers' organisations.

Article 5

Workers' and employers' organisations shall have the right to establish and join federations and confederations and any such organisation, federation or confederation shall have the right to affiliate with international organisations of workers and employers.

Please state the legal provisions relating to the affiliation of workers' and employers' organisations with international organisations of workers and employers.

Article 6

The provisions of Articles 2, 3 and 4 hereof apply to federations and confederations of workers' and employers' organisations.

Please state whether any guarantees prescribed by national legislation which give effect to this Convention and which relate to the establishment, functioning or dissolution of workers' and employers' organisations apply equally to federations and confederations, or whether there exist special provisions with regard to the latter. In the second alternative, please indicate such provisions.

Article 7

The acquisition of legal personality by workers' and employers' organisations, federations and confederations shall not be made subject to conditions of such a character as to restrict the application of the provisions of Articles 2, 3 and 4 hereof.

Please indicate any conditions to which the acquisition of legal personality may be made subject.

Please state, in particular, whether the acquisition of legal personality is optional or compulsory for workers' and employers' organisations.

Article 8

1. In exercising the rights provided for in this Convention workers and employers and their respective organisations, like other persons or organised collectivities, shall respect the law of the land.

2. The law of the land shall not be such as to impair, nor shall it be so applied as to impair, the guarantees provided for in this Convention.

Please give a general indication of the measures of a general character which may apply to workers' and employers' organisations, as, for example, general legislation concerning associations and meetings, laws concerning the safety of the State or a state of siege, penal codes, etc.

Article 9

1. The extent to which the guarantees provided for in this Convention shall apply to the armed forces and the police shall be determined by national laws or regulations.

2. In accordance with the principle set forth in paragraph 8 of article 19 of the Constitution of the International Labour Organisation the ratification of this Convention by any Member shall not be deemed to affect any existing law, award, custom or agreement in virtue of which members of the armed forces or the police enjoy any right guaranteed by this Convention.

Please indicate to what extent the guarantees prescribed by the Convention apply to members of the armed forces or the police.

Article 10

In this Convention the term "organisation" means any organisation of workers or of employers for furthering and defending the interests of workers or of employers.

III.   Article 11 of the Convention is as follows:

Each member of the International Labour Organisation for which this Convention is in force undertakes to take all necessary and appropriate measures to ensure that workers and employers may exercise freely the right to organise.

Please indicate the legislative or other measures taken to ensure the free exercise of the right to organise.

IV.   Please state whether courts of law or other tribunals have given decisions involving questions of principle relating to the application of the Convention. If so, please supply the text of these decisions.

V.   Please supply any general observations which may be considered useful with regard to the manner in which the Convention is applied.

VI.   Please indicate the representative organisations of employers and workers to which copies of the present report have been communicated in accordance with article 23, paragraph 2, of the Constitution of the International Labour Organisation.[1] If copies of the report have not been communicated to representative organisations of employers and/or workers, or if they have been communicated to bodies other than such organisations, please supply information on any particular circumstances existing in your country which explain the procedure followed.

Please indicate whether you have received from the organisations of employers or workers concerned any observations, either of a general kind or in connection with the present or the previous report, regarding the practical application of the provisions of the Convention or the application of the legislation or other measures implementing the Convention. If so, please communicate the observations received, together with any comments that you consider useful.

---

[1] Article 23, paragraph 2, of the Constitution reads as follows: "Each Member shall communicate to the representative organisations recognised for the purpose of article 3 copies of the information and reports communicated to the Director-General in pursuance of Articles 19 and 22."

Appendix 3

Text of ILO Convention No. 98 and Report Form

Appl. 22.98
98. Right to Organise and Collective Bargaining, 1949

INTERNATIONAL LABOUR OFFICE

REPORT FORM

FOR THE

RIGHT TO ORGANISE AND COLLECTIVE BARGAINING CONVENTION, 1949 (NO. 98)

The present report form is for the use of countries which have ratified the Convention. It has been approved by the Governing Body of the International Labour Office, in accordance with article 22 of the ILO Constitution, which reads as follows: "Each of the Members agrees to make an annual report to the International Labour Office on the measures which it has taken to give effect to the provisions of Conventions to which it is a party. These reports shall be made in such a form and shall contain such particulars as the Governing Body may request."

GENEVA
1988

PRACTICAL GUIDANCE FOR DRAWING UP REPORTS

First reports

If this is your Government's first report following the entry into force of the Convention in your country, full information should be given on each of the provisions of the Convention and on each of the questions set out in the report form.

Subsequent reports
In subsequent reports, information need normally be given on the following points:
(a) any new legislative or other measures affecting the application of the Convention;
(b) replies to the questions in the report form on the practical application of the Convention (for example, statistics, results of inspections, judicial or administrative decisions) and on the communication of copies of the report to the representative organisations of employers and workers and on any observations received from these organisations;
(c) **replies to comments by supervisory bodies**: the report must contain replies to any comments regarding the application of the Convention in your country which may have been addressed to your Government by the Committee of Experts or by the Conference Committee on the Application of Conventions and Recommendations.

Article 22 of the Constitution of the ILO

Report for the period.. to ....
made by the Government of...

on the

RIGHT TO ORGANISE AND COLLECTIVE BARGAINING CONVENTION, 1949 (NO. 98)

(ratification registered on ....)

I.   **Please indicate whether effect is given to the Articles of the Convention —**
     (a) by customary law or practice, or
     (b) by legislation.

In the first alternative, please indicate how effect is given to the Articles of the Convention.

In the second alternative, please give a list of the constitutional and legislative provisions or administrative or other regulations which give effect to the Articles of the Convention. Where this has not already been done please forward copies of these various provisions, etc., to the International Labour Office with this report.

II. **Please give any available information concerning the customary law, practice, legislative provisions and regulations and any other measures the effect of which is to ensure the application of each of the following Articles of the Convention. In addition, please provide any indication specifically requested below under individual Articles.**

     If, in your country, ratification of the Convention gives the force of national law to its provisions please indicate, in addition to the constitutional texts from which this effect is derived, any measures which may have been taken to give effect to those provisions of the Convention which may require the intervention of the national authorities to ensure their application.

     If the Committee of Experts or the Conference Committee on the Application of Conventions and Recommendations has requested additional information or has made an observation on the measures adopted to apply the Convention, please supply the information asked for or indicate the action taken by your Government to settle the points in question.

Article 1

1. Workers shall enjoy adequate protection against acts of anti-union discrimination in respect of their employment.

2. Such protection shall apply more particularly in respect of acts calculated to —

(a) make the employment of a worker subject to the condition that he shall not join a union or shall relinquish trade union membership.

(b) cause the dismissal of or otherwise prejudice a worker by reason of union membership or because of participation in union activities outside working hours or, with the consent of the employer, within working hours.

Please indicate how adequate protection against acts of anti-union discrimination in respect of their employment is ensured to workers.

Article 2

1. Workers' and employers' organisations shall enjoy adequate protection against any acts of interference by each other or each other's agents or member in their establishment, functioning or administration.

2. In particular, acts which are designed to promote the establishment of workers' organisations under the domination of employers or employers' organisations, or to support workers' organisations by financial or other means, with the object of placing such organisations under the control of employers or employers' organisations, shall be deemed to constitute acts of interference within the meaning of this Article.

Please indicate how adequate protection is ensured to workers' and employers' organisations against any acts of interference by each other.

Article 3

Machinery appropriate to national conditions shall be established, where necessary, for the purpose of ensuring respect for the right to organise as defined in the preceding Articles.

Article 4

Measures appropriate to national conditions shall be taken, where necessary, to encourage and promote the full development and utilisation of machinery for voluntary negotiation between employers or employers' organisations and workers' organisations, with a view to the regulation of terms and conditions of employment by means of collective agreements.

Please indicate any action taken to give effect to Articles 3 and 4.

Article 5

1. The extent to which the guarantees provided for in this Convention shall apply to the armed forces and the police shall be determined by national laws or regulations.

2. In accordance with the principle set forth in paragraph 8 of article 19 of the Constitution of the International Labour Organisation the ratification of

this Convention by any Member shall not be deemed to affect any existing law, award, custom or agreement in virtue of which members of the armed forces or the police enjoy any right guaranteed by this Convention.

Please indicate to what extent the guarantees provided in the Convention apply to members of the armed forces and the police.

Article 6

This Convention does not deal with the position of public servants engaged in the administration of the State, nor shall it be construed as prejudicing their rights or status in any way.

III.   **Please state whether courts of law or other tribunals have given decisions involving questions of principle relating to the application of the convention. If so, please supply the text of these decisions.**

IV.   **Please supply any general observations which may be considered useful with regard to the manner in which the Convention is applied.**

V.   **Please indicate the representative organisations of employers and workers to which copies of the present report have been communicated in accordance with article 23, paragraph 2, of the Constitution of the International Labour Organisation.[1] If copies of the report have not been communicated to representative organisations of employers and/or workers, or if they have been communicated to bodies other than such organisations, please supply information on any particular circumstances existing in your country which explain the procedure followed.**

Please indicate whether you have received from the organisations of employers or workers concerned any observations, either of a general kind or in connection with the present or the previous report, regarding the practical application of the provisions of the Convention or the application of the legislation or other measures implementing the Convention. If so, please communicate the observations received, together with any comments that you consider useful.

---

[1]Article 23, paragraph 2, of the Constitution reads as follows: "Each Member shall communicate to the representative organisations recognised for the purpose of article 3 copies of the information and reports communicated to the Director-General in pursuance of Articles 19 and 22."

Appendix 4

Ghana Labor Department Questionnaire

Basic Data/Information on Ghana's Labor Relations
1957 - 1986

<u>Part I</u>

1. Ghana Government's stated labor policies — objectives and
    contents of policies with special emphasis on:
    a. Changes or consistency over time (1957 - 1986).
    b. Freedom of Association for workers and their organizations.
    c. Collective bargaining in:
        1) The public sector and civil service.
        2) The private sector.
    d. Role of trade unions in Ghana's development.
    e. Workers' rights to strike in the public and private sectors.

2. The forms of machinery, organizations and processes of
    consultation between the Ghana Government and the labor
    movement, especially the Ghana TUC, on national, political and
    social issues.

3. The Ghana Labor Advisory Committee.

    a. Why it was formed.
    b. Its composition.
    c. Functions: role in labor laws and policies.
    d. Problems.
    e. Achievements.
    f. 2-year Labor Law Codification Program.
    g. Who appoints/elects members of Labor Advisory Committee?

4. Ghana labor laws (on Industrial Relations) "Missing" parts of
    Industrial and Labor Relations Act (No. 56 of 1958):

    a. Section 3 (3) (rules for authorization of Congress expenditure).
    b. Section 6 (auditing of accounts).
    c. Section 7 (powers of auditor).
    d. Section 9 (transitory provisions).

5. Copies/Sources of Parliamentary Hansard (Records of
    Proceedings) on major pieces of labor legislation.

    a. 1958 Act.
    b. 1959 Amendment of the 1958 Act.
    c. 1960 Amendment to the 1958 Act.
    d. 1965 Industrial Relations Act.
    e. 1971 Industrial Relations Amendment repealing parts of the
        1965 Act.
    f. In connection with the above cited pieces of labor legislation,
        did any individual, association, trade union, or group of
        persons institute any court action or legal action? If yes,
        please elaborate on nature of legal proceedings.

6. Labor relations in the public sector.

    a. List of services defined as essential by the Ghana Government
        — additions to or deletions from list.
    b. The Ghana Government's policy with respect to:
        1) Strikes in the civil service.
        2) State enterprises/corporations.
        3) Public utility, e. g., water and electricity.
    c. Methods of dispute settlement in the public sector.

7. Labor unions and politics in Ghana (with emphasis on Ghana
    TUC). Ghana labor laws as they relate to the TUC's sponsorship
    of the Social Democratic Front in the 1979 elections. Did the TUC
    violate any laws? If yes, please elaborate.

8. Functions of the Chief Labor Officer, Registrar of Trade Unions
    and the Commissioner of Labor (1957 - 1986). Any changes in
    functions? Are these the same offices or different?

9.   Basic labor statistics, with sources, on:

   a.   Size of labor force.
   b.   Size of total Ghana population.
   c.   Size of rural population in Ghana.
   d.   Size of wage/salary earning work force.
   e.   Size or percentage of work force covered by collective
        bargaining agreements.
   f.   Size of work force organized by trade unions.
   g.   Minimum wages in Ghana (1957 - 1986).
   h.   Strike rates in the public sector.
   i.   Man-days lost due to strikes in the public sector.

10.   Ghana Government's expenditure on wages/ salaries in the public
      sector.

   a.   Total wage bills.
   b.   Percentage of total wage bills in national budgets for the years
        1957 - 1986.

11.   Existing and past mechanisms for determining minimum wages in
      Ghana.

12.   International Labor Conventions (especially Convention Nos. 87
      and 98).

   a.   Ministries/ Departments responsible for:
        1)   Examination of Conventions and Ministries involved to
             implementation stage.
        2)   Ratification.
        3)   Implementation.
   b.   Number of officials in the Labor Department in charge of
        Conventions.
   c.   Who is responsible in Ghana for submitting Articles 19 and 22
        reports on Conventions to the ILO?
   d.   Role of the National Labor Advisory Committee in
        international labor standards.
   e.   Role of or assistance obtained from the ILO Regional Labor
        Advisers on international labor standards and nature — form
        of assistance.

13.   Ghana Government's participation in ILO activities.

    a.   Major areas or priority of Ghana Government in terms of ILO
        activities.
    b.   International labor standards and technical cooperation.
    c.   The problems of Ghana Government's participation in:
        1)   Governing Body meetings and committees.
        2)   International Labor Conferences.
            a)   Financing/transportation of delegates.
            b)   Other problems.
    d.   Suggestions/rationale for overcoming some of the major
        problems preventing Ghana's full participation.
    e.   What are some of the major areas of ILO's activities
        that Ghana will prefer priority action/attention?

14.   The ILO's technical cooperation activities in Ghana.

    a.   Major projects/programs undertaken.
    b.   Nature of projects/programs:
        1)   Form of project.
        2)   Objective of project.
        3)   Impact of project.
        4)   Current status of project:
            a)   Ended/completed.
            b)   Transferred to Ghana Government.
            c)   Still with ILO assistance, on-going.
        5)   ILO and Ghana Government's contributions in terms of:
            a)   Finances.
            b)   Material contribution.
            c)   Personnel/staff inputs.
        6)   Suggestions for improving efficiency of projects in
            meeting Government's goals.
        7)   Any specific technical cooperation programs in training
            Ghanaians in international labor standards:
            a)   Number of Labor Ministry officials trained.
            b)   Current function/work of trained officials.
            c)   Form of training programs for labor ministry
               officials.
            d)   Local training of officials on standards.

15. ILO's Governing Body Committee of Freedom of Association.

    a. Functions.
    b. Areas/issues of jurisdiction of the Committee of Freedom of Association.
    c. Confidentiality of the Committee's work.
    d. Fairness/unfairness of the Committee's:
        1) Processes/procedures.
        2) Conclusions.
        3) Recommendations.
    e. Government's view of the Committee's structure/membership.

Please provide reasons for Government's views.

16. Trade Union's role in Ghana's development.

    a. Areas of government/union cooperation.
    b. Social welfare functions (noncollective bargaining activities) of Ghana's trade unions.
        1) Areas for improvement.
        2) Policies/plans of Ghana Government to tap unions' resources for national development.

17. Status of:

    a. Ghana National Association of Teachers.
    b. Civil Servant's Association.
    c. Association of Registered Nurses.

Are these collective bargaining agents? If not, how are their members' wages/salaries and terms of work/conditions of work determined?

Part II: Follow-up Questionnaire to Ghana Labor Department

1. Since Ghana has recently ratified five more Conventions, practices tripartism, and consults workers and employers in the area of labor policy and law, what is the Government's view on the possible ratification of Convention No. 144? Does the Government intend to ratify Convention No. 144 or not? If yes, what is being done about ratification now? If no, why does the Government not intend to ratify Convention No. 144?

2.   Ghana's labor policies:

    a.   Ghana Government's labor and industrial relations policies.
    b.   The structure, setup and function/activities of the Labor
       Department.
    c.   An organizational chart of the Labor Department, showing:
       1)   Setup of the Department.
       2)   Ministry Secretary.
       3)   Principal Secretary.
       4)   Chief Labor Officer.
       5)   Other staff.

3.   Concerning the National Labor Advisory Committee for the
    period 1965 - 1986, please provide the following:

    a.   Composition: exact people who represented Government,
       workers (TUC) and employers on the Committee.
    b.   The exact dates or periods or years during which the
       committee operated and was dormant. During periods of
       inoperation, please state why there was no activity and also
       state dates of inoperation.
    c.   For each period of operation/activity, please state:
       1)   Number of times it met.
       2)   Its agenda.
       3)   Outcome of meetings or any changes in labor laws or
          policies they recommended and what happened to
          recommendations.

4.   Present composition of the reconstituted Labor Advisory
    Committee:

    a.   Who represents the Ghana TUC and workers?
    b.   Who represents the Government?
    c.   Who represents the employers of Ghana?
    d.   The independent economists or researchers: Who are these
       independent, experienced labor economists and researchers?
       What is their role, or why are they on the Committee? Who
       selects them?

5.   Are there any stated Government policies, guidelines, rules of
    procedures for the Labor Advisory Committee? Please provide
    copies.

6.   On standards, ILO activities and preparation of reports for the ILO:
    Does your Department or Ministry have an explicitly laid down
    procedure for getting inputs from other Ministries/Departments,
    e.g., Foreign Affairs, Industry, etc.? Who is in charge of this

procedure? Also, the ILO Committee of Experts stated delays in and nonsubmission of reports from Ghana. If delays exist, what are the problems and proposed solutions? Do you have any special problems with interdepartmental relations? What are these?

7.   On strikes: Please provide the major classification of causes.

8.   Minimum wages: Tripartite Committee on Wages: Composition (who is represented), agenda, rules or methods of work, conduct of meetings, terms of reference, mechanism used in Ghana generally to determine the minimum wage. Factors used in calculating/determining the minimum wage. Major/common ones: stated Government policies and objectives on minimum wage.

9.   You stated "financial problem" is the main problem Ghana has in participating in the ILO. Please clarify/provide details.

10.   On both local and outside/foreign training of labor department staff on standards, please provide details of the kinds of training, e.g.:

       a.   When/how training is determined to be needed.
       b.   Frequency of and determination of need for training.
       c.   Who initiates training?
       d.   Rules/procedures used.
       e.   Methods of selecting, appointing or nominating trainees.

11.   Please provide the names, and periods of appointment and reasons for leaving positions:

       a.   Ministers of Labor.
       b.   Permanent Secretaries of Labor.
       c.   Commissioner of Labor/Chief Labor Officer.

12.   Concerning your work and that of other staff on standards or ILO activities, could you provide the following:

       a.   General problems you face, please highlight common, major or frequent ones and explain.
       b.   Suggestions for improving operations in your Department:
             1)   Terms/conditions of work.
             2)   Adequate supplies.
             3)   Work methods, etc.

c. Explain how these will improve efficiency in your Department
    in connection with:
    1)   ILO activities, generally.
    2)   Standards: submission of Articles 19 and 22 reports.
    3)   Improving labor policies, laws and policies.
    4)   Any suggestions, comments you may have on my
         research topic or issues?

Appendix 5

Ghana TUC Questionnaire: 1957–1986

1. Basic labor statistics and sources of data:

    a. Size of Ghana's total labor force.
    b. Size of wage/salary earning labor force.
    c. Size and percentage of labor force unionized:
        1) As members of the TUC.
        2) As members of other unions, e.g., GNAT, Civil Servants Association, etc.
    D. Size of labor force covered by TUC collective agreements.

2. Minimum wage determination in Ghana (and the role of the TUC).

    a. Please describe the mechanisms used in determining minimum wages in Ghana between 1957 - 1986.
    b. Please describe the exact role of the TUC in determining minimum wages.
    c. Please describe the structure, composition (representation of the TUC) and functions of the National Tripartite Committee on Wages.
    d. In Ghana, normally, who initiates new negotiations on minimum wages?
    e. For each minimum wage determined, what were the:
        1) Rates of inflation used.
        2) How were the rates of inflation determined?
        3) What were the other factors used in determining the minimum wages?
    f. Does the TUC have policies, plans, strategies, goals concerning the adoption of minimum wages? Please describe these plans, policies, etc.

3. History of Ghana TUC.

    In connection with the history of the TUC, please supply documents on the information provided. Also, indicate if the information is published by the TUC and the sources used.

      a.   The origins or the birth of the TUC.
      b.   The most significant developments in the Ghana labor
           movement since the TUC's birth.

4.   Structure, composition and functions of the TUC.

      Past and most up-to-date organization structure of the Ghana
      TUC, showing its:
      a.   National unions.
      b.   Local unions.
      c.   Various national offices/ officers.

5.   Please describe the basic decision-making processes within the
      TUC, showing the relationship between the TUC, its national
      affiliates and the local unions, emphasizing the role of the:

      a.   Secretary-General.
      b.   The National Executive Board.
      c.   The Heads/Secretaries General of the TUC 's affiliates.
      d.   Role of Heads of various departments of the TUC.
      e.   Regional/ Local offices/officers.

      You may use the three examples:
      a.   Strikes at local or national level.
      b.   Determination of national economic, social or political
           policies.
      c.   Determination of wages in a collective bargaining agreement.

6.   Please provide the number of TUC affiliates in Ghana between
      1957 - 1986.

      Please indicate/explain why the numbers of affiliates changed and
      when these changed.

7.   Please provide the following:
      Names, duration of tenure, reason for leaving the office for:

      a.   TUC Secretaries-General from its birth to the present.
      b.   Heads of TUC's Executive Board.

8.   Percentage of wages/salaries deducted as union dues.
      Percentage of dues going to:

      a.   National, local and TUC.
      b.   Process of checkoff.

9.   Functions of the TUC.
        Please list/describe:

        a.   Collective bargaining functions.
        b.   Noncollective bargaining functions.
        c.   Does the TUC have a strike fund?

        If no, how does it assist unions in periods of strike?

10.   ILO and International Labor Standards.

        Does the TUC have a department or official(s) assigned to
        International Labor Standards?

        a.   Please describe this department's/official's work.
        b.   Also describe the role to the TUC in:
             1)   The ratification of ILO standards.
             2)   The promotion of ILO standards.
             3)   The application of ILO standards.
             4)   ILO technical cooperation.
             5)   The problems of the TUC in its role in standards and the
                  ILO's technical cooperation programs.
             6)   Does the TUC have any plans, suggestions or solutions
                  for dealing with these problems?

11.   TUC's evaluation or views on:

        a.   The role of the Labor Ministry in labor policies, generally.
        b.   The roles of the Labor Ministry in:
             1)   ILO standards.
             2)   Technical cooperation.
        c.   Does the TUC have any suggestions, plans, etc. for improving
             the roles of the Labor Ministry? Please provide details of such
             plans, etc.

12.   Please list the names and offices held by TUC representatives
        (from 1958 - 1986) on:

        a.   National Labor Advisory Committee.
        b.   The National Tripartite Committee on Wages.
        c.   Have these committees agreed upon terms of reference,
             methods of work and issues of jurisdiction? Please state and
             describe these.
        d.   How did the TUC get its representatives on these two
             committees: by nomination or election?

13.   Two-Year Labor Codification Program.

    a.   What are the objectives?
    b.   When did the program start?
    c.   Who started/initiated it?
    d.   Methods/terms of work of body responsible.
    e.   Accomplishments up-to-date.
    f.   Any TUC memos or position papers submitted or dealing with this program?

14.   About two years ago, the Ghana Government conducted some national job evaluations.

Please describe the goals, methods used and the role of the TUC or its affiliates.

Also, state and explain the TUC's position with regard to this.

15.   Concerning strikes in Ghana, please state and explain the following:

    a.   The TUC's position/general policies.
    b.   The major categories of causes of strikes in Ghana.
    c.   The TUC's solutions, suggestions to improve industrial relations.

16.   Please provide details on how Ghana and the TUC benefit from participating in the ILO's activities and labor standards.

17.   Please list and explain the number of positions held by TUC officials in the ILO, e.g., Mr. A. M. Issifu on the Committee of Freedom of Association, etc. Also, state tenure of office and reason for leaving the office.

18.   Worker participation in Ghana.

Please state and explain:
    a.   Various methods, mechanisms, etc., through which Ghana's workers participate in decisions, job design, national policies, etc., at both national and local levels.
    b.   What are the TUC's policies in the area of workers' participation in management?
    c.   What are the problems identified and solutions in the view of the TUC?
    d.   What are the TUC's views on the role, structure and composition of Workers' Defense Committees?

19. Please state and describe the relationship between governments of
     Ghana and TUC from 1957 up to the present time.

20. The TUC and the SDF (1979 general elections).

     a. Why/how did the TUC decide to support or sponsor the SDF?
     b. What was the form of the TUC's sponsorship of the SDF?
     c. Were the national affiliates, local unions and members of the
         labor movement consulted on the sponsorship issue? How
         was it done?
     d. Did the TUC achieve its objectives?
     e. How were the SDF candidates nominated?

21. Concerning "Union Government" (UNIGOV):

     a. Why did the TUC support it?
     b. Was it able to achieve its objectives?
     c. Would the TUC make similar decisions if it faced similar
         circumstances today or in the future?

22. Please provide TUC memos or position papers on:

     a. UNIGOV.
     b. The National Commission on Democracy headed by Justice
         Annan.

23. Did the TUC submit any memos, position papers to the Ghana
     Government on labor acts/amendments of:

     a. 1958?
     b. 1960?
     c. 1965?
     d. 1971?

     Please provide copies.

24. Is the TUC considering Ghana's ratification of Convention No. 144
     of the ILO dealing with tripartism on international labor standards?

     Please describe and explain the TUC's action.

25. What action did the TUC take at the ILO as a result of the 1971
     Amendment that abolished the TUC?

     Please explain in detail.

Appendix 6

Map of Ghana: The Geopolitical Context of Labor Relations

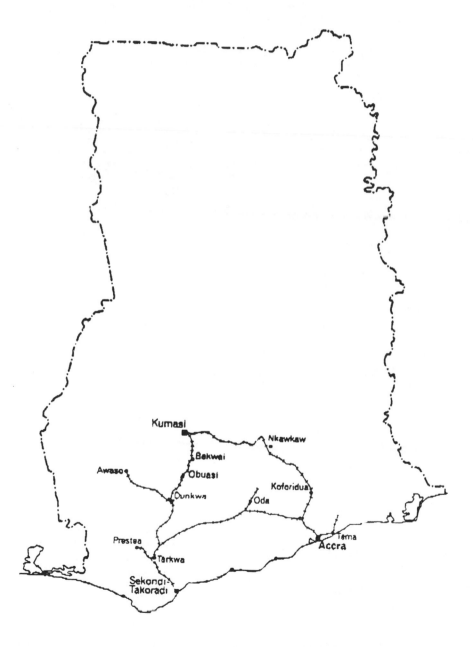

Appendix 7

22 English-speaking African ILO Member States

1. Botswana

2. Egypt

3. Ethiopia

4. Senegambia

5. Ghana

6. Kenya

7. Lesotho

8. Liberia

9. Libyan Arab Jamahiriya

10. Malawi

11. Mauritius

12. Namibia

13. Nigeria

14. Seychelles

15. Sierra Leone

16. Somalia

17. Sudan

18. Swaziland

19. Uganda

20. United Republic of Tanzania

21. Zambia

22. Zimbabwe

---

* This excludes Eritrea, which joined the UN in May 1993 as an independent African nation.

Source: ILO, Washington, DC, 1993

Appendix 8

The 17 Ghana TUC Affiliates from January 1966 to the Present

1. Construction and Building Trades Workers' Union

2. Industrial and Commercial Workers' Union

3. General Agricultural Workers' Union

4. Health Services Workers' Union

5. Local Government Workers' Union

6. Communications Workers' Union *

7. Railway Workers' Union

8. Public Services Workers' Union

9. Mine Workers' Union

10. Teachers and Educational Workers' Union

11. Railway Enginemen's Workers' Union

12. Maritime and Dockworkers' Union

13. National Union of Seamen

14. General Transport, Petroleum and Chemical Workers' Union

15. Ghana Private Roads Transport Union

16. Timber and Woodworkers' Union

17. Public Utility Workers' Union

---

* At its Quadriennial Conference in August 1991, the Posts and Telecommunications Workers' Union changed its name (*Labourscope*, Newsletter of the Ghana Labor Department, No. 51, Dec. 1992: 19).

Bibliography

ILO AND GOVERNMENT DOCUMENTS

ILO International Labor Conference, Thirty-First Session, San Francisco, 1948, *Record of Proceedings*, ILO, Geneva, (1950).
_____ , International Labor Conference, Thirty-Second Session, Geneva, 1949, *Record of Proceedings,* ILO, Geneva (1951).
_____ , *Sixth Report to the United Nations,* ILO, Geneva (1952): 47 - 64.
_____ , "Report of the Committee on Freedom of Employers' and Workers' Organizations" ("McNair Report"), *Official Bulletin,* Vol. XXXIX, No. 9 (1956).
_____ , *African Labor Survey,* ILO, Geneva (1958)
_____ , "The Influence of the International Labor Conventions on Nigerian Labor Legislation," *International Labor Review,* Vol. LXXXII, No. 1 (July, 1960): 26 - 43.
_____ , "Report to the Government of Ghana on Questions of Wage Policy," *Expanded Program of Technical Assistance,* ILO, Geneva, (1962).
_____ , "Report on Workers' Education in Ghana," *Regular Program of Technical Assistance,* ILO, Geneva (1968).
_____ , International Labor Conference, Fifty-Fourth Session, Geneva, 1969 "Trade Union Rights and their Relation to Civil Liberties," ILO, Geneva, (1970a).
_____ , "Third African Regional Conference," Accra, Dec. 1969, *Record of Proceedings,* ILO, Geneva (1970b).
_____ , *ILO Principles, Standards and Procedures Concerning Freedom of Association,* ILO, Geneva (1978).
_____ , African Advisory Committee, Seventh Session, Libreville, January 27 - February 4, 1981, "Ratification and Implementation of International Labor Standards in Africa," ILO, Geneva (1981).
_____ , *International Labor Conventions and Recommendations, 1919 - 1981,* ILO, Geneva (1982).

_____ , *Constitution of the International Labor Organization and Standing Orders of the International Labor Conference,* ILO, Geneva (1982 and 1988).

_____ , *Freedom of Association,* General Survey of the Committee of Experts on the Application of Conventions and Recommendations, ILO, Geneva (1983a).

_____ , *Labor Relations in Africa: English -Speaking Countries,* ILO, Geneva (1983b).

_____ , *Manual on Procedures Relating to the International Labor Conventions and Recommendations,* ILO, Geneva (1984).

_____ , Bureau of Public Information, "The International Labor Organization, Backgrounder," ILO, Geneva (October, 1984).

_____ , *Freedom of Association, Digest of Decisions and Principles of the Freedom of Association Committee of the Governing Body of the ILO,* 3rd Edition, ILO, Geneva (1985a).

_____ , "Report on the Fifth African Regional Seminar on National and International Labor Standards," Lusaka, Zambia, September 23 - October 2, 1985, ILO, Geneva (1985b).

_____ , "Trade Union Participation in Implementing International Labor Standards," Workers' Education Program Course, ILO, Geneva (1986).

_____ , "The Role of the ILO in Technical Cooperation," International Labor Conference, Report VI, ILO, Geneva, (1987).

_____ , *Collective Bargaining and Security of Employment in Africa: English- Speaking Countries*, ILO, Geneva, (1988).

_____ ,*Tripartite Symposium and Structural Adjustment and Employment in Africa,* Nairobi, October 16-19, 1989, ILO, Geneva, (1989).

_____ , *Democratization and the ILO,* Committee of Experts, Report to the 79th Session of the International Labor Conference, ILO, Geneva, (1992).

_____ , *286th Report of the Committee of Freedom Association*, Geneva (March 1993).

Ghana Government, "Seven Year Development Plan," (Annual Plan for the Second Plan Year, 1965 Financial Year), State Publishing, Accra-Tema (1965).

_____ , *Constitution of the Republic of Ghana*, Tema Press, Ghana Publishing Corporation, Tema (1992).

Ghana Labor Department, "Information on Labor Matters, Ghana," Accra (February 1961).

United Nations, "Human Rights: A Compilation of International Instruments," U. N., New York (1983).

U.S. Department of Labor, Bureau of Labor Statistics, "Summary of Labor Situation in Ghana," Washington, DC, (October 1958).

_____ , "Ghana: Country Labor Profile," Washington, DC, (1980).

BOOKS

Agyeman-Badu, Y., and Osei-Hwedie, K., *The Political Economy of Instability,* Brunswick Publishers, Lawrenceville, New Jersey (1982).

Alcock, A., History of the International Labor Organization, Octagon Books, New York (1971).

Amin, S., Neo-Colonialism in West Africa, Monthly Review Press, New York (1973).

Amsden, A. H., International Firms and Labour in Kenya: 1945-1970, Frank Cass, London (1971).

Ananaba, W., The Trade Union Movement in Africa, Hurst, London (1979).

Archer, P., and Reay L., Freedom at Stake: A Background Book, Bodley Head, London (1966).

Austin, D., Politics in Ghana, Oxford University Press, London (1964).

Bangura, Y and Beckman, B., "African Workers and Structural Adjustment: The Nigerian Case," in Ghai, D., (ed.) The IMF and the South: The Social Impact of Crisis and Adjustment, Zed Books, London (1991): 139 - 165.

Ben-Israel, R., International Labour Standards, Kluwer Law and Taxation Publishers, Deventer, Netherlands (1988).

Bentum, B. A., Trade Unions in Chains, Ghana TUC, Accra (1967).

Botchway, F. A., Political Development and Social Change in Ghana: Ghana Under Nkrumah, Black Academy, Buffalo, New York (1972).

Caire, G., Freedom of Association and Economic Development, ILO, Geneva (1977).

Callaway, B., and Card, E, "Political Constraints on Economic Development in Ghana," in Lofchie, M. F., (ed.) The State of the Nations: Constrains on Development in Independent Africa, University of California, Berkeley, Los Angeles (1971): 6 - 92.

Cammack, J., A., Guide to the Industrial Relations Act (Zambia), Zambia Printing Company, Lusaka (no date).

Claude, R. R., and Weston, B. H., (eds.) Human Rights in the World Community, University of Pennsylvania Press, Philadelphia (1989).

Cohen, R. and Goulbourne, H., (eds.) Democracy and Socialism, Westview, Boulder (1991).

Collier, P. and Deepak, L., Labor and Poverty in Kenya (1900 - 1980), Clarendon Press, Oxford (1986): 37 - 42.

Cowan, E. A., Evolution of Trade Unionism in Ghana, TUC, Accra (1960).

Damachi, U. and Fashoyin, T., "Labour Relations in the Nigerian Civil Service," in Gladstone, A., et. al., Current Issues in Labour Relations: An International Perspective, International Industrial Relations Association, Walter de Gruyter, Berlin (1989).

Davies, I., African Trade Unions, Penguin, Baltimore (1966).

Drake, St. C., and Lacy, L. A., "Government Versus the Unions: The Sekondi-Takoradi Strike, 1961," in Carter, G. M., (ed.) Politics in Africa: Seven Cases, Harcourt, Brace and World, New York (1966): 67 - 118.

Erstling, J. A., The Right to Organize, ILO, Geneva (1977).

Ewusi, K., Distribution of Monetary Income in Ghana, ISSER, Accra (Ghana) Technical Publication No. 13 (1971).

_____ , "Ghana" in Blanpain, R., (ed.) International Encyclopedia for Labor Law and Industrial Relations, Vol. 5, Supplement 38, Kluwer Law and Taxation Publishers, Deventer, Netherlands (February 1984).

_____ , Economic Development Planning in Ghana, Exposition, New York (1973).

Forsythe, D. P., (ed.) Human Rights and Development: International Views, St. Martin's Press, New York (1989).

Friedland, W., "Labor's Role in Emerging African Socialist States," in Beling, W., (ed.) The Role of Labor in African Nation Building, Praeger, New York (1968): 20 - 38.

_____ , and Rosberg, C. G., (eds.) African Socialism, Stanford University Press, Palo Alto, California (1964).

Galenson, W., The International Labor Organization, University of Wisconsin, Madison (1981).

Ghai, D. (ed.) IMF and the South: The Social Impact of Crisis and Adjustment, Zed Books, Atlantic Highlands, NJ (1991).

Ghebali, V., The International Labor Organization: A Case Study of the Evolution of U. N. Specialized Agencies, Martinus Nijhoff, Dordrecht (1989).

Gray, P. S., Unions and Leaders in Ghana, Conch Publishers, Owerri: New York (1981).

Haas, E. B., Beyond the Nation-State, Stanford University Press, Stanford (1964)

_____ , Human Rights and International Action, Stanford University Press, Stanford (1970).

Hamalengwa, M., Class Struggles in Zambia, 1889 - 1989, and the Fall of Kenneth Kaunda, 1990 - 1991, University Press of America, Lanham, MD (1992).

Hannum, H., (ed.) Guide to International Human Rights Practice, University of Pennsylvania Press, Philadelphia (1984).

Hansen, E. and Ninsin, K., (eds.) The State, Development and Politics in Ghana, Codesria, Dakar (1989).

Harrod, J., Trade Union Foreign Policy: A Study of British and American Trade Union Activities in Jamaica, Doubleday, New York (1972).

Huq, A., The Economy of Ghana, St. Martin's Press, New York, 1989.

Hutchful, E., (ed.) The IMF and Ghana: The Confidential Record, Institute for African Alternatives, Zed Books, London (1987).

Iwuji, E., "Industrial Relations in Kenya," in Damachi, U., et. al., (eds.) Industrial Relations in Africa, St. Martin's Press, New York (1979): 201 - 239.

Jeffries, R., Class, Power and Ideology in Ghana: The Railwaymen of Sekondi, Cambridge University Press, Cambridge (1978).

Kerr, C., et. al., Industrialism and the Industrial Man, Oxford University Press, New York (1955).

Kimble, D., A Political History of Ghana, Oxford University Press, London (1963).

Kraus, J., "The Political Economy of Industrial Relations in Ghana," in Damachi, U., et. al., (eds.) Industrial Relations in Africa, St. Martin's Press, New York (1979): 106 - 168.

Kusi, N. T. A and Gyimah-Boakye, A. K, Collective Bargaining in Ghana: Problems and Perspectives, ILO, Geneva (1991)

Le Vine, V., Political Corruption: The Ghana Case, Hoover Institution, Stanford University, Palo Alto, California (1975)

Lofchie, M. F., The State of the Nations: Constraints on Development in Independent Africa, University of California Press, Berkeley, Los Angeles, California (1971).

Maitland-Jones, J. F., Politics in Ex-British Africa, Weidenfeld and Nicolson, London (1973).

Ninsin, K. A., Political Struggles in Ghana: 1967 - 1981, Tornado Press, Accra (1992).

Ninsin, K. A., and Drah, F. K., (eds.) The Search for Democracy in Ghana: A Case Study of Political Instability in Africa, Asempa, Accra (1987).

Obeng-Fosu, P., Industrial Relations in Ghana: The Law and Practice, Universities Press, Accra (1991).

Okunade, A., "Human Rights and Trade Unionism in Africa: The Nigerian Experience" in Forsythe, D. P., (ed.) Human Rights and Development: International Views, St. Martin's Press, New York (1989): 650 - 676.

Otobo, D., The Role of Trade Unions in Nigerian Industrial Relations, Mallhouse Press, Oxford (1987).

Padmore, G., The Gold Coast Revolution, Dennis Dobson, London (1953).

Pellow, D and Chazan, N., Ghana, Westview, Boulder (1986).

Ray, D. I., Ghana, Politics, Economics and Society, Frances Pinter, London (1986).

Richard, J., Class, Power and Ideology in Ghana: The Railwaymen of Sekondi, Cambridge University Press, Cambridge (1978).

Roberts, B. C., Labour in the Tropical Territories of the Commonwealth, Bell and Sons, London (1964).

Rodney, W., How Europe Underdeveloped Africa, Howard University Press, Washington D.C. (1982).

Sandbrook, R., Proletarians and African Capitalism: The Kenyan Case, 1960 - 1972, Cambridge University Press, Cambridge (1975).

Sawyerr, A., The Political Dimensions of Structural Adjustment Programmes in sub-Saharan Africa, Ghana Universities Press, Accra (1990).

Shafritz, J., Dictionary of Personnel Management and Labor Relations, Moore Co., Oak Park, Illinois (1980).

Shillinton, K., Ghana and the Rawlings Factor, St. Martin's Press, New York (1992).

Shotwell, J., (ed.) The Origins of the International Labor Organization, Columbia University Press, New York (1934).

Singh, M., History of Kenya's Trade Union Movement to 1952, East African Publishing House, Nairobi, Kenya (1969).

Swepston, L., "Human Rights Complaints Procedures of the International La-
    bor Organization," in Hannum, H., (ed.) Guide to International Human
    Rights Practice, University of Pennsylvania, Philadelphia (1984).
Tettegah, J. K., A New Chapter for Ghana Labour, Ghana TUC, Accra (1958).
Tikriti, A., Tripartism and International Labor Organization, UppsalaUniver-
    sity Press, Uppsala (1982).
Turkson, R. B. "The History of Public Corporations," in Daniels, E and-
    Woodman, C. R., (eds.) Essays in Ghana Law, Ghana Publishing Co.,
    Accra-Tema (1976): 137 - 157.
Valticos, N., International Labor Law, Kluwer Law and Taxation Publishers,
    Deventer, Netherlands (1984).
Van-Hear, N., "Recession, Retrenchment and Military Rule: Nigerian Labor in
    the 1980s," in Southall, R., (ed.) Trade Unions and the NewIndustrial-
    ization in the Third World, Pittsburgh University Press, Pittsburgh
    (1988): 144 - 163.
Woddis, J., Africa: The Lion Awakes, Lawrence and Wishart, London (1961).
Yeebo, Z., Ghana: The Struggle for Popular Power, New Beacon, London
    (1991).
Ziskind, D., Labor Provisions in African Constitutions, Litlaw Foundation,
    Los Angeles, California (1987).

ARTICLES

Bates, H., "Approaches to the Study of Unions and Development," Industrial
    Relations , Vol. 9 (October, 1970): 365 - 378.
Bello, E., "International Labor Law, Social Justice and EconomicDevelop-
    ment in Africa," Osterr, A., Offentl, Recht and Volkerrecht, 31 (1980):
    96 - 126.
Cambridge, C., "Emerging Trends in the Industrial Relations Systems of-
    Former British Colonies," Journal of African Studies (Fall, 1984).
De Schweinitz, K., "Industrialization, Labor Controls and Democracy,"
    Economic Development and Cultural Change, Vol. VIII, No. 6
    (November - December, 1959): 765 - 781.
Fashoyin, T., "Industrial Relations and the Political Process in Nigeria," Inter-
    national Institute for Labor Studies, Research Series No. 69, ILO,
    Geneva (1981).
Fisher, P., "The Economic Role of Unions in Less-Developed Areas,"
    Monthly Labor Review, Vol. 84 No. 9 (September 1961): 951 - 956.
Gray, P. S., "Collective Bargaining in Ghana," Industrial Relations, Vol. 19,
    No. 2 (Spring 1980): 175 - 191.
Hodges-Aeberhard, J. and De Dios, A. O., "Principles of the Committee on
    Freedom of Association Concerning Strikes," International Labor Re-
    view, Vol. 126, No. 5 (September - October 1987): 543 - 563.
_____ , "The Right to Organize in Article 2 of Convention No. 87," Interna-
    tional Labor Review, Vol. 128, No. 2 (1989): 177 - 194.

Kalula, E., "The Influence of International Labor Standards on Zambian Legislation," *International Labor Review*, Vol. 124, No. 5 (September - October 1985): 593 - 609.

Kamoche, K., "Human Resource: An Assessment of the Kenyan Case," *The International Journal of Human Resource Management* Vol. 3 No. 3 (December, 1993): 497 - 521.

Kraus, J., "Strikes and Labor Power in Ghana," *Development and Change*, Vol. 10, No. 2 (April 1979): 259 - 285.

_____ , "Rawlings' Second Coming," *Africa Report,* (March - April 1982): 59 - 66.

Landy, E. A., "The Influence of International Labor Standards: Possibilities and Performance," *International Labor Review*, Vol. 101, No. 6 (June 1970): 555 - 604.

Lewis, A., "Consensus and Discussions of Economic Growth: Concluding Remarks to a Conference," *Economic Development and Cultural Change*, Vol. VI, No. 1 (October 1957).

Lungu, G. F. "The Church, Labor and the Press in Zambia: The Role of Critical Observers in a One-Party State," *African Affairs*, Vol. 85, No. 340 (July 1986): 385 - 409.

Mehta, A., "The Mediating Role of the Trade Union in UnderdevelopedCountries," *Economic and Cultural Change*, Vol. VI, No. 1 (October 1957): 16 - 23.

Mingst, K. A., "Judicial Systems of Sub-Saharan Africa: An Analysis of Neglect," *African Studies Review,* Vol. 31, No. 1 (1988): 135 - 148.

Mutahaba, G., "The Human Resource Factor in African Public Administration," *African Review*, Vol. 9, No. 1 (1982): 32 - 58.

Nwubueze, R. O., "Trends in Nigerian Labor Legislation 1938 - 76," *The Indian Journal of Labor Economics*, Vol. XVIII, Nos. 1 - 2 (April - July, 1975): 1 - 22.

_____ , "Impact of Military Rule on Nigerian Trade Union Movement (1966 -1978)," *Indian Journal of Industrial Relations*, Vol. 16, No. 4 (April 1981): 571 - 592.

Osieke, E., "The Exercise of the Judicial Function with respect to theInternational Labor Organization," *British Year Book of International Law*, No. 47, (1974 - 1975): 315 - 340.

Panford, K., "State-Trade Union Relations: The Dilemmas of Single Trade Union Systems in Ghana and Nigeria," *Labor and Society*, Vol. 13, No. 1 (January 1988): 37 - 53.

_____ , "International Law, Human Rights and Development: A Review Essay," *Bimonthly Review of Law Books*, Rothmans, Boulder Co., (January - February, 1992): 8 - 11.

Pouyat, A. J., "The ILO's Freedom of Association Standards and Machinery: A Summing Up," *International Labor Review*, Vol. 121, No. 3 (May - June 1982): 287 - 302.

Samson, K.T., "The Changing Pattern of ILO Supervision," *International Labor Review*, Vol. 118, No. 5 (September - October 1979): 569 - 587.

Sawyerr, A., "Thirty Years of Industrial Relations in Ghana: 1941-1971," *Verfassung Und Techt in Ubersee*, 11 Jahrgang, 3 Heft (1978):   331 - 345.

Servais, J., "ILO Standards on Freedom of Association and their Implementation," *International Labor Review*, Vol. 123, No. 6 (November - December 1959): 765 - 781.

Shivji, I. G., "The POs and NGOs: Reflections on the Place of the Working People in the Battle for Democracy, *Codesria Bulletin*, No. 4 (1990).

Tewson, V., "Trade Unions in the Colonies," *New Commonwealth*, No. 27 (April 1, 1954).

Twumasi, Y., "The Newspaper, Press and Political Leadership in Developing Countries: The Case of Ghana, 1964 - 1978," *Gazette*, Vol. 26 (1980): 1 - 16.

Yesufu, T. M., "Management Policies for Industrial Peace in Nigeria," *The Journal of Business and Social Studies*, Nigeria, Vol. 1, No. 1 (September 1968): 35 - 47.

Zeytinoglu, I. U., "The Impact of the ILO's Freedom of Association Standards on African Labor Laws," *Comparative Labor Law Journal,* Vol. 8, No. 1, (Fall 1986): 48 - 83.

UNPUBLISHED WORKS

Adu-Amankwah, K. "The State, Trade Unions and Democracy in Ghana, 1982 - 1990," MA Research Paper, Institute of Social Studies, The Hague (December, 1990).

Agyeman, O., "A Case Study of the Ideo-Praxis of Pan-Africanism," Ph.D. Dissertation, York University, Downsview, Ontario, Canada (1980).

Arthiabah, P. B., " The Ghana TUC and Workers: Its Relationship With Past Governments and Contributions to National Development," Paper presented to The Symposium on the Life of Kwame Nkrumah, Institute of African Studies, University of Ghana, Legon (May 27 - June 1,1985).

Ewusi, K., "The Development of Manufacturing Industry in Ghana and the Government's Role in it," World Employment Program Working Paper, ILO, Geneva (January 1976).

Kalula, E., "Labor Law and Policy in a Post-Colonial State: Aspects of Trade Union Incorporation in Zambia," Ph.D. Dissertation, Warwick University, Coventry, U. K. (1988).

Kraus, J., "Strikes and Labor Power in Post-Colonial African State: The Ghana Case," Institute of Social Studies, The Hague (1977).

Panford, K., "Political Corruption, Economic Crisis and Political Instability in Ghana," Sociology Department, MacMaster University, Hamilton (Fall 1980).

_____, "Structural Adjustment, the State and Workers in Ghana," (forthcoming, 1994).

_____ , "The Influence of the International Labor Organization on African Workers' Union and Collective Bargaining Rights: A Case Study of Ghana," Ph.D. Dissertation, Law and Public Policy Program, Northeastern University, Boston (1989).

Index

Abban, I. K., Justice, 143
Accra-Tema: and overcentraliza-
tion, 96; location of industries,
96
Acheampong, Ignatius Kutu, Head
of State *(Ghana)*, 30, 63, 121,
125-129, 143, 155
Adebo Commission *(Nigeria)*, 18,
112
Adjei, Ako, Labor Minister
(Ghana), 18, 52, 65-67, 112
African-American Labor Center,
159, 165
African Socialism, 5, 18
Akuffo, Frederick, General, Head
of State *(Ghana)*, 30, 128
American Federation of Labor and
the Congress of Industrial Or-
ganizations *(AFL-CIO)*, 90,
159
Amissah, Kojo, Archbishop
(Ghana), 126
Ampah, Kwaw, Secretary-General
(Ghana TUC), 53
Ananaba, Wogu, 8, 19, 37, 50, 62,
89, 94, 112, 118, 130, 148
Anglophone Africa, 73, 79, 93,
111, 140. *See also* English-
speaking Countries
Arbitration, 41-42, 54, 58-59, 122,
147
Armed Forces Revolutionary

Council *(AFRC)*, 30
Association of Local Unions
(ALU, Ghana), 125
Association of Recognized Professional Bodies, 97
Assumptions: about the ILO, 137;
about unions, 89; about workers, 86, 153; impact of unions,
160; of policies, 145, 160; values and ideological preferences, 2; within the ILO, 70;
workers' participation, 13
Austerity policies, 29
Automatic checkoff, 45, 49, 65

Baako, Kofi, Minister *(Ghana)*, 52
Babangida, Ibrahim, President
(Nigeria), 65, 94, 113, 154,
155
Baiden, J. K., 121, 126
Bentum, Benjamin, Secretary-
General *(Ghana TUC)*, 17, 99,
111, 124
Boateng, D.S., Minister *(Ghana)*,
114, 149
Botchwey, Kwesi, Minister
(Ghana), 164
British, 70, 72-76, 90, 95; and the
right to strike, 73; and tripar-
tism, 71, 84; authorities, 43,
73, 78, 147; colonial govern-
ment, 83; colonial labor laws,

About the Author

KWAMINA PANFORD is an Assistant Professor in the Department of African-American Studies at Northeastern University. He has spent several years of research involving field work in Ghana and a year's employment at the ILO's Geneva head office. Dr. Panford specializes in international labor relations, comparative socio-economic development and international human rights.